Social geography of the United States

Social geography of the United States

J. Wreford Watson,
Convenor, Centre of Canadian Studies and Professor of Geography
University of Edinburgh

Longman
London and New York

Longman Group Limited London

*Associated companies, branches and representatives
throughout the world*

*Published in the United States of America
by Longman Inc., New York*

© Longman Group Limited 1979

First published 1979
ISBN 0 582 48196 1 cased
ISBN 0 582 48197 X paper

British Library Cataloguing in Publication Data
Watson, James Wreford
   Social geography of the United States.
   1. Anthropo-geography – United States
   2. United States – Social conditions
   I. Title
   301.29'73   GF503

   ISBN 0-582-48196-1
   ISBN 0-582-48197-X   Pbk

Printed in Great Britain by
Richard Clay (The Chaucer Press) Ltd, Bungay, Suffolk

Contents

List of illustrations

Preface

People make places. The North America of the Indians was very different from what it became under the Whites: and that part of it developed by the Americans differed in striking ways from portions left to Canadians and Mexicans. Americans secured the heartland of the continent, gripped by the dream of a free, dynamic, competitive and democratic society, with an ever higher standard of living for the common man. They matched the opportunities of a rich environment with the genius of an even richer mind. But success cost conflict. The clash of culture, race riots, alienation, and depravation soon marked the land. Hence, social factors came to dominate the scene, and geography took on the lineaments of society.

Social geography is an analysis not only of how people make place, but of how they think they do so: it is concerned with the perceptions behind the patterns. To get at these, it should tap various sources and use a variety of approaches. Crucial to geography is to *savour* a place – or rather, savour the difference between places. This comes with personal acquaintance and observation, or, short of that, with reliance on accounts based on experience and understanding. Yet to live in a place can be to be blind to it, especially in terms of other areas: comparisons and contrasts are essential. Personal prejudices, though taken account of, must be weighted by dispassionate assessment: facts and figures are of the essence.

This book concerns itself with individual views, but also with an impersonal overview of the American scene, using the speeches and reports of eminent persons who either created geography in their day or illuminated it; together with the appraisal of novelists and poets, with a strong sense of place, who described and interpreted it, and at the same time with the statistics and statistical analysis that gave an objective model of the whole. It also refers to acts of government that actually changed the geography of the land, and stamped the American image on America.

The attempt has been made to adapt method to subject. The Indian problem is taken up mainly through peoples' images and government policy; the negro question through the voice of individuals and the testimony of statistics; the clash of cultures by way of the regional novel supported by impersonal surveys; poverty and crime from the weight of statistics. The statistical approach is used of youth, sex, and age in the American population. Status divisions are given force through novelists of the poor and of the rich. The social geography of the city appeals to a wide range of support, from the research of scholars, the novelist's insight, and the speeches of city fathers to the say of statistics and the arguments of enaction. The great debate between individualism and the community goes back to what individual men and communal leaders actually did – or are doing. The deep concern for conservation, welfare, and above all – well-being, looks at the debate of educators and congressmen, and appeals to those acts of government by which Americans are reshaping the American environment.

Thus, consideration of fact and perception, of behaviour and belief, of personal interpretation and public action, of statistical analysis and the 'great American dream', are all used, so as to bring out the realities of man and environment in the making of America.

Acknowledgements

The author is greatly indebted to Miss Margaret Watson, DA, illustrator, for the background work put into the making of the graphs and maps that illustrate the text.

He is also in debt to Miss Dorothy McLennan, secretary, for the preparation of the manuscript and to Mr and Mrs Ernest Nevitt for their kind hospitality and stimulating discussions when the penultimate chapter was being written at their summer cottage in N. Ontario.

Finally, the author wishes to thank his wife, without whose help in motoring him across America and back, in obtaining information and in reading and contributing ideas to the book, he would hardly have attempted, much less proceeded with, this account of the American image as it has stamped itself on the landscape of America.

The Author and Publishers are grateful to the following for permission to reproduce copyright material:

The Association of American Geographers for map by D. W. Meinig from *Annals* Vol. 55 (1965); Ballinger Publishing Company for fig. 2.4 Ch. 2 by C. S. Sargent from *Urban Policy Making and Metropolitan Dynamics*, ed. J. S. Adams, Copyright 1976, Ballinger Publishing Co; Professor W. Bunge for p. 150 and p. 166 from *Human Geography in a Shrinking World* eds. Abler, Janelle and Philbrich, Duxbury Press (1975); United States Department of Justice for fig. p. 177 from *U.S. Department of Justice Annual Report* 1975; Economic Geography (Clark University) for fig. 2 p. 61 *Geographical Perspectives on American Poverty* by de Vise, ed. Peet from *Economic Geography*; The New York Times for fig. from 'The Second Regional Plan' *New York Times* 15 June, 1969, © 1969 The New York Times Company. Reprinted by permission; Author, William B. Stapp for fig. p. 76 from *Environmental Education*, Gale Research Co. (1974); United States Department of Labor for fig. p. 9 of *Labor Force Projections to 1985*.

1

The importance of the social factor: problems and prospects

The geography of any country is what people see in it, want from it and do with it. In few places has that been more apparent than in America. Before European invasion, a sparsely settled area, it is now the fourth largest country in the world with 220 million people. This has resulted from a social explosion almost without parallel. As a consequence, the landscape has become dominated by the social factor. A social geography of America has evolved, reflecting the structure of society, the ends people have, and the means at their disposal. Essentially, this geography has been made through solving problems, and exploiting prospects.

The problem of the American image

First and foremost is the problem created by America's image of itself. This grew out of two things: the breakaway from the Old World, and the breakthrough to the New. There was the rather negative attitude of breaking away from, renouncing and even repudiating the past, and the more positive aim of breaking through to something different and new in the future. Both of these aspects of how America saw itself are important for geography. Breaking away meant leaving behind Old-World uses of land and patterns of settlement. Though, to begin with, the manorial system was represented, it gradually broke up, especially as agriculture became more commercialized and specialized. The old tenurial holdings, tied cottages and farm villages disappeared. Even in the South, where tenantry is still characteristic, owner-occupation has become more dominant. New land-survey systems were devised, which, at any rate in the North and West, were based on the planner's drawing board, and laid down with geometrical precision. Cities, too, developed on the grid system and, within these limits, were shaped by the competition for land. There was a new emphasis on land-values, and a new ordering of settlement in terms of individual status.

The American stress on newness

Whatever was *new*, indeed, the new itself became increasingly the hallmark of America. 'He is an American', said Crèvecoeur at the Revolution, 'who, leaving behind him all his ancient prejudices and manners, receives *new* ones from the *new* mode of life he has embraced. Here individuals of all nations are moulded into a *new* race of men.' Crèvecoeur (1782:1963) specifically linked these images with the landscape, pointing out that America had broken away from the dominance of institutions, like castle and cathedral, to become centred in the works of the individual, like farms and businesses.

The sense of a new American order was nowhere greater than on the frontier. 'American development has been continually beginning over again', wrote Turner in 1893. 'This perennial rebirth, this fluidity of American life, this expansion . . . furnish the forces dominating the American character.' They certainly came to dominate the landscape. Turner was writing about the challenge of the frontier, and of winning new land. And for a long time this represented a major part of the geography of newness, the urge to find more land and develop it, possibly in new ways. The national and foreign demand for cheap food led to the clearance of three-quarters of the forest, and the breaking up of four-fifths of the sod – major geographical changes – in the development of farmland. Increasingly, this was done on a very large scale through extensive mechanization. This was described by Moody in 1879, who wrote 'within the past year or two a new development in agriculture has forced itself upon public attention'. This consisted of farm companies buying up blocks of from 20,000 to 100,000 acres of land, using gangs of a dozen or more ploughs to break up the soil, and teams of harvesters to cut the wheat, all under expert agricultural managers.

Changes like these have obviously affected the landscape to a tremendous extent, reducing the number of units of production but increasing their size, cutting down on the number of producers, making the machine dominate the scene, and providing a higher personal standard of living by way of houses, cars, aeroplanes, schools, telecommunications, roads, parks, and so forth, than anywhere else in the world.

Newness also made a great deal of difference to *urban* geography, in the forefront of change. Nathaniel Hawthorne (1851:1964) makes one of his characters, Holgrave, cry in *The House of the Seven Gables*, 'Shall we never get rid of the Past!' and to hope:

> We shall live to see the day, I trust, when no man shall build his house
> for posterity. If each generation were expected to build its own houses,

that single change, would imply almost every reform which society is now
suffering for. I doubt whether even our public edifices – our capitols,
state-houses, court-houses, city-halls, and churches – ought to be built of
such permanent materials as stone or brick. It were better that they
should crumble to ruins, once in twenty years, as a hint to the people to
re-examine and reform the institutions which they symbolize.

In another generation, Henry James was to write of the extraordinary
rapidity with which American cities changed. They had a positive thirst for
newness. 'One story is good only till another is told, and skyscrapers are the
last word in ingenuity only until another word be written.' This is still true
today. Citified America is growing at 1.8 per cent per annum compared with
America as a whole, at 1.1 per cent. Furthermore, the newest part of urban
areas, that outside the central cities, in the huge sprawl of the suburbs into the
countryside, is growing at 2.4 per cent. Such rapid expansion of the urban
fabric is one of America's greatest problems: new schools, new shopping
centres, new hospitals, new housing, new roads have to be built at a phenomenal rate. All this goes with the state of mind which, in Henry Adams's
famous phrase, made 'the American stand in the world a *new order of man*'.

   The American sense of destiny was part of the American image. The first
British settlers in both Virginia and New England had a strong belief that
they were helping to make destiny. This might be no more than 'building a
foundation for posterity', in the words of Captain John Smith, or it might be
following the conviction, such as Edward Johnson held, that 'Christ creates a
New England to muster His forces in . . . intending to make [it] the very
wonder of this Age'. The American Revolution deepened this sense of destiny.
In justifying America's split from England, Thomas Paine wrote, 'the time
likewise at which the continent was discovered, adds weight to the argument
[for separation], and the manner in which it was peopled, increases the force
of it. The Reformation was preceded by the discovery of America, as if the
Almighty graciously meant to open a sanctuary in future years. . . .' George
Washington, before retiring from the first presidentship of the newly founded
state, wished to congratulate his fellow citizens 'on the glorious events which
Heaven has been pleased to produce in our favor'. Another of America's
founding fathers, Jefferson, spoke of America, in his Inaugural Address, as 'a
rising nation . . . advancing rapidly to destines beyond the reach of mortal
eye'. He himself helped destiny forward by extending America's boundaries
from the Mississippi to the Rockies in one great leap, through the Louisiana
Purchase of 1803.

   The ordinary American was often in front of his leaders. When the
Indian Line, dividing White from Indian territory, stood along the
Appalachian divide, Americans had poured across it to the Ohio; when the
Indian Line was moved to Ohio, pioneers were already along the Wabash. As
Billington (1960) repeatedly points out in his *Westward Expansion* the 'colonies

of the West showed a dangerous tendency to take matters into their own hands'. The Southwest was opened up by 'aggressive expansionists, eager to overrun international boundaries in their search for wealth'. The Northwest was invaded by swarms of 'lawless adventurers staking out their tomahawk

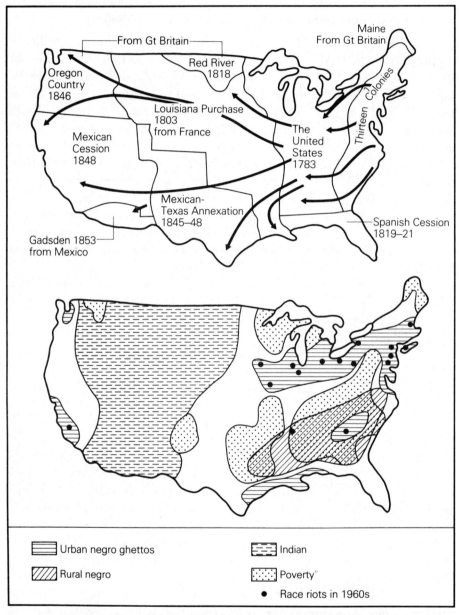

Fig. 1.1 *Growth and conflict.* A sense of 'manifest destiny' prompted the United States to take over the heart of North America from Britain, France, Spain and Mexico, but expansion led to clashes of race and culture and economic and social inequalities.

claims . . . firm in the belief that every American had an undoubted right to pass into every vacant country . . .'. even though it might have been designated Indian Territory, by official treaty.

They swept aside not only the treaty agreements with the Indians but the legal claims of Britain in Canada, of Spain in Florida, and the Mexicans in Texas and California. In the 1845 crisis over Oregon, in which Britain was trying to preserve its rights, based on early partitions with Spain, O'Sullivan, a famous American journalist wrote, 'Away, away with all these cobweb tissues of rights of discovery, exploration, settlement, contiguity, etc.' These were nothing as compared with 'the right of our manifest destiny to overspread and to possess the whole of the continent which Providence has given us for the development of the great experiment of liberty and self-government entrusted to us'.

This sort of image gave Americans a sense of superiority that tempted them into imperial expansion. It created a very grave problem of international relations which has been with America ever since – the problem of whether to isolate itself from foreign involvements or become leaders in world affairs. American expansion has certainly been one of the great makers of American geography, and, indeed, of the geography of the world.

Thus, it may be seen that the American image has had a great deal to do with the American scene. The way Americans have viewed themselves has affected their use of America. Consequently, the American image is the basic frame of reference of American geography. It forms the parameters in which specific problems and prospects are set. For example, the longing to do a new thing, and the sense of becoming a new people, created growth and expansion that then caught up many other ideas and sentiments into the American way, each one of which raised further national issues. The rapid growth of America (see Fig. 1.1) pushed by an almost excessive individualism and vested with a high sense of destiny, led to bitter competition for the land with Indians, enslaved the Negro, exploited the immigrant, produced sharp clashes in religion, induced grave economic inequalities, brought America into conflict with other nations, and jeopardized the environment throughout much of the continent. These and other problems were the cost of expansion. Nevertheless, expansion opened the prospects of high standards of living, and the strength to serve people in need throughout the world.

The Indian problem

Not unnaturally, the question of how to behave towards the Indians became one of the first and most pressing issues that faced the European invaders of North America. It straightaway posed itself to the Americans as they took over from the British in the march across the continent. The Americans, of course, inherited many of their ideas and policies from colonial days. However, it is important to realize that they had just thrown off colonial control, and that they had done so in a bitter civil war. The Americanism that had been prepared to take on the English did not hesitate to tackle the Indian. In the spirit of the War of Independence, men contested whatever land they could win: if the English had had to go to the wall, so much more the Indian.

The attitude reinforced the aggressiveness which had, in fact, already grown up. When the Narragansetts sent a bundle of arrows tied up in a snake's skin to warn off the Plymouth settlers, they drew counter-threats upon themselves: the settlers 'sent them a rounde answer that, if they had rather have warre than peace, they might begin when they would'. Americans saw comparatively empty land in front of them, and were determined to put it to good use. Even if we accept the most generous estimate of the native population at the time when the Whites arrived, which Dobyns and Thompson have put at 12 millions north of the Rio Grande, it would still give a density of only 3.3 persons per square mile. At the lower, and probably more realistic, estimate of some 6 millions, there would have been less than 1 person per square mile. Of course the densities varied enormously from the passably peopled parts along the Atlantic Coast Plain, in the Lower Great Lakes–Mohawk Valley, in the Ohio Basin, and the Gulf Coast Plain, to really empty areas in the drier Great Plains and the desert basins of the trans-Rocky West. But even in areas like Virginia where the Indians practised agriculture as well as hunting and fishing, and had many small villages, there were still great stretches of comparatively unused country that made the *wilderness* more impressive to the first settlers than *made land*. Captain Smith (1624:1967) remarked of Virginia, 'The land is not populous . . . for they [the Indians] make so small a benefit of their land. Within thirty leagues of sailing we saw not any, being a barren country.'

At the time that America gained its independence there were (1790) over 3,900,000 settlers, living between the Atlantic coast and the Ohio, giving a density of 4.5 people per square mile. The land had been rapidly taken up, and the pressure of white encroachment was beginning to bear down on the Indians. Frequent conflicts broke out, and the Indians were pushed back first beyond the Appalachians, next to the Ohio, following that the Mississippi, and eventually the Rockies. The Indian population fell drastically. Jefferson, quoting the Virginia enumeration of 1669, said that, within a man's lifetime 'the tribes . . . were reduced to about one-third of their former numbers. Spiritous liquors, the small-pox, war, and an abridgement of territory to a people who lived on the spontaneous productions of nature, had committed terrible havoc among them.' This havoc continued until a low point was reached in 1850 when the numbers, for the whole of the United States, had dropped to only 250,000. The Indians had been steadily driven off their lands and confined to smaller and smaller areas (mostly in the arid West) which were not economic for white men to colonize. The whole geography of Indian America was changed. Their most populous parts, east of the Mississippi and south of the Great Lakes, had become virtually depleted, while their least settled areas, in the High Plains and Intermontane Basins became, perforce, their main abiding place. This was the result, not of natural influences, but of social forces taking over the most favoured areas for the Whites, and leaving the least productive districts to the Indians. After the Indian wars finally ended, in the 1870s, numbers increased until today they are over 800,000. Indians now have a rate of increase above the national average, which should bring their numbers to 1,250,000 by AD 2000. However, this would still leave them a very small minority, about 0.41 of the then total population. They would still be confined mostly to the West.

The negro problem

The white sense of destiny that had driven the Indian west, replaced him by the Negro in the East and South. The desire for rapid development, coupled with an extreme shortage of labour in colonial days, led to the use of imported African slaves. The American feeling of superiority confirmed this practice, even though Americans had come into being fighting for freedom. Slavery remained. By the time consciences began to stir, and the importation of Negroes to America was forbidden in 1807, the negro population was self-perpetuating: most Negroes had big families. The infamous practice of breeding slaves, to beat the ban on importation, forced numbers up still more. By 1850 when the Indian population had reached its nadir of only 250,000, the number of Negroes had climbed to over 3,600,000. Most of these were east of the Mississippi and south of the Ohio and Delaware: that is, in areas once most well peopled by Indians. Thus, through white intervention a complete reversal in geography had taken place: brown skins had given way to black, though white supremacy was still maintained.

Having slaves gave status. On the other hand it gave offence, especially to those looking for a New Eden. Soon the situation divided the Whites; and the Civil War broke out. The results of this still further affected negro geography. Freed at last, Negroes began to move. The map of negro distribution saw a shift from country to town, and then from southern to northern town, and next from northern to western town. Once confined to the Southeast, the Negro filled the United States. But he had not escaped conflict: it followed him into every town where, as Jefferson feared, 'deep-rooted prejudice entertained by the Whites, ten thousand recollections by the Blacks of the injuries they had received', parted one group from the other and led to one of America's major problems, the black ghettos. With the continuing growth of the negro population, now reckoned to be about 25 millions, many black ghettos, like Harlem, are cities in themselves. Continued mass immigration of Whites from Europe which came to offer strong competition with the in-migration of Negroes, for jobs and homes, in all the great metropolises, further aggravated the situation. In striving to gain acceptance for themselves with native-born Americans, a lot of foreign-born Whites added to the forces of prejudice and segregation.

The problem of the foreign-born

The fact that many – and indeed for a long time, most – Americans were born abroad and had to make their adjustment to their new homeland when they were already set in their ways and ideas, has always been a major American issue. A great number came without English, with little education, made self-conscious by different clothes, foods, games, and habits; fearing non-acceptance they tended to seek their own company and to congregate in ethnic quarters. This was not unnatural since they met with prejudice, even in high places. No less a man than Jefferson (1785:1964) wrote:

> *Here I will beg leave to propose a doubt. The present desire of America is to produce rapid population by as great importations of foreigners as possible. But is this founded in good policy? The advantage proposed is the multiplication of numbers. But are there no inconveniences to be thrown into the scale against [this] advantage. . . . It is for the happiness of those united in society to harmonize as much as possible in matters which they must of necessity transact together. Every species of government has its specific principles. Ours perhaps are more peculiar than those of any other in the universe. It is a composition of the freest principles of the English constitution with others derived from natural right and natural reason. . . . [But immigrants] will bring with them the principles of the government they leave, imbibed in their early youth; or, if able to throw them off, it will be in exchange for an unbounded licentiousness, passing, as is usual, from one extreme to another. It would be a miracle were they to stop precisely at the point of temperate liberty. These principles, with their language, they will transmit to their children. In proportion to their numbers they will share with us the legislation. They will infuse into it their spirit, warp and bias its directions, and render it a heterogeneous, incoherent, distracted mass.*

Jefferson then asked was it not safer to wait on the natural increase of the native-born population (which was, of course, still predominately Anglo-Saxon and Protestant in his day)? Would not the native American way of life, if continued without adulteration from external sources, be 'more homogeneous, more peaceable, more durable'?

It was not to be. The Anglo-Scottish dominance had passed by the end of the Civil War, though all its great leaders – Lee, Lincoln, and Grant – were of that extraction. Between that war and the First World War there was a tremendous influx of Europeans, a big invasion of Canadians and Mexicans, and a not inconsiderable incursion of Asians. By 1920 about one in six Americans was foreign-born. This proportion fell off rapidly thereafter, especially during the Great Depression of the 1930s and the Second World War: America then changed its immigration policy to take in only selected individuals whose skills, capital, health, and character might contribute to the nation. Today only one in twenty Americans is foreign-born. However, native-born people of foreign parentage still account for 11 per cent of the population.

Actually, most Americans have accepted the problems involved in immigration, for its *advantages*, confident in the belief that America would act as a melting pot to fuse together all differences and create a typically American way of life. And the mix did occur. Immigrants moved throughout America and carried their cultures with them, at the same time adopting American ways. Mobility thus helped, and is still important in bringing differences together, and making people aware of each other.

Religious and other cultural problems

Since people came to America to be different, whether as individuals or as groups, they set up churches and other institutions based on their own ideas. This meant an early, and a continued, proliferation of sects, often very much at odds with each other. Religion has been one of the most divisive forces in America and is responsible for a geography of innovation, competition, and separation probably without equal. The 'New Light' movement early split up Boston, and led to the colonization of Rhode Island. The leaders, Mrs Hutchison and her brother, Mr Wheelright, were, according to Governor Winthorp, 'disenfranchised and banished'. The Puritans were likewise harsh on the Baptists and the Quakers, most of whom fled the early settlements, and dispersed further inland, or moved to Pennsylvania. According to Ziner, (1961) 'Quakers caught by the Puritans had their ears sliced off, their cheeks branded with hot irons, or were beaten insensible, flayed with tarred ropes, stripped of all possessions – even blinded and hanged'. No wonder they migrated further west! Later the Mormons, also forced to suffer for their new-found faith, made the great trek half across the continent to Utah. Religious dissension often meant geographical dispersal.

However, it should be pointed out that all this competition, fierce though it was, released a new creativity among the American people. It was all part of that newness which had come to be their image, here translated into newness of soul. In 1906, William James wrote:

> *We are now witnessing a very copious unlocking of energies by ideas in the persons of those converts to 'New Thought', 'Christian Science', 'Metaphysical Healing' . . . etc. The common feature of these optimistic faiths is that they all tend to the suppression of . . . 'fearthought' [i.e. the 'self-suggestion of inferiority'], so that one may say that these systems all operate by the suggestion of Power.*

That power has made a tremendous impact on the landscape by the geography of new sects and new institutions, American in concept and practice. New denominations are founded and then these are divided up and subdivided.

American religious geography presents a fantastic array of churches. Not content with having Baptists, as such, America has: (1) the American Baptist Association; (2) the American Baptist Convention; (3) the Baptist General Conference; (4) the Baptist Missionary Association of America; (5) the Conservative Baptist Association of America; (6) the National Association of Free Will Baptists; (7) the General Association of Regular Baptists; (8) the General Baptists of America; (9) the National Baptist Evangelical-Life and Soul-Saving Assembly of the USA; (10) the National Primitive Baptist Convention; (11) the Northern Baptist General Convention; (12) Primitive Baptists (not in Association); (13) the Progressive Baptist National Convention; (14) the Southern Baptist Convention; (15) the United Baptist Church; (16) the Free Baptist Church; (17) the United Free Will Baptist Church. Thus, even faiths that have a nation-wide distribution have nevertheless become subject to regional fission and racial division.

Regionalism is strong. Certain sects have come to dominate the institutional geography of large areas, like the Episcopalians in Virginia, and the Unitarians and the Christian Scientists in New England, Catholics in Maryland, the Mormons, Seventh-Day Adventists, and Jehovah's Witnesses out West, and so on. Some regions are noted for a plethora of sects, like Pennsylvania and, later, California. In any case, religion has written itself into American geography in an indelible way.

The problems of status in America

Further division in America has stamped itself upon the landscape through differences of status, class, and income. This has become highly geographical. Americans translate social difference into geographical division. Every American city is split into status areas. This is part of their free, individualistic, competitive system. The chief aim of personal competition in America is to achieve social status, it is to arrive at as high a position in the social scale as possible, and protect that place through a system of social grouping.

'Although social-class categories are not sharply defined', writes Warner, (1965) one of the great students of class in American society, 'there is in American communities a clear understanding of the social differences, values and behaviour which compose a class system.' This works itself into the geography of the land since 'social distance is achieved in such ways as the use of geographic distance and institutions based upon spatial factors'. Classes strive for, or are relegated to, what society regards as the best or the worst environments. Upper classes get the heights, lower classes 'live on the river-banks, in the foggy bottoms, in the regions back of the tanneries or near the stockyards, and generally in those places that are not desired by anyone else'. Hills do not *make* upper classes, or bottoms lower classes; relief, drainage, and climate are important not because they determine society, but because society picks them out in determining what are the most-valued or least-valued environments. Hence, social factors become the measure of physical features, to dominate the geography of the land. Going beyond the poor of the cities, to the poor of the nation, poverty became entrenched among the dismal swamps of the Atlantic Coast Plain, the piney sands of the Piedmont, the rugged hills and plateaux of Appalachia, the cut-over barrens of Michigan and Minnesota, the deeply-ravined Ozarks or the dustbowl of Oklahoma. The least-favoured environments were the lot of the least-competitive communities.

Although the *problems* of America may be grave, its *prospects* are exciting. With its stress on new ideas, and out of a sense of destined responsibility, it has been applying its resources, technology, and organization to the lot of the person, to personal standards of living, and to an improved environment for each person in city and countryside. As a result, the American has never had such an opportunity to help other people in the world before. Exploiting such prospects is changing the whole geography of the country.

The prospects of the full society

All elements of society are now being given freedom to contribute to a fuller development of the community. In particular, women, youth, and the aged are having much more say.

Women have come to the fore. They now number more than the men: over 110 million strong they are larger than most of the world's nations – about the equal of Germany and Britain put together! Moreover, they are expanding at a greater rate than the men – 1.4 per cent per annum compared to 1.1 per cent. This has created great changes. It has made a huge dent on male predominance. Turner made much of the maleness of America in the forging of the frontier. American expansion was headed by the explorer, the trail-blazer, the axe-man, the ferry-man, the trader, the speculator, the cow-puncher, the prospector, the coach-driver, the railroad gang – and so on. These were all men on the make and they made America an aggressive, expansionist nation. They pushed the destiny of America forward because that was the best chance of making their own way ahead. Even as late as the 1911 census, America was distinctly a masculine country: it was only after the First World War that the sexes began to balance out. Now the United States is more female than male, and the age of male dominance is over.

Newness and destiny are imaged increasingly in the progress of women. The female labour force is now 38 per cent of the nation's total and is expanding at the very great rate of 4 per cent per year, which is much higher than that of the population as a whole. The woman's view of life, her say in factory and office, in recreation and public affairs, and indeed in the *mores* of the entire country, are now shaping up a new America.

This is true of the youth also, and of the youth culture that is having such an impact on the landscape, with youth clubs and conventions, the vast expansion of youth education and recreation, and the movement of youth about the countryside in prodigious numbers. Today, 91.1 per cent of immigrants are under 45 years of age. Of all persons 26 per cent are under 17 years. The median age of America is only 28 years. The young in America are a powerful force. They are of the future. They stress the image of newness. They have a strong sense of 'going places' which, for the more articulate, expresses itself in a new manifest destiny.

Yet the aged also have powers. This is likely to increase. Age expectancy between 1960 and 1975 had put a year on to the life of each man, from 66.6 to 67.6 years, and over 2 years on the life of each woman, from 73.1 to 75.3 years. The increasing affluence of the American people means that these are years of higher disposable income – hence the enormous importance in the landscape of trailer camps, cottage colonies, and apartment districts for the retired, indeed of virtually whole cities for America's senior citizens.

All these changes add up to the full society where there is much more prospect for each segment of the community to have its say and to contribute its share to a more rounded and better balanced society.

The prospects for individual living standards

The fuller society gets its strength from the better-developed individual. The United States is concentrating more and more on raising personal standards of living. Through heightening productivity per person it has been able to provide comfort, ease, health, education, and recreation for its people far in excess of most other countries in the world. What huge gains it has made since the Revolution! This is brought out if we compare it with the greatest country of that day, China, which then had 300 million people compared with America's 3 million. But although the Chinese nation grew until it has over 800 millions today, it did not show the same general progress as the United States. Growth is not only a matter of population, but of productivity. And here, America shot ahead. Compare the two nations today. China with 21 per cent of the world's population produces only 13 per cent of the world's grain; in fact, it falls short of its need, and over the last decade has had to import from 6 to 9 million tons a year, 3 to 4 million from the United States: America with 6 per cent of the world's population produces over 20 per cent of the grain. In terms of per-capita food production, America raises, with 1,005 kg a head, more than five times as much as the Chinese, with 190 kg. In the vital matters of oil and steel, China accounts for some 1 and 2.8 per cent, respectively, but America for 20 and 21 per cent of the world's total. China still relies to a surprising extent on manual labour, America on machines, and automated machines at that.

These differences result, of course, from the phenomenal per-capita output of the United States, an output that is increasing at a faster pace with each decade. For instance, between the mid-1940s at the end of the Second World War, and the mid-1970s, coal production had risen from about 5 tons to nearly 20 tons a day; while farm production had increased even more, from feeding eleven people for every farm worker employed, to feeding forty-five. Indeed, American production is so great that it can afford to switch its work force from the primary sector, now only employing 5 per cent, to tertiary activities (business, services, and service industries) supporting 65 per cent of the people. The American is now concentrating on consumption rather than production, on enjoying what he can get out of America – on having a home of his own, his own car, telephone, and other amenities, and time off for recreation and enjoyment. The fact is, America has now entered the post-industrial stage of development, where people are not out just to make a living, or even a good living, but want a good life. It is what to do with goods rather than to make goods which is now important. Retired people, the great consumers, will soon outnumber all the primary producers in America. They have a great deal to spend. Since the personal disposable income in AD 2000 will be nearly three times what it is today (the median family income will then be over $23,000 a year) people will make a tremendous demand on goods, not only from the United States, but from many parts of the world. Thus, the impact of American consumption will change geography around the globe.

America already has a larger share of the world's wealth than any other people. Americans eat better than others, with a daily food intake of about 3,300 calories, compared with 3,200 for Western Europe, 2,450 for

Japan, and 1,700–2,000 for South Asia. They have the highest standard of living in the world, with a per-capita income that is a fifth higher than Sweden, the highest in Europe, twice that of Japan, the highest in Asia, and eleven times that of Libya, the highest in Africa. These are almost unbelievable gains, especially when it is remembered that they have been made by comparatively few people in a relatively short time.

Prospects in the built environment

Most of the gains made by Americans have been poured into the city. Today 74 per cent of the people live in cities. What is more significant, 68 per cent live in large, metropolitan cities. Thus, the environment for eight out of ten growing Americans is a man-made, a *built* environment. In that built world, individuals and groups vie with each other for what they want: the city is thus an amalgam of competing differences. The result has been suburbs for the rich and downtown slums for the poor, Irish quarters and Jewish quarters, and ghettos for the Africans. Grave inequalities have developed. Yet if the American aim is the good life these should be reduced, if not made to disappear. Hence, there is a powerful move throughout America at urban renewal which will not only renew the worn-out fabric of, but create new ideas for, the American city.

All American cities have resulted from conscious planning, since they had literally to be planted in the wilderness. Many of them, like Philadelphia, were planned with the highest social motives as places for good living. Most of those built after the American Revolution were affected by the urban renewal then going on in Georgian Britain, based on neoclassical lines, including a rectilinear layout of broad streets opening out at regular intervals to beautiful squares or 'ovals'. Many American cities, like Washington, were planned by leading European architects who were able to do something much more spacious and gracious in the New World than in the Old. L'Enfant's plan for the capital was the envy of his contemporaries.

Yet, in spite of all this, the American city became warped increasingly by economic competition and the status struggle, to produce living disparities that were the despair of the planners. In fact, planning for the community interest tended to lapse in favour of development for individual gain. This does not imply that America became simply the prey of big 'developers'; almost all Americans were party to the speculation in land and property that brought about the collapse of the central areas and the explosion of the suburbs, now an overall American pattern.

Today, there is a rebirth in America of that state of mind which not only accepts but believes (to quote Weaver, (1964)) in

'the substitution of public for private decisions in the use of land

resources. The community has developed the principle, that land may be taken and used for the general benefit. Americans are no longer interested in living in a series of suburbs surrounding the ruins of their old central cities. To abandon our central cities (in the metropolitan sprawl) would be to forsake the cornerstones of our culture. Through planning and urban-renewal programs we want to revitalize the city centre',

and also control the surburban surrounds. In this way, the built-environment could offer Americans that personal well-being it now has the power to achieve. Instead of shaping people to the city, the city will be reshaped for the needs of the people. This is an exciting prospect.

Prospects for the natural environment

The making of America was from the beginning a part of desert-making; as soon as the tree was cut down and the sod broken, erosion began, floods increased, dust storms multiplied, pollution spread, and the desert was let in. Few Americans saw this, partly because they could always move on to break new ground. But the 'back to nature' movement, inspired by Thoreau's *Walden*, and Emerson's essay on *Nature*, made people not only care a lot more about nature, but become anxious that there was less and less nature to get back to! Hence, the rise of the conservation movement in the United States which is now so powerful that it is remaking the geography of the nation. Views such as those of Collin, aired in the late eighteenth century that 'Our stately forests are a national treasure' and should not be abandoned to the axe or saw, were strengthened in the mid-nineteenth century by the powerful work of Marsh who pleaded that 'some large and easily accessible region of American soil should remain as far as possible in its primitive condition. . . as an asylum where indigenous trees, plants, and beasts may dwell and perpetuate their kind'.

In the latter half of the nineteenth century action began to be taken. In 1872, national 'Arbor Day' was established to foster replanting trees. In the same year, a more positive step was made when the forest at Yellowstone was turned into a park 'for the benefit and enjoyment of the people'. In 1885 the Department of Agriculture started a Division of Economic Ornithology that was eventually to become the US Wildlife Service, and in 1886 a Division of Forestry was set up, made a separate Bureau in 1901, and now enlarged and strengthened as the US Forest Service. Still another major advance was made in 1916 with the setting up of the National Park Service. Today it controls fifty national parks, totalling over 22 million acres. In 1964 the Wilderness Act was passed to establish wilderness areas where truly wild regions of the country would be preserved, only to be reached by horseback, canoe, or on foot. Here parts of the original US

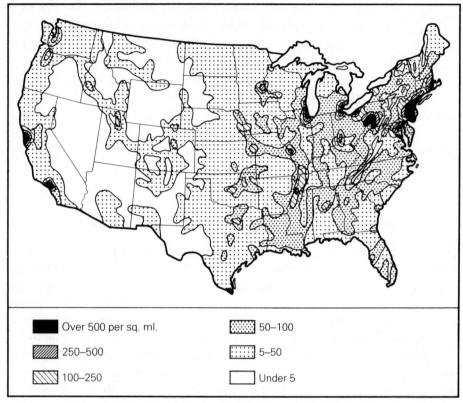

Fig. 1.2 *United States population in the 1970s.* This is the clearest reflection of how man has used the advantages and has had to respect the limits of the environment.

landscape have been kept as forever contributing to the geography of the land. Over 14 million acres of wilderness have been preserved in this way. Public rangeland, covering over 160 million acres, is also being managed for the people so as to maintain America's grasslands as a part of the new 'conservation geography'.

However, a much greater problem than preservation is resuscitation. The American way of life has put enormous pressure on the land which, in turn, has created erosion and pollution. Jeanne Davies writes:

> *One aspect of America's landscape problems is directly related to its affluence. Only a country with a high economic standard of living is afflicted with litter. In many less economically developed nations the newspapers, bottles, and cans that we throw away are carefully hoarded and re-used until they are beyond any utility. People in these countries could not imagine a place where automobiles, stores, and furniture end in a junkyard, a county's landfill, or on a city street.*

To try to prevent the rapid deterioration of its environment, the United States government eventually created the Environmental Protection Agency (EPA) guided at the highest level by the President's Council on Environmental Quality, set up in 1969. In 1970 the Environmental Quality Act gave the nation very considerable powers over the use of land, water, and other resources. The prospects along these lines are putting America in the lead in environmental improvement, providing models copied throughout the world.

Prospects for world betterment

Increasingly, the United States is using its wealth and power under a new sense of destiny to better living conditions throughout the world, recognizing that no country can solve its own problems without respect to other countries. Although General Washington, the father of the nation, advised Americans not to get entangled in foreign disputes, the United States could not, in fact, keep out, and both in the First and Second World Wars had to lend its enormous strength to restore and maintain the peace of the world. Under Roosevelt and Eisenhower, America reversed its policies and took an active part in world affairs. Extensive political alliances were strengthened by massive economic aid. The North Atlantic Treaty Organization and Marshall Aid helped to restore Western Europe to security and prosperity. The South East Asia Treaty Organization sought to do the same for areas on the opposite shores of America across the Pacific. Other treaty alliances, such as CENTRO, linking Turkey, Persia and, at one time, Pakistan, and ANZUS, joining Australia, New Zealand, and the United States, provided additional support for world peace. Finally, in the Western Hemisphere, America led in the formation of the Organization of American States (OAS) to try to prevent the disruption of the Americas from without or within.

Yet probably a far greater prospect for world peace and well-being lay in the programme of American aid in money, technology, education, and leadership which has been extended with extraordinary liberality to all members of the so-called free world. Government help is matched by private effort, through missionary societies, philanthropic organizations, and educational institutions. In some years agricultural aid programmes, which now amount to over $8 billion, cost more than the profits earned from agricultural exports. In addition, economic and technical aid grants, bank credits, loans, and other forms of help, of over $10 billion a year in the 1960s, increasing to more than $12 billion a year in the 1970s, have enabled many parts of Asia, Africa, and Latin America to revolutionize their agriculture, initiate industry, improve trade, and raise standards of living. The so-called 'Green Revolution', a major breakthrough in the production of high-yield varieties of rice and wheat, which has profoundly affected the geography of

Asia and Latin America, was inspired, devised, researched, organized, and supported by the United States, and may well be its greatest gift to mankind. Even though America has far fewer former colonies to which it might be supposed to owe an obligation than Britain, France, Belgium, or Holland, yet its total aid to the world is more than that of these ex-colonial powers combined. Thus, the United States makes an enormous impact on the social geography of the world in agricultural and urban settlement, routeways, telecommunications, power and irrigation projects, and public works, visible in the landscape.

Conclusion

All these facts reveal that social aims and ideals profoundly influence geography. Since America has been and is one of the most dynamic societies in the world, it has stamped its image on the landscape in no uncertain way. Some aspects of the American image, such as its breakaway mind, its passion for newness, and its high sense of destiny have been of particular importance in the geography of the country. They have created grave problems as, for instance, the clash of cultures between Whites and Indians, Whites and Africans, and among Whites themselves with different ethnic origins. Religious divisiveness and class divisions, together with the whole tradition of violence in America, have created marked geographical patterns. So have the attempts to solve the problems. Here, the prospects for the future suggest radical and sweeping changes in such spheres as rural resuscitation, urban renewal, the management of the environment, and betterment in the whole standard of living. These are offering prospects for a new geography – in which, not only Americans, but people helped by American aid all over the world, will benefit. The shape of this new American geography should therefore be of world-wide interest; it may well become the geography of the future.

References

Billington, R. A. (1960) *Westward Expansion, a History of the American Frontier*, 2nd edn, Macmillan N.Y., p. 210.

Crèvecoeur, J. H. St. J. de (1782:1963) *Letters from an American Farmer* (1782) Signet edn, N.Y. (1963) Letter III, 'What is an American?', pp. 60–99.

Hawthorne, N. (1851:1964) *The House of Seven Gables* (1851) Riverside edn, Cambridge, Mass. (1964), p. 269.

Jefferson, T. (1785:1964) *Notes on the State of Virginia* (1785) Harper edn, N.Y. (1964), pp. 82–3.

Smith, J. (1624:1967) *The General Historie of Virginia, New England and the Summer Isles* (1624) Harper edn, N.Y. (1967), p. 138.

Warner, W. L. (1965) *American Life, Dream and Reality*, Pheonix Books Chicago, p. 129.
Weaver, R. C. (1964) *The Urban Complex*, Doubleday, N.Y., p. 38.
Ziner, F. (1961) *The Pilgrims and Plymouth Colony*, Harper, N.Y., p. 120.

The Indian question

Introduction: the image of the Indian

Relations with the Indians were among the first things that moulded the geography of the United States: here the white man's image of himself and of the Indian, and the Indian's image of the white man and himself were of vital importance. The white man's contact with the Indian occurred during one of the greatest explosions of creativity known to man, with the rise of the Renaissance and the Age of Discovery. Europeans had combined the civilizations of Palestine, Greece, and Rome in a new order which was buoyant, optimistic, arrogant, and on the advance. Europe's great men, during the exploration and colonization of America, ranged from Columbus, through Shakespeare, to Spinoza and Velázquez: geographer, dramatist, philosopher, and painter. 'What a piece of work is man! How noble in reason, how infinite in faculty. . . .' The England that was ultimately to give rise to the United States stood at its apogee. Here, in Trevelyan's words, 'Shakespeare chanced upon the best time and country in which to live, in order to exercise with least distraction and most encouragement the highest faculties of man.'

In Shakespeare's time, Indians were still an oddity. To see so much as a wooden effigy of one, people would put out ten times the money they would offer to 'relieve a lame beggar'. The British had got their ideas from Columbus, Cabot, and Cartier and also from conquistadores like Cortes and Pizzaro. Reports varied from Indian nations with great wealth, to tribes in abject poverty; and from friendly folk to cruel monsters. In King Henry VII's reign, natives were brought from Newfoundland 'which were clothed in Beestes skinnes and ete raw fleshe, and were rude in their demeanure as Beestes'. This was in 1502–03, 100 years before the settlement of New England. During those years the view strengthened that most Indians were poor, primitive, ignorant, and vicious. This gave the Europeans an immense feeling of superiority, so that the Pilgrims did not hesitate to go to America, even though they thought it full of

> *savage and brutish men, which range up and downe, little otherwise than as wild beasts . . . being cruel, barbarous, and most treacherous, furious in their rage and merciles where they overcome; not being contente only to kill but delight to tormente men in ye most bloodie manner . . . fleaing some alive, cutting of ye members and joynts of others by peesemeale, and, broiling on ye coales, eat ye collops of their flesh in their sight whilst they live; with other cruelties horrible to be related.*

Actually, the earliest reaction of the Indian to the White was one of friendship and goodwill. His image of the white man was such as to inspire awe, admiration, and even adulation: Whites were thought of as little short of gods. In John Smith's *Generall Historie of Virginia*, etc. he said of the Susquehannocks that 'they were with much ado restrained from adoring us as gods'. He remarks on how 'civil' they were 'to give entertainment'. French and Spanish records also speak of the Indian's desire to please. Paul le Jeune, in the Jesuit Relations, stated: 'Mind is not lacking among the savages of Canada, but education and instruction. They are tired of their miseries and stretch out their hands to us for help.' Columbus said of the Indians he first met: 'They are most wondrously timorous. . . . Since they have become more assured, they are artless, and generous with what they have . . . and show us much lovingness as though they would give their hearts.' The Indians in Haiti 'believed very firmly that I [Columbus] came from the sky'.

Their timidity suggests that the Indians felt inferior compared to the white man, yet they did, in fact, treat them with great dignity, and even with a measure of sterness. This arose from a strong sense of self-respect. The Indian image of themselves (as gathered from early white accounts), was of a contained and self-controlled people, with concern for each other's needs and rights, but capable of pride and revenge. Smith wrote of the Virginia Indians, '. . . they have amongst them such government, as that their magistrates for good commanding, and their people for due subjection and obeying, excel many places that would be counted very civil'. However, Smith also calls the Indians inconstant, crafty, quick in apprehension, and cautious – as human as the rest of us!

In general, then, Whites had immense confidence in themselves and their views, and treated Indians, even at their best, as their inferiors: Indians may have justified this opinion by their initial deference to the Whites, but nevertheless, from their own sense of what men were due each other, came to expect courtesy, if not respect, from the Whites. These images profoundly affected the reactions between Whites and Indians and so influenced the geography of their relations.

Problems immediately arose as the Whites went into the land.

Should the Indians be left alone, or should they be converted and made like white men? Ought the white men to move in among them and live side by side, or should they displace them? These soon became very hot issues. Had the Indians a right to keep the white men out? By what right did Whites take over? Should Indian land be bought or fought for? If America were Europe's second chance, should the Indians be allowed to stand in the way: what was their place in the new Canaan?

The situation was aggravated by the fact that what is now the United States seemed such an empty region, open and ready for white development and settlement. This was a major reason why the Pilgrims left Holland (which had given them a refuge from persecution in England) because, as Bradford said, they looked across the Atlantic to 'those vast and unpeopled countries of America, which are fruitfull and fit for habitation, being devoid of all civil inhabitants'. Emptiness cried out to be filled!

Leacock (1951) prefaces his history of Canada with a chapter on 'The empty continent'. As he points out '. . . enormous stretches of territory were made up of unbroken forests, impassible except by lake and stream, where the voyager might wander for days without meeting or expecting to meet, the face or trace of other human beings. Even more lonely . . . were the wide savannahs, the open prairies that stretched to . . . the Rockies.' He then quotes an English traveller who, as late as 1870, wrote of the West, '". . . there is no other portion of the globe, in which travel is possible, where loneliness can be said to dwell so thoroughly". Such, and no more . . .', Leacock concludes, 'is the meaning and extent of the Indian ownership of North America.'

The emptiness of the continent seemed providential. It offered an unparalleled opportunity to those who, in Cotton Mather's famous words, fled 'the Depravations of Europe to the American Strand'. There was a chance to make a new life in new circumstances. Furthermore, in moving into the land, Whites not only found new scope for themselves but could give a better hope to the Indians. The white man was doing both himself and the Indian a favour in opening up and developing the continent! Thus, when Captain John Smith set out his reasons for settling Virginia, he said; 'So then here is a place, a nurse for soldiers, a practice for mariners, a trade for merchants . . . and that which is most of all, a business (most acceptable to God) to bring such poor infidels to the knowledge of God.' Sir George Peckam went further and urged that in addition to converting the Indians, England should bring them on 'from unseemly customs to honest manners, from disordered, riotous routs . . . to a well-governed commonwealth'.

The general idea was, then, that the Indians were of little consequence and should not impede the settlers who, as a more advanced people, had the right to take over from primitive ones, provided they shared with them the benefits of civilization. If, however, the Indians resisted, they should be put aside and their lands expropriated for better purposes. These views profoundly altered the geography of the Indians in North America.

The aboriginal geography

Part of the difficulty between White and Indian lay in their different stages of culture. It was a thousand years or more since the Whites had depended on hunting and fishing in the way that the Indians did, and they could not put themselves or their minds back into that early state. As Franklin said (though at a much later date): travel a thousand leagues west, go a thousand years back. And that was what the Europeans were doing – on coming to America they were going back to the Stone Age. No wonder they showed little patience with the Indians; they had got beyond that stage themselves centuries ago.

It is, of course, a fact that most of the Indians in what is now the United States remained quite undeveloped until the white man arrived in America. Thus, although they came late in time, most of them between 15000 and 10000 BC, they brought with them very early ideas and customs, equivalent to those of the Old Stone Age in Asia and Europe. Consequently, they did not have the technology or organization to make use of the opportunities presented to them. Quite the contrary: they were at the mercy of problems such as distance, terrain, frost, and drought, which they had to face. They did little to change the face of the land in what became the United States, though in Mexico they did evolve a considerable civilization of their own. In the semi-arid interior and on the Great Plains they tipped the balance between grassland and forest, helping the grasses to expand at the expense of trees; and in the humid and more temperate East they opened up the forest with their primitive fields and villages. But by and large they were the creatures of their environment, responding to rather than changing tundra, taiga, wood, grassland, and desert. Indian cultures, then, tended to mirror, to a remarkable degree, the natural environments which they found: in early America men very largely reflected nature. Furthermore, many wanted to keep things this way when challenged by the Whites to make more use of the land – another factor in White – Indian tension.

Most of the Indians came into the continent from Siberia, via the Bering Strait. The trail of old stone tools, in what is often called the Lower Lithic age in American archaeology, continued from Siberia up the Yukon across to the Mackenzie, then it split into several paths as the migrants fanned out. Some groups hugged the edge of the Shield and moved from lake to lake until they came to the St Lawrence. Others left the Great Lakes to drift southeast by the Mohawk–Hudson and the Ohio to the Atlantic Coast Plain, or pushed on, directly south, following the Mississippi to the Gulf of Mexico.

These were all forest lovers, who lived by hunting elk, mammoth, and bear. Others moved up the tributaries of the Mackenzie through the Rockies to the Columbia Basin and the Pacific coast, where they fished for their living. Tribes also migrated from the Columbia to the Great Basin and so to the Southwest, heading for the warmth of California. These desert dwellers made a meagre living by collecting seeds, nuts, and fruit, and trapping small animals. Still other Indians, hunters of the grassland, took the track of the Great Plains, from Alberta to Texas, living on mammoth and early kinds of bison.

All these migrations were from a narrow apex in Alaska to the broad base of the continent between the gulfs of California, Mexico, and the St Lawrence. The routes led people to fan out and get further and further away from each other: consequently, the deeper they penetrated America the more isolated they became. Doubtless this meant avoiding conflict, but it also denied them that clash of ideas which has helped to stimulate progress. They only got to know about new inventions and different techniques very slowly. They kept to their own ways for thousands of years. This background made it difficult for them to adjust to Whites, and created in European settlers an impatience with their views.

The biggest gap between them and the British (and later, the Americans) was the lack of cities. What became the United States witnessed the less developed peoples of the continent. Even the mixed agricultural and hunting economies of the East, and the fishing communities of the Pacific Northwest, were short of what the Whites regarded as civilized, while the hunting groups of the interior plains, and the food-gatherers of the desert basins, seemed quite backward.

The hunters and gardeners of the Northeast

These included such well-known peoples as the Penobscots and Pequots of New England, the Iroquois of Upper New York State, the Manhattans of Lower New York, the Susquehannocks and Delawares of Pennsylvania, the Lenape and Nanticoke of New Jersey–Maryland, and the Powhatans of northern Virginia. These Indians dwelt in villages and small towns, in clearings in the forest, with gardens where tobacco, beans, squash, and maize were grown. Most families lived in temporary dome-shaped houses of bent poles covered with bark or mats. There were small smoke-houses in which joints of game were smoked: the meat was thus preserved from going bad and could keep people until new animals were trapped. There were also sweat-houses, into which heated stones were thrust: water thrown over these created steam that helped to cleanse the body. A series of cleverly designed traps set in the forest killed bear, fox, and racoon. Weirs were built across streams and fish speared in the rapids. Fish were also caught by line and hook.

Moose and deer, and in Virginia, wood-buffalo, were killed by bow and arrow. There was little hunger, and though living was by no means easy, it was good. As Thomas Morton wrote in *New England's Canaan* (1632): 'Since it is but foode and rayment that men need . . . why should not the Natives of New England be sayd to live richly, having no want of either.' Part of their success, in Morton's eyes, was that 'they love not to be cumbered with many utensilles . . . or superfluous commodities'.

This was because they moved about a lot: men constantly banded together to go out hunting, tribes would often break up in the summer and move into the hills in separate bands to follow the game that migrated with the receding snows, and from time to time a whole settlement would be abandoned, as game was exhausted or the soils were taxed, in favour of a new location. Whites found this difficult to understand.

Such a life required a lot of space. Tribal territories were large. They were also vaguely defined – a fact that caused frequent confusion when white men negotiated for land. Population density was low. Much country, though needed for this semi-nomadic kind of life, was empty. People lived in small, widely separated centres, and fanned out in the areas between. War occasionally broke out over spheres of hunting, and young men were trained in arms. This gave a discipline to their society, which was remarked on by almost all white settlers. In the case of the Powhattans and the Iroquois, discipline was used to weld tribes together in confederations that ruled wide regions and exerted a great deal of influence. The British alliance with the Iroquois was a major factor in the defeat of France and in opening the way for American expansion beyond the Appalachians.

The Iroquois were the most advanced and well organized of the northeastern tribes. They lived in large villages, made up of long rectangular buildings housing related families, protected by high wooden palisades. Woman played a notable part; they owned the homes and gardens, and, since descent was through the female, chose the leaders. If the men chosen did not give good leadership, they could be replaced. The Iroquois were particularly ferocious in war, and revengeful upon their enemies. They used their power in the so-called Beaver wars to capture the fur trade of the Lower Great Lakes, first for the Dutch and then for the British at New York. At the end of the Revolutionary War they concluded a treaty with Washington that reserved some of their land to them in perpetuity, although most of them migrated to Canada, settling along the Grand River, Ontario.

The hunters and farmers of the Southeast

These Indians were more dependent on their crops, lived in larger settlements, and developed their crafts to a higher degree than other forest Indians. They cleared a good bit more of the forest, had farmlands that extended for miles outside the town, and planted out orchards. Their houses were well built of wood and thatch, and were neatly organized around a large square centred in a council house. Each town had its chief, and alliances of towns formed quite formidable confederations, accounting for considerable population, production, and wealth. There was a strong sense of social values, and civil authority prevailed over military.

However, in spite of a generally more sedentary life many tribes were subject to a good deal of movement. This surprised and irritated the Whites, who did not know how to deal with it. The Jesuit missionary to South Carolina, Rogel (1964) though at first praising God when he saw 'each Indian married to only one wife, in charge of his own field, and maintaining his house and rearing his children with much care', later grew frustrated because 'when the acorn harvest arrived all of them left me alone and went into the woods, each one by himself'. He saw 'little disposition in them for their conversion since they are so scattered, being without fixed abode for none out of twelve months of the year'. He wrote to the Governor, '. . . it is necessary first to give orders that the Indians join together and cultivate the land to secure enough sustenance for the whole year'.

However, the so-called Five Civilized Tribes – Creek, Chickasaw, Choctaw, Cherokee, and Seminole – soon adopted a fully sedentary, settled, agricultural form of life. They abandoned the hoe for the plough, they learned to domesticate cattle, they built saw-mills, and developed spinning and weaving. They not only emulated the white colonists but matched them in performance until the Whites, alarmed at their progress, and the rapid increase in their population, decided to push them out. As will be seen later this created major issues in White–Indian relations.

The hunters of the Plains

The Plains Indians lived a simpler and a harder life – at least until they learned from the white men the use of the horse. Population was sparse, since a large area of land was needed to supply enough game for a tribe. Even though buffalo roamed in great numbers, to hunt them on foot was difficult and dangerous. Fires were lit to stampede the herds into ravines or over cliffs, where the buffalo were killed or wounded by their precipitous fall, or could be finished off in their panic. Roosevelt, in his *Winning of the West*, was not far wrong in talking of a 'dozen savages who hunted at long intervals over a territory of a thousand square miles . . .'. The tribes were nomadic wanderers, following the seasonal migration of the game. They were extraordinarily dependent on the buffalo, wearing buffalo cloaks, using the leather for tents, ropes, and bags, and making bow-strings from the gut. They had to travel light. They lived in easily erected tents. They had little luggage. They could not carry pots around with them – their containers were leather. When they struck camp, they folded up all their movable goods, packed them on the travois, and harnessed dogs, or sometimes their women, to make the move to the next site.

When subsequently they got the horse, they became more mobile and far more lethal. They could stampede buffalo herds and shoot them down from horseback. Food and clothing were always in plentiful supply, and the Plains Indians lived well. Nevertheless, the very success at the hunt kept them from agriculture. Only the Mandans of the Missouri tried to augment their diet by cultivating maize and beans, and became semisedentary. The Sioux, Blackfoot, Sauk, Fox, Pince Nez, Cheyenne, and other tribes kept up their nomadic life. As a consequence, they seemed to the Whites to be very wasteful of land, leaving parts of their hunting grounds unused at every season of the year and often for years on end. This invited the Whites to move and take up the empty areas.

Roland (1973) has pointed out that since there 'was no chance to accumulate material possessions [on the Plains] and little prestige was attached to them, the way to renown was through prowess in hunting and courage in fighting. The important thing was the individual's exploit for glory's sake. . . .' Armed with the horse, the Plains Indian was a match for most of the early white settlers, and since the settlers killed off the Indian's game, the Indian often retaliated by killing off the settler. On the Plains were some of the worst conflicts between White and Indian.

The fishermen of the Pacific Northwest

These were among the most prosperous of Indians at the time of their discovery by the Whites. They included the Quinault, Chehalis, Nootkas, Salish, Chinooks, and Hupas. Unlike the tribes of the interior Plains, they put great stress on property and material wealth. There was, of course, a lot of natural wealth at hand, in the immense forests of Douglas fir, western cedar, and redwood, and in the hordes of salmon that spawned in the rivers, and the herring and halibut along the coast. The people had such an ample supply of food in fish, fruit, and nuts, that they did not turn to agriculture. They built stone traps and weirs to help them fish the rivers, and made long dugout canoes in their chase after halibut. They had a great array of fish spears, harpoons, and nets. With large stone-headed axes they cut down trees and erected big, roomy, solid houses of logs, roofed with bark. Cedar bark was used for manufacturing cloaks, blankets, mats, containers, rope, and snares. Copper hooks, knives, pots, and plates were signs of wealth. Population was able to grow without the threat of famine, large villages of 2,000–3,000 people were developed, in permanent sites by river or sea, and a considerable degree of specialization of labour occurred, resulting in many arts and crafts. The carving and painting of huge totem poles, and the making of painted masks, often of the most striking design, represented a high level of imagination and skill. Chiefs were proud of the arts they could display, and proved their status by the system of the Potlach in which they not only showed off, but gave away, their treasures in fantastic rites of hospitality. As Josephy (1972) points out: 'On such an occasion the chief would free or kill his slaves, cut up or throw away his large plates of copper, distribute piles of blankets, burn his store of fish wealth and perhaps his own house. The more wealth he divested himself of, the greater was his prestige and that of his clan.'

This was another Indian custom that Whites found hard to understand. It was so opposed to their own custom of saving and adding to what a man got, and of making capital out of wealth, and putting that capital to work. It seemed an extraordinary waste of resources – resources which white men could turn to such profit!

The Indians of arid America

These Indians were the last that the Americans came upon, at least in the continental USA. These were two kinds, primitive hunters and food-gatherers like the Paiute, and quite sophisticated agriculturists, using irrigation, such as the Hopi and the Pueblos. Where tribes were not aware of the riches that water could bring them, fed from eternal snows, they were very restricted by the desert environment. Such people were among the poorest, weakest, and least populous in America, making very little impact either on the land or on other folk. They lived in very small groups, constantly on the move, making only temporary shelters at their round of stops, had no pottery, wore little clothing, and possessed few tools or household utensils. Seeds, nuts, grubs, and rodents were their mainstay. They made cloaks and blankets of rabbit skins. They often went cold and hungry in the winter. When the white men came through, these Indians preyed on them, usually by the theft of horses or cattle. 'The desert Shoshones and Paiutes', Stewart (1964) writes, 'were poverty-stricken and often hungry. They had little sense of private property, and lifted what they could [from the white settlers], on the ancient principle of belly-need.' These very different views about property bedevilled White–Indian relations.

Farming, fixed settlements, arts and crafts marked the Pueblo and other Indians who discovered the value of irrigation. Throughout the Upper Grande and the Colorado numerous streams came down from mountains capped with snow. In the dry Southwest they tended to make steep-sided ravines or gorges, which then issued in broad fans into either major valleys or the sides of desert basins. By throwing a dam across the stream at the apex of the fan, and then distributing the water in channels down the widening cone, a permanent and controlled supply of moisture was available for crops of corn, beans, squash, and cotton. Turkeys were domesticated, and their feathers used for cloaks. People lived in caves on the sides of the gorges, or in house-colonies, with one set of houses built on another, made of stone or sun-baked brick, and covered with dried mud. Storage cists lined with stone slabs kept a surplus of grain through the winter. Huge pots were also built for storing grain or holding water. Shortly before their discovery by the Whites, these advanced Indians of the Southwest were expert in pottery, basket-ware, textiles, and jewellery. Their bracelets and necklaces of turquoise set in silver attracted Spanish expansion into the area, Coronado thinking that at last he was about to find the seven lost cities of Cibola which had for so long lured explorers on, beyond one horizon after another.

The Pueblo towns and their irrigated lands were highly organized, under civil and military priests. This theocracy directed everything, and made it difficult for white men's ideas to be accepted. Once again, the two cultures were very much at variance. Pueblos, Hopi, and Zunis praised communal ways, conformism, obedience, loyalty, and discipline and denigrated the white qualities of individualism, non-conformity, competition, and aggression. It was difficult for each side to understand the other.

White–Indian relations

White and Indian soon had to learn to exist with each other, but since Whites differed greatly in their ideas about the Indians, and Indians in their reaction to the Whites, it was virtually impossible to work out any overall policy to govern their relations. A few well-meaning Whites wished to treat the Indians as equals, most Whites hoped they would step aside and allow the settlers in but were ready to fight them if they showed any resistance, while some Whites were prepared to exterminate them. In the same way, some Indians were ready to become as Whites, most gave way to the Whites but only reluctantly and after a lot of argument; quite a number wished to fight it out. All these views had their champions.

Four ways of relating to the Indians were tried out, often simultaneously. These were (1) cohabitation; (2) separation; (3) extermination; and (4) assimilation. Cohabitation was attempted in early colonial times, but had largely been given up in favour of separation in late colonial and early American days. Extermination was never followed as a matter of policy, but was often practised, and was a side-effect of the Indian wars in the opening of the American West. Assimilation was increasingly seen as the way out, and has been put into effect in a concerted manner in this century.

Cohabitation

This was never very successful. It was all right in the days of fishing and the fur trade, but became increasingly difficult with the advance of agriculture, trade, and industry. Seas and lakes were unfenced and here Indian and White could fish side by side as long as the Whites got the choice of quayside bases. Similarly, when Indians learned commercial trapping they could go on with that occupation, especially in muskrat swamps, and live at or near the trading post. But where the forests and the wildlife on which the Indians depended were cut down and shot out by the Whites, then the two communities could scarcely live side by side: the Indian had to retreat with the retreat of the woodland. And in the West, as the buffalo range was fenced in by the homesteader, the Indian hunter had no chance – unless, of course, he became a farm worker or a cowboy. Attempts were made, as in the famous Stockbridge experiment, in New England, to teach the Indians to farm and have Indian and white farmers develop the land together, but they failed. Few Indians took to farming.

The trouble was: (1) the Whites saw themselves as a new Israel entering Canaan, a new chosen people going into a promised land, superior, and with a superior destiny; and (2) there was so much empty land to be taken up that the Whites felt justified – much as modern Israel in Palestine – in taking over.

The reference to Palestine is not without its point, because it occurred to John Cotton, who harked back to the days when the Jews first entered the Holy Land. Preaching from the text, 'I will appoint a place for my people Israel, and I will plant them, that they may dwell in a place of their own, and move no more', Cotton claimed that there were three ways God could make room for His people: (1) by casting out their enemies before them in lawful wars, though this 'depends on a special commission from God or else it is not imitable'; (2) by making God's people find favour with the natives and be asked 'to come and sit down with them'; or (3) by giving His people the liberty 'to inhabitate . . . wherever there is a vacant place'. The sermon comes to its crux:

> *Abraham and Isaac, when they sojourned amongst the Philistines, did not buy the land to feed their cattle, because they said* There is roome enough. *And so did Jacob pitch his Tent by Sachem. There was roome enough, as Hamar said. And in this case if the people who were former inhabitants did disturb them in their possessions, they [the Israelites] complained to the King, as of wrong done unto them: as Abraham did because they took away his well. For his right thereto he pleaded . . . his own industry and culture in digging the well. Nor doth the King reject his plea with 'what had he to doe to digge wells in their soyle?' but admitted it as a Principle in Nature, That in a vacant soyle, he that taketh possession of it, and bestoweth culture and husbandry on it, his right it is. If therefore any sonne of Adam come and find a place empty, he hath liberty to come, and fill, and subdue the earth there.*

This sermon has more to do with, or perhaps one should say did more for, American geography than almost any other factor, geology and climate not excepted. Here was the image of the American as the new chosen people, the new Israel, going into the new Canaan; and God help those who were against him! Cotton's words have been repeated again and again, and are still echoed, over 300 years later, in our own day and generation. Recently McKenna (1972) wrote: 'The savages of N. America had no right to appropriate all the vast continent to themselves, and since they were unable to inhabit the whole of these regions, other nations might without prejudice settle in some parts of them, provided they left the natives a sufficiency of land.'

Separation of Indian from White

This seemed the best way of solving the problem. To have Abraham be *among* but not *of* the Philistines never satisfied either party, as witness the bitter and prolonged wars between Israel and Philistia. To have Whites slip in among the Indians, yet not really live with them, did not work out either. Whites may have thought they could do this because there was 'room enough': much of the land appeared to be empty. And yet it was not – not for the Indian. Though he did not use the land all the time, he needed each part in its season; the ridges in the summer, the shoulders of the hills in autumn, the bottom lands in winter, and the valley terraces in spring. All observers noted this sort of movement; few seem to have understood it. Speaking of the Powhatans, an agricultural people that lived in villages surrounded by gardens, Smith wrote: 'At their hunting [seasons] they leave their habitations, and reduce themselves into companies, and go to the most desert [isolated] places with their families. . . .' Their villages were then all but empty. On the other hand, when they returned for the maize harvest, their hunting grounds were deserted.

At some time or another, then, some part of their lands would be unused, yet all parts were always considered useful, i.e. liable to be used. The Whites wanted the riverside and seaboard sites; the Indians had to retire inland or up to the hills. If they did not, they were forced to. Friction led to war. This continued well into the eighteenth century throughout the Thirteen Colonies. John Adams, writing in 1812, said, 'I can remember the time when Indian Murders, Scalpings, Depradations and conflagrations were . . . common on the eastern and northern Frontier of Massachusetts. . . .' These Indian attacks were in reprisal for the white invasion of their lands, and drew down counter-attacks from the Whites. In the Pequot War virtually the whole tribe was exterminated, and its lands were taken over by the Whites. In King Philip's War the several tribes that banded themselves together under that luckless 'monarch' were devastated, and their lands appropriated. The

The Indian question

Puritans were the fiercest exterminators of the Indians, since their faith made them regard the natives as nothing but 'limbs of Satan', but in Virginia, war against Powhatan tribes, in North Carolina against the Tuscaroras, and in South Carolina against the Yamassees, substantially reduced these people, and their lands were occupied by the Whites.

The trouble was that the Whites did *not* come upon 'unpeopled countries'. Quite the reverse: so far as the British were concerned they moved into the most populous, developed, and well-organized part of North America, north of the Rio Grande. For many Indians this had been the end of their long migration, moving down and across the continent from its Alaskan bridgehead. Here they settled down, learned agriculture, built villages, and – in the case of the Iroquois, Powhatans, Creeks, and Cherokees – leagued themselves into quite effective not to say powerful confederations. They naturally resisted the European invasion: the struggle that ensued was for some of the best parts of America.

The wars were so wearying that the British tried to solve the problem by separating the Indians from the Whites. They put the remnants of the Indian tribes east of the Appalachians into reservations, and, drawing a line down the Appalachian divide, proclaimed all the land to the west as Indian territory. This divide became known as the *Proclamation Line*, and was meant to put the two nations apart, Whites on the east, and Indians to the west. The concept of the two-nation state emerged, in which, through their apartness, each would respect the other – only it was understood that the Indian nation would be under the American state. But the idea of a two-nation country did not prove acceptable. Too many Whites wanted to press on across the Appalachians, to be stopped by the Proclamation Line. Indeed, many of even the officials regarded the line as 'a mere provisional arrangement'. De Vorsey (1961) has shown how group after group transgressed the line, particularly as the wealth of the Trans-Appalachian Plains became known. This wealth compared favourably with many parts of the east coast: in the late eighteenth century, as Henry Adams said, 'the New Englander began to abandon his struggle with a barren soil, among granite hills, to learn the comforts of easier existence in the valleys of the Mohawk and Ohio'. Although the official policy might be peace by separation, the private settler was intent on infiltration, even at the price of war.

It was at this point that Americans took over from the British. At once they were in a dilemma. They had just fought a war with the British for the freedom of the individual, and they could therefore scarcely debar the individual from using that freedom to wrest what he could for himself from the Indian: on the other hand, it was imperative to keep good relations with the Indian in an area where authority was so weak that the British were allowed to maintain their posts in the very territory they had lost, in order to keep law and order until the Americans took over.

Naturally, the Indians were confused and nervous at the new course of events. Some of them like the Senecas, the Delawares, the Cherokees, and Choctaws asked that former rights, obtained from the British, should be preserved and in 1789 the US Congress promised that: 'The utmost good faith shall always be observed towards the Indians; their land and property shall never be taken away from them without their consent; and in their property, rights and liberty, they shall never be invaded or disturbed, unless in just and lawful wars.' This sounded good but 'just and lawful wars' were often appealed to, as an excuse to go on driving the Indians from their homes.

Western space roused a sense of progress: here it was the European could at last become American, here men could do the really new, here destiny met a man. Geography awoke the image; the image made a new geography. The most powerful minds were wedded to the West – Jefferson, Jackson, Monroe, Roosevelt. Jefferson seemed to see two possibilities: the more advanced Indians might stay side by side with the Whites, but the others would be driven – and therefore perhaps ought to be helped – into remoteness; up to the mountains, out beyond the frontier, or even into Canada. 'On those who have made any progress', he wrote, 'English seductions [to take their land] will have no effect.' He instanced the Creeks who 'have good Cabins, enclosed fields, large herds of cattle and hogs, spin and weave their own clothes of cotton, have smiths and other of the most necessary tradesmen, write and read, and are on the increase in numbers'. But there were many other Indians who had made no such progress. These, 'the backward, will yield, and be thrown further back. These will relapse into barbarism and misery, lose numbers by war and want, and we shall be obliged to drive them, with the beasts of the forests, into . . . the mountains.' Rather than have this happen through war and want, Jefferson opened the way for their retreat by using his purchase of Louisiana to move the Indians across the Mississippi.

In the Old Southwest, the Cherokees and Creeks at first stood firm, resisting the claims of the Whites for more land. Their stand led to a historic judgment by Chief Justice Marshall on their behalf, the essence of which was that they were nations within the nation, and therefore entitled to their apartness in the form of separate homelands. In his summing up, Marshall stated:

> *This bill is brought by the Cherokee Nation, praying an injunction to restrain the State of Georgia from the execution of certain laws of that State which . . . go directly to annihilate the Cherokees as a political society, and to seize, for the use of Georgia, the lands of the Nation which have been assured to them by the United States in solemn treaties repeatedly made.*

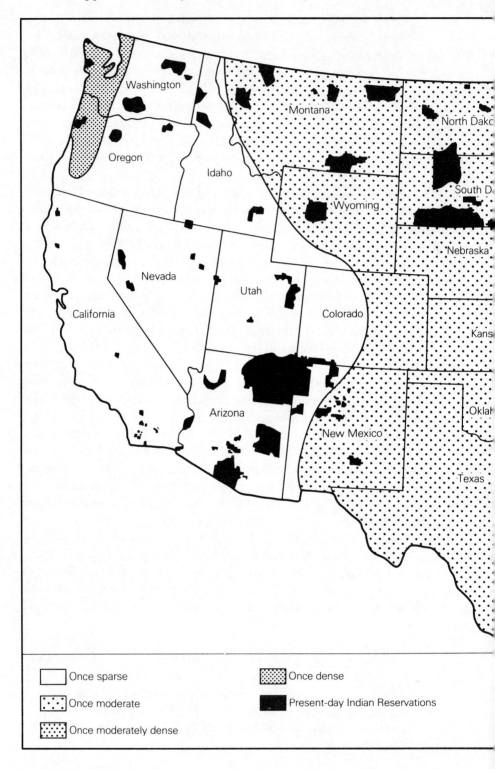

Once sparse

Once moderate

Once moderately dense

Once dense

Present-day Indian Reservations

Fig. 2.1 *Indians past and present.* The geography of American Indians has been completely reversed by US geography; where the Indian population was once moderately dense, east of the Mississippi, it is now sparse; where once sparse, west of the 'break of the plains', it is now dense by comparison.

The Cherokees, Marshall insisted, 'have uniformly been treated as a State from the settlement of our country. The treaties made with them by the United States recognize them as a people capable of maintaining the relations of peace and war. The acts of our government plainly recognize the Cherokee Nation as a State, and the courts are bound by those acts.' This had obviously galled the State of Georgia, which did not think of the Cherokee territory as in any way being equivalent to a State (such as Georgia itself had become). Marshall acknowledged this by saying that the Cherokees 'may, more correctly perhaps, be denominated a domestic dependent nation'. Nevertheless 'their territory was separated from that of any State [in this case, Georgia] within whose chartered limits they might reside, by a boundary line, established by treaty; and, within their boundary, they possessed rights with which no State [of the USA] could interfere'. He concluded: 'The Cherokee nation, then, is a distinct community, occupying its own territory, with boundaries accurately described, in which the laws of Georgia have no right to enter but with the assent of the Cherokees themselves or in conformity with treaties and with the acts of Congress.'

Here the principle of apartness, of separate but equal treatment, was given its finest and clearest statement. A country could have several nations living within it, each of which should have its rights, provided that overall unity and standards were maintained.

However, Marshall's judgment was ignored, and under President Jackson – the first western executive – the Cherokees, Creeks, and other nations of the Old Southwest were forced to move across the Mississippi. The tide of American sentiment against the Indian swept away theories like the two-nation state, White and Indian living side by side. Even Christian leaders preached dispossession. Thus, Tomothy Flint (Flint, 1964) a missionary from Massachusetts wrote in the mid-nineteenth century:

> Our industry, fixed residences, modes, laws, institution, schools, religion rendered a union with them [the Indian nations] as incompatible as with animals of another nature. Either this great continent, in the order of Providence, should have remained in the occupancy of half a million of savages, engaged in everlasting conflicts . . . or it must have become, as it did, the domain of civilized millions. It is in vain to charge upon the latter race [the Whites] results which grew out of the laws of nature and the Universal march of human events.

As a result of this, only forty small reservations were left in the whole of America east of the Mississippi, including a few for the last remnants of the Cherokee, Choctaw, Creek, and Seminole, and a few more for the Iroquois, but negligible bits and pieces for other groups.

Since this area had been the most populous in Indian America, north of the Rio Grande, before the white men came, the white invasion completely reversed the geography of this immense region (see Fig. 2.1). The Indian presence was gone. The social geography of America was wholly changed.

Extermination of the Indians by the Whites

War and want, Jefferson said, would put an end to most of the Indians. This kind of fatalistic attitude spread to become in a sense an answer to the Indian problem. That problem would disappear with the disappearance of the race. However, a few Whites went further and tried to remove the Indian. Many individuals decided that separation or assimilation were not enough: whatever the government policy was, they would deal with the Indian in their own way. To these men, used to shooting things out among themselves, it was nothing to shoot an Indian. In the words of Guthrie's pioneers in *The Way West* 'the Indian was no different from a varmint'. Whites shot at them as they might at wolves. Brackenridge spoke of 'those animals, vulgarly called Indians'. He wrote scornfully of the Indian's right to the soil, or of the authority of the chief to give Whites title to Indian land. 'I would as soon admit a right in the buffalo to grant lands as in any of the ragged wretches called chiefs and sachems. What would you think of going to a big lick [where beasts collect to lick saline water] and addressing yourself to a great buffalo to grant you land?'

This equation of Indians with animals grew, of course, from the white man's image of himself as the earthly paragon. That image was the problem, and not the Indian: from that image flowed the drastic geography that sought to eliminate the Indian from the scene.

In Jessamyn West's (West, 1975) novel, *The Massacre of Fall Creek* – which she claims was based on historic documents – she has a white man, George Benson, scorn Indians who stood in his way. '"They're animals", he said, "They're worse than animals. Animals don't torture each other. . . . Nothing's safe as long as they lurk around. There's land and to spare west of here."' The Bensons had come over the Appalachians into the Ohio Basin, which they were taking over as their own, pushing the Indians out. '"What are they doing", Benson goes on, "still squatting right here on our doorstep? This is our home now, not their hunting ground. They ought to be given their walking papers, and the only walking papers they understand is lead."' He urged another white neighbour, Jud, to help him push the Indians out or eradicate them. Jud was of the same mind. He upbraided chief Red Cloud for hunting so close to the Whites. Red Cloud retorted:

> *'We were here before you were born.' Jud didn't waste breath on this old argument: who was here first, cut no ice. What cut ice was who would be here last. Why couldn't the Indians see this. They could die in*

their tracks saying, 'We were here first.' Did they expect white men who
had never owned an acre or been allowed to run a deer to go back,
hangdog, to an English squire and say, 'We've come home. Somebody
was there first'? No, siree! They couldn't push the Squire around, but
. . . they could push the Indian. And if he wouldn't push, why, shoot
him.

But to turn from novels, even if they should be based on history, to
facts. There are many records of the ordinary white person simply shooting
the Indian out of his way. For instance, a story of Kit Carson comes to mind,
in which he describes how a group of white men, thrusting into the
Sacramento Valley, heard that they might be ambushed. They therefore took
another path. Here they ran across a lone Indian who stood in their way. This
man

commenced firing arrows at us very quickly. We retreated beyond the
range of his arrows when I dismounted and, taking deliberate aim, fired
at him. The shot took effect, and he was quickly scalped. He had a fine
bow and a beautiful quiver of arrows, which I afterwards presented to
Lieutenant Gillespie. He was a brave Indian and deserved a better fate,
but unfortunately he had placed himself on the wrong path.

A somewhat similar story is told by George R. Stewart (Stewart, 1964) in his
The California Trail where he describes a particular group of wagons

destined for trouble. With them was John Greenwood who had a
consuming desire to kill an Indian. On September 6, as the group were
riding along, an Indian suddenly stood up from the sage brush,
frightening John Greenwood's horse, which reared and almost threw
him. John was furious at being humiliated and cried out he would kill
the Indian. There was a moment's confusion. John seized the rifle; the
others protested; the Indian raised his hand in sign of friendship;
someone called to him in alarm; sensing trouble, he turned to scuttle off.
But the rifle spoke, and the Indian fell, face forward.

The Indians were in the wrong path. They stood in the way of
'manifest destiny'. They obstructed 'the new order of men'. The American
image had no place for them, other than as the flotsam of the receding tide, to
be swept aside.

In 1857 the policy was announced that Indians should cede their
general entitlement to land in return for specific reserves, together with
federal grants and services. It was stated that 'reservations should be
restricted so as to contain only sufficient land to afford the Indians
comfortable support by actual cultivation, and should be properly divided
and assigned to them, with the obligation to remain upon and cultivate the
same.' Huge Indian territories were carved up into small reservations and

once more the geography of the Indian was completely changed.

However, although Jefferson had warned long ago that the Indians were being 'reduced within limits too narrow for the hunter's state' and that therefore 'humanity enjoins us to teach them agriculture and the domestic arts', this effort had not gone very far, and a great number of the Indians were still, by the mid-nineteenth century, hunters and nomads. A lot of them would not be confined to the reservations, but still tried to hold on to their hunting lands or, if forcibly herded into reservations, often broke out.

This 'recalcitrance' on their part infuriated many Whites, and gave them the excuse to compel the Indians by force of arms to go into and remain in the reservations assigned. When they refused, tension mounted, and tempers ran high. Whites would not tolerate Indians using land, as hunters, which could be turned over with much more profit to farmers. 'The Indian will not labour [i.e. plough] and he should give up the land to those who will work it. The tools to the man who not only can but will use them!' This common idea was spelled out at the highest level by President Monroe in his famous statement:

> The hunter-state can exist only in the uncultivated desert. It yields [elsewhere] to the greater force of civilized population; and of right it ought to yield, for the earth was given to mankind to support the greater number of which it is capable; and no tribe or people have a right to with-hold from the wants of others, more than is necessary for their support and comfort.

Here was the white man's charter for dispossession.

It was out of this situation that general talk of extermination started to rise. Those Indians who refused to be confined to their reservations, but who remained as nomads and hunters on land that was fit for farming, were hunted down. The saddest chapter of White–Indian relations came to be written. 'The people who rejoice in the prospect of extermination', as Dunn put it in his now famous *Massacres of the Mountains*, 'in the belief that "the only good Indians are dead ones" now came to the fore.' That quotation was not from the mouth of some common ignoramus, but from the lips of a high-ranking officer, General Sheridan. (Attributed to a speech at Fort Cobb.)

It was in the Mountain West that trouble came to the boiling point. Here most of the Indian hunting lands whose bounds had been quite vague, were cut down to specific reservations. Many Apaches refused to give up their traditional freedom and be ponded into reserves, particularly as these were too restricted and often in poor country. They fought for their rights bitterly. As a result 'people who have been willing to extend sympathy and assistance to other Indians, have stood aghast at the murderous work of the Apaches, and given their opinion that nothing but the extermination of the tribe could ever rid the country of a constant liability to outrage and devastation'. Both on the Mexican and on the American side the call went out to exterminate those Apaches who would not conform to the law. The Mexican State of Chihuahua 'promulgated a law offering $100 for the scalp of every Apache warrior, $50 for the scalp of a squaw, and $25 for that of a child'. This hardly differed from the wolf-bounty offered in ranching counties! When General Carleton (Hawgood, 1963) took over the American side of the frontier, in 1862, he 'devoted his attention to the subjugation of the Indians.' He required the Navaho–Apaches to go to a reservation at the Bosque Redondo, on the Pecos River. His message to them was clear: 'Go to the Bosque Redondo, or we will pursue and destroy you. We will not make peace on any terms.' The natives were forced to comply, or else be shot. Many hid themselves in the mountains. The orders then went out to each command: 'The men are to be slain whenever and wherever they can be found. The women and children may be taken prisoners. . . .' Carleton made a league with the Mexican governor, saying, '"If your excellency will put a few hundred men into the field . . . we will either exterminate the Indians or so diminish their numbers that they will cease their murdering and robbing propensities and live at peace." The war was conducted on strictly extermination principles.'

The 'greater force of a civilized population', to use President Monroe's term, came to win out, but often in the most barbaric ways! Naturally, Indians resisted these tactics fiercely, and then even fiercer retaliation was called out from the Whites. Massacres occurred on both sides. One of the worst took place at Sand Creek, in New Mexico, on 29 November 1864. In the enquiry afterwards, Lieutenant Connor testified as follows:

> *About daybreak we came in sight of the camp of the friendly Indians aforementioned, and were ordered by Colonel Chivington to attack the same, which was done. The command of Colonel Chivington was composed of about 1,000 men; the village of the Indians consisted of from 100 to 130 lodges or . . . from 5–600 souls, the majority of which were women and children. In going over the battleground the next day I did not see a body of man, woman, or child but was scalped, and in many instances their bodies were mutilated in the most horrible manner. I heard one man say that he had cut out a woman's private parts and had them for exhibition on a stick. Other men had cut out the private parts of females and stretched them over their saddle-bows, or wore them over [the peaks of] their hats while riding in the ranks. . . .*

The last great conflict was perhaps the saddest of them all, ending in a massacre of a branch of the Sioux at Wounded Knee. After the assassination of Sitting Bull, this tribe had left with its chief, Big Foot, to seek a refuge in an unsettled district called Pine Ridge. The US government sent out word to apprehend them, and ordered Big Foot to a military prison at Omaha. The Indians were easily rounded up. They pitched camp in a valley, with the US soldiers on the ridge. The Indians were told to hand in their arms. Most of them did so, but one or two disobeyed. When their guns were seized one of them went off. The shot led to a panic, and the soldiers fired into the mob, killing men, women and children. Long after, Black Elk, a survivor, said: 'I did not know then how much was ended. When I look back now . . . I can see the butchered women and children lying heaped and scattered all along the crooked gulch. And I can see that something else died there in the bloody mud. A people's dream died there. The nation's hoop is broken and scattered. There is no center any longer, and the sacred tree is dead.'

The assimilation of the Indian by the White

The centre had died. The idea of nationhood had gone. The nation's hoop, the binding force of belonging to a nation, was broken. Nothing could have seemed truer than these prophetic words. The Indians became split up into comparatively small and isolated reservations, away from each other and from the mainstream of American affairs. They were so reduced in numbers that by the end of the nineteenth century there were less than 250,000. New York City, with a population of 2 millions at that time, had eight times as many people!

Few Americans, of course, had ever believed in extermination, but most were relieved when the Indian simply began to vanish. A different attitude started to grow up, in which it was hoped the Indian could be integrated with the White in the general life of the country.

There were good examples of this having happened over time and in different parts of America. Quite a number of Six-Nation Indians in up-state New York had turned to white man's farming, lived in white man's houses, and worshipped in the white man's faith. Moreover, many individual Indians were leaving the reservations and living in the growing towns like Rochester and Buffalo where there was a great demand for labour. Indian pickers helped in the New York fruit belt.

Perhaps more significant was the way in which the Creeks and Cherokees developed. Forced off their original lands at last by the 1830 law, they moved to the newly formed Indian territory of Oklahoma. Here they started afresh, building up farming communities again, although in a much drier climate. Gradually their population increased until there were over 56,000 when, in 1901, they accepted the offer of becoming American citizens. A few years later, in 1907, Oklahoma became a fully fledged State of the Union, and the Indians played their part in its development. 'Since then', as Roland (1973) points out, 'the Indians have become fully integrated: many hold public offices, and all have a voice in community affairs through their votes. Their children attend public school; a good number of them go to college and to careers as doctors, lawyers, and businessmen.'

Assimilation was a move towards togetherness by both Indian and White. Many Indians were attracted by the good wages to be earned by working on ranches and farms, and in city depots and mills. Others wanted the white way of life with its freedom for the individual to take his own path and to go as far as he could go. Still others envied the education which for the white man seemed to be the key to advancement. For some it was simply discontent at the cramped and confined kind of life on the reservation. All too frequently Indians eked out a very lean and restricted living by reliance on government grants. There were cases where groups 'passed their time moping in their tents, while barely existing on government welfare. In the circumstances what hurt the band was the deterioration that comes with nothing to do, the loss of dignity and the loss of purpose.' (Haycock, 1972.) Those who sought something different, went to work 'outside', or eventually left to live with the Whites.

Meantime, white men increasingly felt that the separation of the races was no real solution to the problem of White–Indian relations. After the Civil War 'the Whites began to press systematically for Indian integration'. In this they were affected by moves for black integration. Having fought a war to give the Negroes full rights as American citizens, the Union realized it could hardly do less for the Indian. Moreover, there was a strong move to Americanize immigrants by having them learn English, follow American ways, and live among American people. Why not do the same with Indians?

It was not enough to have Indians learn English at reservation schools, though this began to happen in the late 1880s. In 1879, Richard Pratt started the Carlisle Indian School in Pennsylvania, where Indian children were brought in to a white settlement and were boarded in white peoples' homes. Similar schools sprang up elsewhere and tried to make good white men of the Indians.

Meanwhile, at a higher level, major changes were happening. In 1871 Congress decided not to recognize the Indians any more as independent nations. Perhaps if Indians lost their sense of separate nationhood, they would become absorbed into the American nation. Congress next tried to shed its special responsibility for Indians by devolving these upon the states. The idea of a two-nation country was given up. Indian communities were to think of themselves as part of their local society.

Indians still lived and worked as groups. But they could only be Americans as individuals. If their dependence on the group were replaced by self-reliance they would the more easily accept the American way. The strength of America was in individual liberty; its success, in liberating individual initiative. To reach this goal among Indians it was necessary to break the traditional modes that limited the autonomy of the individual. The American image of himself as the new man wanted to make new men of the Indians. In 1884, the Coke Bill was presented to Congress claiming 'that the best method of placing the Indian on a right footing among us, and patient effort to accomplish this result, have united in the belief that the allotment of land to individual Indians by secure title would prove one of the most powerful agencies in the advancement of the race'.

Here was a proposal to change the entire geography of Indian settlement, breaking up the land communally held and managed by the Indians, and allotting it in severalty, that is, among the several individuals comprising the group. Land in severalty had long ago broken up the feudal system; it might lead to the demise of the Indian pattern. This was justified in terms of ideals that had made Americans out of Europeans. Had not Crèvecoeur said Americans were different in that 'we are all animated with the spirit of an industry which is unfettered and unrestrained, because each person works for himself'. Jefferson had written, '. . . before the establishment of the American States nothing was known to history but the man of the old world, crowded within limits either small or overcharged, and steeped in the vices which that situation generates. But here everyone may have land to labor for himself. . . .' Steeped in this image, the promoters of the Coke Bill could not but argue, 'The great mass of men work from the imperative necessity for self-support. . . . We have placed the Indian . . . in such a position that he has neither the necessity for self-support nor any proper protection in the result of his labour.'

Although the Coke Bill was not enacted – one of its clauses would have allowed Indians not in reservations to claim individual farms from the public domain, a claim that was much resisted – similar measures came into effect under the Dawes Severalty Act of 1887. Shortly after this, the attempted breakup of the Indian reserves began. Each Indian household was allotted the 160 acres assigned to white homesteaders, became subject to the land laws of its state, and was regarded very much as any and every other American citizen. The US government ceased to pay out the tribal handouts to the new landowners, who were 'left to take care of themselves'.

However, although the Dawes Act did in a sense make white men out of Indians, it still left them by themselves. True, Indian landowners often sold out, and, with the proceeds, moved to town: white speculators also bought up Indian allotments. But the kind of assimilation where a separate Indian geography, even if Americanized, would have disappeared altogether in favour of a complete mix of Indian and White, did not take place.

Indians did succeed in making use of their land in white men's ways, but the result of this success was to add to their problems: it made them more populous, and thus crowded them together in their own areas, more than ever. By the early twentieth century the Indian population started to rise, quite dramatically, and Indian lands began to be overpopulated. The Indian Reorganization Act of 1934 helped those Indians still staying on their lands to educate themselves to white men's standards and to form chartered companies and trade for themselves. This certainly helped, and economic development went ahead. The Navahos struck oil, and also started irrigation works. The Sioux improved their grazing lands and leased them out to individual stock growers. The Seminoles and Apaches made tourist centres of their reserves. But this was not the same as moving in among, and becoming assimilated by, Americans.

During the Second World War many Indians moved into white towns to get jobs in war industries. This started off a major drift from the reservation, and from the Indian allotment, into the white community. In 1948, a *relocation programme* was inaugurated by the federal government to give aid to individual Indians in the American West moving into cities like Denver, Los Angeles, and San Francisco. In 1951 this was expanded into a general relocation plan, and cities like Chicago, Salt Lake City, and Oakland were assisted in giving employment and housing to Indians and their families. Thousands of Indians took this opportunity of getting established among the Whites. At last assimilation had come: or had it?

Self-assertion by Indians

Operation relocation soon met with Indian resistance. Many Indians suddenly grew aware of what this meant for their culture: the American Indian would vanish from America to become an Indian-American. A strong surge of self-assertion stopped the atomization of Indian geography, and its gradual disappearance, subsumed in the lands and settlements of the American majority. A fierce upsurge of nativism occurred, with the natives themselves wanting to be different and apart.

Actually, of course, there had long been resistance to assimilation; the new movement, spearheaded by Red Power, was an old cry. In Grinnel's *Pawnee Hero Stories* he recorded a conversation with a Pawnee chief about early contacts between Indian and White. The chief began:

> *I heard long ago there were no people in this country except Indians.*
> *Before I was born . . . men that had white skins visited us. A man came*
> *from the Government. He wanted to make a treaty with us, and give us*
> *presents; blankets and guns and flints and steel knives. The Head Chief*
> *told him that we had no need of these things. He said, 'We have our*
> *buffalo and our corn. These things the Great Spirit gave to us and they*
> *are all we need. See this robe. It keeps me warm, even in winter. I need*
> *no blanket.'*

The white men had with them some cattle and the Head Chief said,
'Lead out a heifer here on the prairie!' They led her out and the Chief,
stepping up to her, shot her through behind the shoulder with his arrow,
and she fell down and died. Then the Chief said, 'Will not my arrow
kill? I do not need your guns.' Then he took his stone knife and skinned
the heifer and cut off a piece of fat meat. When he had done this he
said, 'Why should I take your knives? You see, my brother, that the
Great Spirit has given us all that we need; the buffalo for food and
clothing; the corn to eat with our dried meat; bows, arrows, knives and
hoes; all the implements which we need for killing meat or cultivating
the ground. Now go back to the country from whence you came. We do
not want your presents and we do not want you to come into our country.'

It was a far cry from this to the situation in the mid-twentieth century, described in *Time* (August 1960) where it was stated that: 'Most Indians have never seen a horse except in the movies, and most are afraid of buffalo and wouldn't know how to butcher one.'

The contrast between past and future began to worry many thinking Indians. They certainly wanted to benefit from the white man's life, and, for example, go to the movies, but they did not want to lose their own heritage. The result has been a new assertion by the Indian of his image.

One sign of this is an awareness of his identity through his cause and tradition and race as a whole. In *Time* (19 May 1967) it was stated that '... for the first time Indians have begun to think of themselves not as members of disparate tribes, but as a single group.' In this, they see themselves as a distinctly underprivileged group in a society which is the most affluent in the world. After a lot of pressure, this was at last recognized by the Whites. For instance, President Lyndon Johnson (Johnson, 1967)

acknowledged that Indians are the most impoverished section of the
American population. 90 per cent of their housing is substandard;
unemployment is about 50 per cent; the high school dropout-rate is 60
per cent; the income for reservation Indians is one third of the national
average; and finally, the average life expectancy of reservation Indians is
forty-two years, in contrast with a national average of sixty-two. The
President pledged to offer new opportunities for Indians.

Later, this was turned into a policy to build up the reservations as active centres of Indian life. In 1971, an Indian, Louis R. Bruce, was named for the first time as head of the Bureau of Indian Affairs. The geography of the Indian was to be that of self-determination. Each Indian group was resuscitated and given power to take over the administration of any federally supported project within its jurisdiction.

As before, however, there has been more talk than action, and hence Indians have tried to activate affairs by bringing their wants and needs sharply before the Whites. Violent incidents have highlighted their determination, such as the occupation of Alcatraz Island, America's most hated gaol, in 1969-71; the invasion of the Bureau of Indian Affairs in Washington in 1972; and most critical (because most symbolic of all) the bitter stand at Wounded Knee in 1973. Indians demanded a renegotiation of the Indian treaties with a return of lands lost to them since the original treaties were made between Indians and the United States. They also wished to democratize tribal government and receive federal aid directly instead of through federal officials. And finally, for those Indians off the reservations who were living in Indian ghettos in white cities, they called for proper training, work, and housing programmes, fully the equivalent of white ones. The *American Indian Movement* was formed in 1968 to achieve these and other aims. It soon became a militant pressure group that, while it achieved much, also gave much offence. Not least it offended some of the tribal leaders. In 1973 the Chairman of the Oglala Sioux threatened to throw the AIM out if they interfered with the running of his reservation. The challenge was taken up by the activists, who surged into Wounded Knee, the very site of the last of the Indian massacres. The federal authorities were at once involved in trying to restore peace, but were presented with the demands for the renegotiation of the Sioux treaty of 1868, and for the acceptance of equal relationships between Indian nations and the US government.

Thus, Indians are asserting their right to an independent separate existence, seen in a geography of voluntary apartness, as they try to revive the nations of the past, and at the same time develop a new consciousness of the Indian race as a whole.

Society and geography

Throughout this long history, social forces have worked themselves out in geographical patterns.

Americans have created a geography of the Indian very different from what prevailed in the days before the Discovery. After taking over from the British, they drove west, expanding the white frontier at the expense of Indian territory. Hence, they took over most of the Indian country and used it for white settlement. As a result, they entirely reversed the aboriginal geography of what became the USA.

To begin with they adopted the British colonial policy of a two nation state, dividing the country up into settlers' land and Indian territory. However, they kept on reducing Indian territory from (1) the crest of the Appalachians, 1783; to (2) the Ohio River, 1798; to (3) the Mississippi River, 1803; to (4) the Rocky Mountains, 1845.

With the drive of settlers to Oregon, 1845, and California,

1849-50, the concept of keeping the West for Indians was given up. Indians were forced to surrender a general title to the land, and to accept restricted areas, or reservations, where they had to live. Separation of Indian from White became the guiding principle. But squatters, mining companies, and road and railroad builders frequently invaded Indian reservations, even where these were delimited by treaty. Consequently, most US treaties with Indians were broken. Indian lands became very fragmented.

A mass redistribution of Indians occurred, which wholly altered the balance of Indian population. The most populous parts, aside from the small area round Puget Sound, had been in the East, especially in (1) the Lower Great Lakes and Mohawk Valley; (2) the mid-Atlantic Coast Plain; and (3) the plains flanking the Southern Appalachians. These well-settled and comparatively well-developed regions were almost completely emptied of their native inhabitants, except for remnants of historic federations and small groups of 'Christian' Indians. A forced migration of Indians took place where tribes were removed to areas utterly remote from their homelands, first across the Ohio and Maumee, then across the Mississippi, next the Missouri, and finally the Rockies.

West of the Rockies lay a mountainous and desert region very thinly settled by rather primitive Indians. This area is now the principal district of Indian settlement, with the largest Indian nation left, that of the Navahos, over 100,000. Hence, Americans have quite reversed the pattern of Indian distribution.

The United States at first continued to accept separate development, but tried to make it more equal, by 'bringing on' Indians in their reservations through ranching, agriculture, arts, and crafts. Subsequently, they tried to break down the idea of independent Indian nations, and to assimilate the Indians with the Whites, especially in their relocation policy of helping Indians off the reservations into white cities.

Operation relocation is resisted by many Indians in favour of a voluntary apartness in which Indians, while accepting all the technological and organizational advancement made by Whites, still retain their own culture. They want to make a go of their reservations, renegotiate former treaties, get back lost land where they can, and devlop their own pursuits. They would then hope to influence white culture through their own, and thus evolve a multicultural country, with each race maintaining its own image and sphere, but trying to create an image for America as a whole.

References

Carleton (1963) In Hawgood, J. A. (ed.) *Massacre of the Mountains*, Dunn, J. P. (1886) Eyre & Spottiswoode London, pp. 310, 314-15, 333, 335-6.

De Vorsey, L. (1961) *The Indian Boundary in the Southern Colonies, 1763–1775*. Univ. N. Carolina Pr. Chapel Hill, W.C., pp. 62-4.

Flint, T (1964) In Washburn, W.E., *The Indian and the White Man*, Doubleday Anchor, N.Y., p. 126.

Haycock, K. G. (1972) *The Image of the Indian*, Waterloo Lutheran U. Waterloo, Ont., p. 81.

Jefferson, T. (1785:1964) *Notes on the State of Virginia* (1785) Harper edn (1964) N.Y., p. 91.

Johnson, Lyndon (1967) In Oswalt, W.H., *This Land Was Theirs*, Wiley London, p. 515.

Josephy, A. M. (1972) *The Indian Heritage of America*, Jonathan Cape London, p. 76.

Leacock, S. (1951) *Canada, the Foundations of Its Future*, Seagrams Montreal, pp. 19-22.

McKenna, J. A. J. (1972) In Haycock, op. cit., p. 69.

Rogel, J. (1964) In Washburn, op. cit., p. 173.

*****Roland, A.** (1973) 'The first Americans', *Dialogue*, Vol. 6, No. 2, pp. 19, 18.

*****Stewart, G. R.** (1964) *The California Trail*, Frontier Lib. London, pp. 99, 96.

*****West, J.** (1975) *The Massacre at Fall Creek*, N.Y. Harcourt Brace–Fawcett, pp. 31, 10.

---

*The sequence of page numbers at the end of the reference corresponds to the sequence of quotations in the text.

The Negro problem

No better case exists of the way in which society makes geography than the negro problem of America. The Negro was transplanted from Africa to the Americas against his own wish by the will of the Whites who used him to open up and exploit the land. Even after Britain gave up the system the United States carried it on. The freedom which meant so much to Americans made free with the American Black and created what became an almost insupportable situation. Here again the white man's image of himself as destined through his superiority to govern the New World made him do with it what he liked, even at the expense of others.

The introduction of the Negro and the rise of slavery

In a sense it was because the Whites could not solve the Indian question that they brought the negro problem on themselves. In early colonial days the settlers had tried to use Indians as workers and servants, even to the extent of making slaves of those rebel Indians who were captured and subdued. But the Indian hated manual labour. He was too proud and independent to remain a slave. He could always flee into the forest and join his fellows, in the freedom of the wilderness. Nathaniel Hawthorne contrasted the strict modes and set ways of the Puritan township with the 'untamed forest' where people could 'roam as freely as the wild Indians, whose customs and life were alien'. The colonist therefore turned to the negro slave as the answer to his needs. Transplanted to N. America, Negroes became a significant part of the American landscape. This was especially true of the Southern Colonies where many settlers were landed gentry who disdained work, but who could only run their plantations with a great deal of labour.

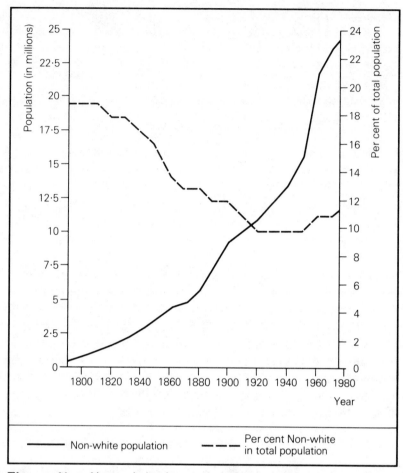

Fig. 3.1 *Non-white population from 1790 to 1975.* Non-white population at the founding of the United States was low in number but fairly high in percentage. As Indians decreased, Negroes grew in number and now make up the bulk of the nearly 24 million non-whites. However, their percentage has remained low in the twentieth century owing to white immigration and the growth of the white native-born population.

Here again, differences in mind made all the difference to the landscapes concerned. The mental climate of the North did not welcome 'gentlemen', in the sense of men unused to work; it favoured those who would pitch in and help in one capacity or another. Work was the air they breathed.

Work, for the night is coming
When man's work is done.

The Puritan leader, Robinson (see Miller and Johnson, 1963) went so far as to say, 'However great or rich soever, a man could not keep a good conscience before God who made labour but an accessorie, and not a principal and that which takes up his ordinate time.'

The reverse might have been said of the Virginian gentleman who eschewed work on principle, and took up his 'ordinary' time with the social round. 'To him the practice of hospitality is at once a duty, a pleasure, and a happiness', said the French visitor, Chevalier (1836). 'He is better able to command men than to conquer nature and subdue the soil.' These latter tasks were left to the slaves. As Jefferson (1785:1964) explained, in his *Notes on Virginia*, 'In a warm climate, no man will labor for himself who can make another labor for him. This is so true, that of the proprietors of slaves a very small proportion indeed are ever seen to labor.'

The appeal to climate as a justification for the use of Africans was often made. (Had it been sustained, the case for social geography would have been less effectual: but it failed.) The Whites in the Southern Colonies came from Britain where the summer temperature averaged between 60° and 65°F; the Blacks were brought from Africa where all-year temperatures were above 65° and hot season conditions were over 90°F. *Ergo*, Blacks could stand heat better than Whites. Jefferson claimed that, constitutionally, they were better able to work and survive in a hot climate. They had more or larger sweat glands than the Whites and their bodies could thus find greater relief from excessive heat. 'This greater degree of transpiration renders them tolerant of heat and less so of cold than the whites.' Such an idea spread and became a firmly held conviction. It greatly helped to create an image in at least the Southern mind which was to shape the scene in a profound way. Debow implied that one reason why the South had drawn so few immigrants from Europe, particularly when the Gulf States were being opened up, was the hot climate; most Europeans avoided the heat. Those Whites who had become native to the region thus had no pool of immigrants to draw on, but had to rely on black labour. Indeed, it became the general view throughout the South, as Harvey Wish (Wish, 1950) indicates, that 'the slave was an indispensable source of labor, suited for the enervating 90 degrees in the shade of the Southland'.

This became expressly stated in the Dred Scott case, involving a Missouri-born Negro who had lived for a considerable time in the free North. On his return to his native state, Scott was treated as a slave again. He appealed against this, but Chief Justice Taney (US Govt., 1857) turned down his plea. In doing so he felt bound to explain why slavery was necessary in the South, and why the Southern States could not come to regard Negroes as ordinary citizens of a state, with a right of appeal. Claimed the Judge:

> *When we look to the condition of the negro race in several States, at the time the U.S.A. was formed, it is impossible to believe that these rights [of State citizenship] were meant to be extended to them. It is very true that in that portion of the Union where the labor of the Negro was found to be unsuited to the climate and unprofitable to the master [i.e. the*

North] but few slaves were held at the Declaration of Independence; and when the constitution was adopted, it [the practice of slavery] had entirely worn out in one of them, and measures had been taken for its gradual abolition in several others. But this change had not been produced by any change of opinion in relation to this race; but because it was discovered, from experience, that slave labor was unsuited to the climate and production of these States: for some of the States, where it had ceased to exist, were actively engaged in the slave trade, procuring cargoes of slaves on the coast of Africa, and transporting them for sale to those parts of the Union, where their labor was found to be profitable and suited to the climate. . . .

In fact, however, slavery had much less to do with the climate of the country, than with the climate of the mind. A great number of poorer Whites *did* work in the heat, and worked far more effectively than the Negro. Indeed, it was claimed that one White could do the work of three Negroes in the field. Black America resulted from mental outlook, not environmental decree. The landscape of slave lines, and slave coffles, slave markets, and slave gangs arose from the mindscape of master ownership, use, and supervision.

The image of white supremacy rapidly grew up. As McKitrick (1963) points out in his *Slavery Defended* not only the owners but churchmen and scientists believed in a basic gulf between the two races. 'The institution of Slavery', the Rev. Stringfellow is quoted as saying, 'has received the sanction of the Almighty.' The sanction of science was no less emphatic. 'The species of the genus homo', wrote Dr Cartwright, 'are not a unity but a plurality . . . [in which] the black species was so unlike the others – Caucasian and the Mongolian – as to be . . . like the brute creation.' The danger of questioning slavery 'lies in the ignorance of Scripture, and of the Natural History of the negro'. Even as rational a person as Jefferson, surely one of the adornments of the Age of Enlightenment, found himself persuaded by his own argument to claim that, on balance ' . . . the blacks, whether originally a distinct race, or made distinct by time and circumstances, are made inferior to the whites in the endowments both of body and mind'. He went on to say that this helped explain, although it should not justify, slavery. Even when he urged upon his fellows the gradual emancipation of the blacks from slavery, he seemed loath to accord blacks that kind and degree of freedom where, for example, they could marry white women. 'When freed', he wrote, 'the black slave is to be removed beyond the reach of mixture.' Somehow or other he was to be kept from 'staining the blood of his master'.

It was when personal issues like this were raised that emotion clouded the mind. Jefferson was distressingly aware of this, particularly when he thought how emotions were passed on. He wrote:

The whole commerce between master and slave is a perpetual exercise of the most boisterous passions, the most unremitting despotism on the one part, and degrading submissions on the other. Our children see this, and learn to imitate it. The parent storms, the child looks on, catches the lineaments of wrath, puts on the same airs in the circle of smaller slaves, gives a loose to the worst of passions, and thus nursed, educated, and daily exercised in tyranny, cannot but be stamped by it with odious peculiarities.

For these reasons Jefferson suggested a scheme by which the slaves should be repatriated to Africa, and their place taken by hired labour imported from Britain. He became anxious at the growing frustration and anger of the Negroes. 'The spirit of the slave', he warned, 'is rising from the dust.' Their very backwardness demanded charity: they should be freed as an act of philanthropy. Otherwise they might take freedom into their own hands. 'Indeed, I tremble for my country', Jefferson cried out, 'when I reflect that God is just; that his justice cannot sleep forever. . . .'

Although people might fear the consequences, they still continued to rely on slavery, and, through this, to change the peopling and settlement of America. It is a commentary on the times that the very year which saw the setting up of a representative legislature in Virginia, 1619, also saw the first sale of slaves. Twenty negroes were landed at Jamestown, on 20 August.

The impact of the Negro on the American landscape

So great is the influence of the Negro on America that it makes American geography significantly different from that of its neighbours, Canada and Mexico. In Canada the Negro is a small minority, for the most part absorbed into his community. 'Africvilles' there were, as at Halifax, but today these are few and far between. In Mexico, the Negro was liberated much earlier than in the United States, he became dispersed, often he married with Indian or White and lost his separateness. It is the apartness of the Negro in America that sets America apart in the continent.

This goes back to the white master and his power to make the geography of the land. That geography was in fact a whole complex of things, all reflecting the social forces at work up to the Civil War. It included: (1) the nucleus of white master and black domestics at the plantation house; (2) the slave lines; (3) squatter settlements of freed slaves, usually at the edge of town; (4) the town and the town houses of the planters, together with their servants; and (5) the hamlets of the poor-Whites on the fringes of the plantations or in the back-country, remote from town.

The sites of town, plantation and hamlet still exist, but a new social geography sprang up with the abolition of slavery, that saw the shrinking and, in some cases, the break up of the plantation, an explosive dispersal of the

Negro, and the Africanization of many of the towns. The Negro vied with the poor-White, leading him to retreat up-state still more or to migrate.

The plantation nucleus

Going back to the planter as decision-maker, we still find his mansion the key to much southern geography. It is true that, as Cash (1941) says, there were probably not more than 500 major landholders in the South at the Revolution and not more than 5,000 substantial ones in a population of 2 million Whites. Even if we allow for a significant increase of plantations up to the Civil War – S. Carolina alone was said to have had 33,000 by 1860 – they would still have housed a minority of the Whites. But these were the Whites that made the majority of the decisions, they had the main control of affairs in their hands. Moreover, although their numbers did not bulk large in the population, their estates bulked large in the landscape. They made a terific geographic impact, out of all proportion to their numbers. They not only had big estates, but they had well-placed estates, with mansions crowning the main heights in the otherwise featureless plain so that all eyes were constantly drawn up to them. One could not pass into or out of a town without being aware of them. In sailing up the rivers one came on one of their great houses at every main bend, commanding every fine viewpoint.

Furthermore, many of these landlords had plantations which were scattered through the state, or even in several states, and consequently their presence was felt over a very wide area. They might visit some of these plantations only occasionally, none the less they were the life and fortune of all their slaves and retainers throughout the year in each of these far-flung centres.

One does not suggest that the Virginia aristocrat was any more wealthy or powerful than the New England merchant or capitalist. In fact, he probably had much less money. But he had much more land and this made his wealth more *evident* in the landscape.

Here lay the real contrast between North and South. Northern wealth went into trade and industry; Southern wealth went into land. This was a difference of mind – but that mental difference meant a vast amount in geography.

Parkins (1938) makes a great deal of this in his book on the South. In 1800, when the first census of occupation was made, there were nearly five times more merchants and bankers in the North than there were in the South. The South had 48 per cent of the population but only 28 per cent of the industries – and most of these were domestic industries. 'They turned to manufactures through necessity, not from choice. Land was the magnet.' Parkins describes the scene very well.

The abundance of cheap fertile land and its acquisition were talked about in every city and country house in the South. Moving lines of settlers were daily sights on all the trails, which soon became well-traveled roads, that led westward through mountain passes to the fertile plains of the Mississippi – the wealthiest part of America. Is it surprising that manufacturing, mining, trade and commerce received less attention than agriculture?

And the situation accentuated itself with time. In 1850, the South was turning out less than 14 per cent of the manufactured goods of the USA, although its population still accounted for about 40 per cent of the total.

The country gentleman made himself felt not only by the large amount of land he had, but by the spacious and gracious way in which he used it. Here again he set his stamp on the landscape in a unique way. His house, which was itself built on generous proportions in order to hold the many friends and relatives that Southern hospitality delighted in entertaining (with high-ceilinged rooms and great halls, glittering with crystal chandeliers) was surrounded by formal gardens, done after the French or Italian styles, and could only be approached through wide parks of sunny sward, elegantly dotted with large oaks or clusters of chestnut trees, like the ducal parks of England.

The house and grounds looked all the finer and more handsome because they stood out in strong contrast to the small, unpainted huts of the slave lines. Contrast was the key to the Southern scene.

One might have contrasted the slave lines with the fine stables, for example, or the well-tended kennels. These, too, made their visual, concrete impression and for a season of the year were the very focus of the planter's life as he rode with hunter and hound after fox or racoon, his red coat conspicuous for miles around.

There was the contrast, too, between the slave lines with nothing to differentiate one house from another, and the whole suite of buildings associated with the manor. For round the manor house clustered church and school, the parsonage, the doctor's house, and the house of the chief factor. Not far off would be the mill and the miller's house and the homes and workshops of the carpenters and smiths. The manor was like a sun in a whole solar system. And yet the planter was usually not content with this. He often had a large town house, and a factor's house and warehouses in town.

His daughters, dressed in the latest Parisian styles, would go to town finishing schools where in the words of a late eighteenth-century advertisement (Cooke, 1962) they were introduced 'in the most refined of circumstances to the arts of sewing, embroidery, music and painting, combined with dancing, beadwork and papyrotamia'. And in case no one now knows what papyrotamia was, it consisted of 'cutting out paper designs so fashionable for valentines'.

The boys were usually sent to a military academy, and although this tradition was by no means confined to the South, there it had its widest and highest development. A Southern gentleman had to ride and shoot, he had to know his history and geography; above all, he had to be a leader of men. He was taught to accept the dictum of Southern leaders like George Fitzhugh who wrote, 'The gentlemen of the South have the lofty sentiments and high morals of a master race', and so he asserted himself as one of a line of masters. And it was, of course, due to the astonishing success of the handful of aristocrats as the undoubted leaders of their countrymen that this small élite had such a tremendous say in affairs.

As the novels of Faulkner show, even after they were defeated and their banners trailed in the dust the great aristocratic people like Sartoris, straitened in circumstances and reduced in power though they might be, still had an immense hold on the imagination and mind and loyalty of their country, notwithstanding the rising sway of families like the Snopes, moving up the ladder from landless folks to men of property in the new democracy that followed the Civil War. Men continued to be thrilled by the glorious if vain attempts of leaders like Bayard, asserting their astonishing and magnetic authority at the high crisis of their times – such as the Civil War, and later the First World War – even if they saw the Snopeses of the world creep into control through the inexorable levelling of life and the encroachment of universal mediocrity.

But the Sartoris of today can really keep up his manor house only as part of a going commercial estate or through earnings from a profession or business in town. The modern manor has to be run by its owner or manager as a farm business. Where this is done, it still exists and has a proud place in the landscape. Yet even so it is shorn of most of its former significance. Where it was part of a whole complex of buildings that formed the nucleus of the entire plantation, it now stands alone except for an attached steading. As J. B. Jackson (Jackson, 1972) points out, Abolition abolished 'one of the traditional community forms of the South: the plantation headquarters [which] . . . ceased to be the recognised center for sociability, for barter, and for local administration'. The nucleus broke up with the breakdown of the old plantation system.

The explosion of the slave quarters

Abolition also abolished the slave lines. These had formed a veritable village, not far from the plantation nucleus. But the chief desire of the free Negro was to get away from his past, and to have a place of his own. Hence, plantations were divided up into tenancy farms, and the Negroes became dispersed throughout the landscape in small houses on small farm lots. A tremendous change in the geography occurred out of this one social force that spurred the Negro away from the plantation headquarters to be on his own. Thus, from a highly nucleated pattern, settlement changed to a highly dispersed one: there can be few better examples of the importance of social geography in the shaping of the countryside. This dispersal was followed by stores, halls, schools, and churches, which now pepper the rural South. The negro general store at the local road-meeting and the negro church, oriented to its own small group of followers, still characterize negro geography. Where store and church coincided in their choice of location a small negro hamlet would grow up that now boasts a garage and service station, a meeting hall for dances and other social occasions, and perhaps a country doctor and his clinic. Yet this return to partially nucleated settlement is negro centred, and not, as before, centred on the white man's mill, store, clinic, quayside, or what have you.

However, many Negroes moved off the land altogether and drifted into the white man's town, which, as a result, soon became Africanized. This does not imply that the town did not have its Africans before liberation: it did, but they were mixed in with the Whites to a large extent and not segregated into negro districts. It is not always realized that segregation followed liberation. This resulted both from white and from black reactions to the new society.

Africanization of the town

Although town life was never as significant in the South as in the North, it served very essential business and social needs. It had the banks, mortgage companies and trading houses, the schools, the theatres and other places of amusement on which the plantations depended. Most planters sent their children to finishing schools and academies in town and spent part of each year in town for the social round, living in their own town houses. Naturally, they took their servants with them and these lived in domestic quarters behind the town house. The cooks and cookhouse, the laundry-maids and laundry, the coachmen and stables, the butler and house servants with their rooms all had to be catered for. Their children grew up and played with the white children in the back yard. Negroes went from each town house to the local white stores to buy goods or do messages for their masters. The white storekeeper had negro help that generally lived behind the store. Negro artisans, brought from the plantation or hired locally, had to put the town house in order and paint and repair it if necessary: these, too, lived in alleys between the white homes. Thus, there was a great social mix with people of all classes and both colours living within sight and sound of each other. The only change from this pattern were the shack-villes of freed slaves who lived as squatters in those places like the river swamps, gullied-out creeks, or railway sidings that the Whites did not bid for.

Here, on land for which taxes were seldom paid, they lived in communities with only the most primitive of facilities. Yet they had their freedom, and clung to it. And this freedom made their squatter towns quite different from the slave camps on the plantations because it enabled them to build saloons, brothels and gaming houses, dance halls, Sunday-school halls, and gospel halls, in a great proliferation of their own institutions. A vast number of evangelical sects sprang up with new ebullience, each with its own little meeting places. A new joy took hold of space and made a new geography.

Many of the sects were distinctly African, like the Bethel Methodist African Church, founded as early as 1794, or the African Methodist Episcopal Zion movement begun in 1821. The freed slave was not going to sit in the side aisle of a white church; he put up a church of his own. This might be the replica of a white man's church, but it might also be an African church, having little if any connection with an established denomination. Gradually the old religious rhythms and symbols and performances of their African days came back and asserted themselves. As Wish (1950) says, 'West Africa had [had] its cults of religious dancing under priests governed by a hypnotic rhythm, marked by hand-clapping, shouts, drum-beatings, and the hysterical acts of the possessed'. These ancient habits woke again. An eighteenth-century diarist, Mary Chestnut, wrote about black religion in her day. The preacher

> became wildly excited. He fell on his knees, facing us with eyes shut. He clapped his hands at the end of every sentence, and his voice rose to the pitch of a shrill shriek. Sometimes it sang out like a trumpet. The negroes sobbed and shouted and swayed back and forth, some with aprons to their eyes, most of them clapping their hands and responding in high shrill tones, 'Yes God', 'Jesus', 'Saviour', 'Amen, Lord'.

With liberation, an ever-increasing tide of free Negroes invaded the towns. The poorer ones added to the rapid expansion of squatter districts. Those with some education and means moved into town and tried to buy up property. This great influx changed the social balance, and, in doing so, altered the face of the town. Certainly the great negro drift made American towns quite different from Canadian towns: similar physical environments saw quite different social uses. Whites became afraid that they might be swamped. They began to resist the penetration of the Negro into town. Also, they ceased to bring with them a whole negro retinue when they 'did the season' in their town houses. They began to use white artisans to put these houses in shape. A swift polarization between White and Black took place. The Whites kept the Negro at a distance. Public places, such as parks and concert halls, were barred to Blacks. Public utilities were either pre-empted by the Whites or divided between White and Black. Separation became the order of the day. As we have seen, this was fortified by Jim Crow laws that formally segregated Black from White. Black ghettos began to grow up, either in the worn-out parts round the centres of the towns, or in shack towns at the city fringe. Riverside, canal-side, and railway-side strips of black settlement ran through the urban scene. A new negro geography emerged which became the basis for the present-day pattern.

Institutional geography soon showed this up. Even the Christian Churches, even educated circles, were involved in it, and gave way to it. White churches excluded Negroes from membership. Hence, a whole new church geography sprang up with, as indicated, African replicas of the white denominations, together with new African sects. This strained relations with more liberal elements in the North, so much so that nation-wide communities were split. The Southern Baptist Convention, the Southern Methodist, and Southern Presbyterian Churches broke off from the North. Religion became gripped by debate and division. Likewise, colleges set themselves apart, and most of them did not take Negroes in. Although Bowdoin was the exception and registered Negroes as early as 1826, it was Northern; the first Southern university to take in negro students was North Carolina, but this did not occur until 1951! In America, many colleges are denominational, and have taken on the positions of those churches to which they are affiliated. They tend to be very conservative.

The breakaway of the Southern Churches led them to become more and more reactionary, and the Methodists and Baptists, in particular, took a narrow and rigid line on subjects like the inspiration and literal interpretation of the Bible. They believed that Africans were the sons of Ham, cursed eternally, as the Book of Genesis said, to be a servant of servants (Gen. 9, 25).

Their fundamentalism opposed Darwin's ideas of evolution by which it could be shown that the Negroes had evolved, equally with the white man, from our simian forefathers. Actually the Negro has made some advances that mark him out as physically most remote from the apes: he has a much more pronounced heel than any other race, lower brow ridges and a higher brow. In these respects he is more 'advanced' than white men. In terms of physical evolution there is no justification whatsoever for regarding him as an inferior race.

Darwinism, and the teachings of Huxley, and later of Kropotkin, were anathema to Southern Methodists and Baptists. Perhaps it was unfortunate in the light of the suspicions and tensions between South and North that the chief American proponent of Darwin was Professor Asa Gray of Harvard, the great Northern University. Southerners reacted more strongly than they might have, because they were reacting, not so much against Darwin, as against Northern support of Darwinism. Darwinism was identified with 'damned-Yankeeism' and therefore became taboo. In 1880 the celebrated Woodrow case brought things to a head. Dr James Woodrow, accepting the theory of evolution, tried to teach it at Columbia College in South Carolina. As Cash (1941) says, he at once found himself denounced from one end of the South to the other both as un-Christian and as un-Southern. He was adjudged guilty of heresy by the Southern Presbyterian Church, and driven out of his post.

The emphatic teaching of Southern fundamentalism was set forth by no less a person than Alexander Stephens, the Vice-President of the Southern Confederacy, who claimed, 'Our new government is founded upon . . . the great truth that the negro is not equal to the white man.'

Although the defeat of the Confederacy by the Union led to the repudiation of such views, their influence remained. Indeed, the Union might well be accused of carrying out on a social level what it had fought against on the political level. The North and West did not take the Negro into their bosoms but, though giving him his legal entitlement to freedom, would not allow him to make free with the social situation. Segregation sprang up and became entrenched in the North and West: it was a nation-wide phenomenon. The negro ghetto evolved in every city, even where there were no laws or covenants that specifically separated Black from White.

The geographical spread of the Negro in America

In a land-hungry but labour-starved country, slavery caught on quickly, in spite of the protest of men of conscience. Maryland, which was founded on the freedom of conscience, was one of the first colonies to confirm (1664) that negro slaves were slaves *durante vita*, and that their issue should be 'slaves as their fathers were, for the term of their lives'. Laws such as this gave security of ownership to the planter. Southern colonies like Georgia that did not happen to follow suit felt out of the running. Georgia, which originally prohibited slavery, argued in 1750 for its introduction as a 'convenience and encouragement to the inhabitants'. It seemed that no part of the plantation region could afford to be without its slaves. In the meantime the actual shipping of slaves had been made more profitable by an agreement between 'the Queen of Great Britain, being desirous of coming into this commerce' and the King of Spain, allowing Britain to expand the trade into Spanish territory and buy slaves from Spanish America for transhipment to the Southern Colonies. Cuba became a major centre of transhipment and its use assisted the rapid spread of slavery in the Gulf States up to the 1812–14 war.

Decline of slavery in the North

By this time many people in the North were alarmed at the territorial spread of slavery. The Northern abolitionists had gradually been gaining in influence. Delaware State, on the boundary between South and North, decided in 1776 to forbid the import and sale of slaves, though it did not free existing slaves. Seven other mid-Atlantic and New England States abolished slavery in the late eighteenth century, including Vermont, 1775; Pennsylvania, 1780; Massachusetts and New Hampshire, 1783; Connecticut and Rhode Island, 1784; and New York, 1799. It was strongly argued that in all the land west of the Appalachians, won from the British, in which the individual states had waived their claims in favour of the federal government, there should be no slaves. In 1787 Congress decided in its famous Northwest Ordinance that 'there shall be neither slavery nor involuntary servitude in the said territory' (Ohio to the Great Lakes). This one piece of social legislation thus had major geographical significance in setting bounds to the extension of slavery in the United States.

Expansion in the Southwest

The invention of the cotton ginning mill, and of new spinning and weaving machines, gave cotton the edge over linen as a lightweight serviceable textile, and the export of cotton from the South to New England, British, and West European factories led to a swift expansion of cotton planting. This rapidly exhausted the soils in the older cotton-growing areas of the Southern Coast Plains and the Piedmont and led to the strong demand for new cotton territory west of the Appalachians. The States set up in this region, namely Alabama, Tennessee, Mississippi, and Louisiana, all demanded the use of slaves.

Congress became alarmed at the growing extent of the slave trade. Faced with Southern opposition it could not abolish slavery, but in 1808 it prohibited the further importation of slaves. This was well-intentioned and did indeed put a formal end to one of the worst scandals in the world, but only to bring in things more scandalous: the breeding and the smuggling of slaves. Thwarted by the new law, some unscrupulous slave owners began to breed slaves in the United States for sale, thus circumventing the ban on importation. Although some states like Alabama took 'full power to prevent slaves being brought into this State as merchandize', the individual states permitted migrant owners, wishing to settle in their bounds, to bring in their slaves. A landholder in one state only had to get property in another to be able to transfer his slaves and thus in effect treat them as merchandise. Moreover, illegal slave-running, mainly from Cuba, continued for many years. The last ship to land slaves, the *Clothilde*, came into Mobile as late as 1859.

West, beyond the Mississippi

The habit of taking slaves west as landlords moved to new lands led American planters emigrating to Texas, then in Mexico, to bring their slaves along. Mexico had already liberated its slaves, and objected to having slavery reimplanted on its soil. But Mexico City was remote from its outer provinces. On the other hand, the black prairie soils which lay in a great arc around the Gulf, from Alabama down to southern Texas, were close to the advancing Americans and invited them to cross the Sabine River into Mexican territory. The conflict over the extensions of slavery into Texas was one factor in the insistence of the American settlers in liberating Texas from Mexico and running it as the Lone Star State until the United States agreed to annex it.

The swift advance of slave-using planters anxious to extend cotton-planting on to the virgin soils of the Gulf and the lower Mississippi Plains was watched with unease by Northerners, who feared that slave work might undermine work done by the free. After the Louisiana Purchase of 1803, a vast tract of land was opened up for development between the Mississippi and the Rockies. The North was determined to keep this free. Most of it, however, was tributary to New Orleans, at the mouth of the Mississippi, in the South. Southern planters moved into the area up the Arkansas River and then up the Lower Missouri, and soon there was pressure to establish a State of Missouri. The notorious 'Missouri compromise' was reached allowing Missouri to enter the Union as a slave state, but prohibiting slavery further north. The black population crept out from the coastal plains up the Mississippi-Missouri out on to the Great Plains. There the tide halted for a time, since, as has been noted, land west of Missouri had been designated Indian territory and was to be inviolate.

The far West

Meanwhile the Mexican War of 1846-47 brought up the problem of the far-western extension of slavery from Texas through New Mexico to California. The thought that a tier of Southern slave states might be extended across the country in the newly won land was anathema to Northern thought. By the compromise of 1850 it was agreed that California and the other lands ceded by Mexico should remain free, and consequently slavery was boxed into the states east of the Rockies and south of the Missouri and the Ohio.

Here again, social decisions had profound geographical consequences. The arguments between white factions, and the compromises made by Congress, came to write the basic geography of slavery in the United States. Slavery was held essentially to the subtropical humid lands of the Southeast and South where the plantation system flourished on cheap labour, particularly in producing the great cash crops of the South – sugar, tobacco and cotton. In those areas where the white homesteader wanted land for his family farm and where the traditional patterns of European agriculture – wheat raising, fat-stock farming, and dairying – were being established, strong opposition to slavery kept the United States open for vast numbers of European immigrants.

Following the liberation of the slaves after the American Civil War 1861–65, new social factors came into play. Reconstruction legislation by Congress was passed to give Negroes their right to hold property and vote. There began to be a shift from the rural areas to urban centres and an attempt to enter urban callings, creating a distinct change in the negro landscape. However, Southern Whites resisted such a change, trying to keep the Negroes as tenants or sharecroppers on the land. The infamous 'Black Codes' were passed by the Southern States to limit the freedom acquired by the negro freedmen. For example, licence fees were required to set up as artisans, merchants, or professional men, fees which were quite beyond the means of the Negro: consequently the Negro could not get on in town except as an unskilled labourer. Tied apprenticeships prevented the movement of young people away from new-style masters. Although a Civil Rights law was passed in 1875, it was largely made null and void by state segregationist regulations. For example, railway cars became segregated in Tennessee in 1881, and thereafter laws were passed separating Blacks from Whites in Florida, 1887; Mississippi, 1888; Texas, 1889; Louisiana, 1890; Alabama, Kentucky, Arkansas, and Georgia, 1891; South Carolina 1898; North Carolina, 1899; and Virginia in 1900. It is shocking that such measures should have been taken as late as the twentieth century.

Confusion reigned as a result of conflict between the 'Black Codes' of the Southern States and the Thirteenth and Fourteenth Amendments, together with the Civil Rights Acts 1866–75 of Congress. The United States expressly forebade any state to 'make or enforce any law which shall abridge the privileges or immunities of citizens of the United States' and gave Negroes 'full and equal benefit of all laws and proceedings . . . as are enjoyed by White citizens.' The Fifteenth Amendment (1870) was passed to grant Negroes universal suffrage. Even this was frustrated. In 1890, 20 years later, the Mississippi Constitutional Convention excluded Negroes from political life by insisting on literary tests for the right to vote: other Southern States followed suit, including South Carolina, 1895; Louisiana, 1898; North Carolina, 1900; Alabama and Virginia in 1901; Georgia, 1908; and Oklahoma as late as 1910.

The flight north

The way in which the Southern States continued to get round the laws of Congress showed up badly against the cooperation of the Northern States. Consequently, many Negroes began to leave the South and migrate to the North. Here again social ideas came profoundly to influence geographical realities. The Negro obtained an image of the North as the land of freedom and moved out to it. One of the great mass movements of modern times was set in motion. It was slow to get under way because the need for Negroes in the North was at first not great. Widespread immigration from Europe supplied ample - and cheap - labour. Negroes were sometimes used as 'scab' labour to break a strike, and of course this did not make them popular. They had to accept jobs even cheaper or dirtier than those taken by the humblest peasants and proletarians out of strife-torn Europe. But, they kept coming. Southern counties that had been predominantly Negro in 1861 became increasingly White by 1901. The great concentration of Blacks in black America had gone. The black population was becoming more widely spread. The 50,000 that left the South for the North in 1879 had become 500,000 in 1923.

It is ironic that black fortunes rose during the agonies of the American nation as it passed through the First and Second World Wars and fought the bitter wars of Korea and Vietnam. At these great periods of crisis there was a desperate need for manpower, both for the armed forces and also for support industries on the home front, creating an altogether unprecedented demand for negro participation. Negro migrations on a scale and at a tempo never before known in the United States took place during and after both wars, mainly to the North and West but also to the cities of the South.

It is significant that Bontemps and Conroy (1945) entitled their collection of stories on negro migrants to the North *They Seek a City*. 'The stream of fugitives', they point out was always there and

> *continued to pour out of the Slave States. After emancipation the stream became a flood. It backed into Kansas City and St Louis and rose like a tide in Ohio, Michigan, and the Indian Territory [of Illinois and the new Northwest]. It reached New York and Boston on the east coast, San Francisco and Seattle on the west. But this was not [simply] a stream of fugitives. This was a migration [of settlers]. The pre-Civil War migration of fugitives had followed the rivers, the steamboat lines and the wagon-paths from South to North. With the railroads came lateral east-to-west migrations. The biggest movements occurred in periodic waves. The Fugitive Slave Law of 1850 brought to a peak the travel on the Underground Railroad. Freedom [after the Civil War] touched off the great push of 1870. Another big one followed the Chicago World's Fair of 1893. A huge one paralleled World War I, and still another began with the Second.*

During the Second World War well over 1 million negroes migrated north and in the following decade this increased to over 2 millions. Altogether $4\frac{1}{2}$ millions have left the South, principally for Northern cities, since 1940. Up until the First World War over 80 per cent of all American Negroes still lived in the South. By 1960 only 52 per cent remained there. However, as we shall see, life in the northern and western cities was not as free as it was thought to be and the migration came to a close in the 1970s. A balance was struck between North and South.

In the meantime the Negro had hit the big city in a big way. Blacks have become more urbanized than Whites, with 80.7 per cent of them in cities, compared with 72.4 per cent Whites. In particular, they have gone for the centre-city precincts of the great metropolitan communities where they now make up 56.5 per cent of the population. Washington, DC, is today three-quarters black. Newark and Atlanta are more than half black. Fourteen other major cities are between 40 and 50 per cent negro, including Baltimore, Cleveland, Detroit, St Louis, New Orleans, Birmingham, and Richmond. Chicago is more than a third black. At the current rate of increase these will all be two-thirds black by the end of the century – unless they reorganize their boundaries to take in the suburban communities into which so many Whites have fled. A new geography of America is being made that has spread the

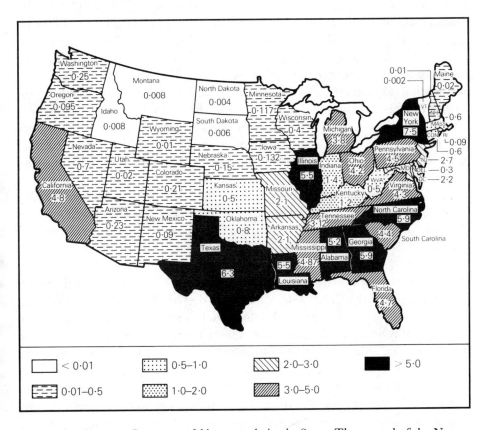

Fig. 3.2 *Percentage of Negro population by States.* The spread of the Negro across America faces every American. The negro presence is still strong in the South, but has extended to the industrial north-eastern and north-central states and also to the Pacific West. It is particularly strong, as negro ghettos, in the great metropolitan cities.

negro problem across the nation (see Fig. 3.2): every American now shares it and must do something about it. In the main, however, what he does is to keep the Negro apart in his ghetto.

The contemporary negro situation

But the ghetto is a *mediaeval* form! It is an Old-World creation, by which the Jew was segregated from the Christian. Yet the American image, according to Americans, has been to create a 'new order of man'. That was what the American Revolution was for. Lewis remarks on 'the image of the American as Adam, [where] the American myth saw life and history as just beginning. It described the world as starting up again under fresh initiative, in a divinely granted second chance for the human race, after the first chance had been so disastrously fumbled in the darkening Old World.' New in making the Black equal? New in acknowledging a newness for the Black as well as for the White? The newness was for Whites only. It gave *them* freedom to be different, to assert *themselves*, to live the life *they* wanted, to be *their own* new Adam rid of the sins and failings of the old. But what did the American Revolution do for the Blacks who, by then, were also American, who had put in more years on the continent since the day they had been brought to Virginia in 1619 than the Pilgrim Fathers and their descendants! White and Black had to be thought of as equal human beings. It had to be realized that they were of one blood. It was not only unjust but absurd to think of them apart.

Nevertheless, they were apart – and still are. As Baldwin (1963) suggests, they may as well be living in *Another Country*. The facts are, there is in America a country other than that of 'the American myth', other than that of the new Adam going into possess a new Eden, other than the home of the brave and the land of the free. It is a country of frustration, anger and hate. Anger blazes on almost every page of Baldwin. Emotive adjectives of hate and violence, mixed with those of desolation and despair, build up an atmosphere of bitter conflict, as effective as the story itself. In the first part of the book a Negro, Rufus Scott, is in a New York cinema listening to the '*violent* accents of an Italian film' when a man felt him over: he 'scarcely had the energy to be *angry*, but *bared his teeth*'. He stumbled out into the street, 'one of the *fallen . . .* entirely *alone*', and looked in at a night club. Here the 'music was being hurled at the crowd like a *malediction* in which not even those who *hated* most deeply any longer believed'. He recalled his girl-friend, Leona, with her '*sad-sweet*, poor-white smile'. To remember her brought to mind 'the *rage* of his father' . . . 'the white policeman who had taught him how to *hate*' . . . a young saxophone player who had 'hurled his *outrage* at them with his contemptuous pagan pride', playing out the experience of his own short past 'in the gutters of *gang fights* or gang shags . . . where he had received the *blow* from which he would *never recover* . . .'

Thus, in a matter of half a dozen pages, more than a dozen adjectives or nouns of violence and hate, hurt and misery have been introduced: they pile up one on the other to form a huge ground swell of condemnation - this is what the American myth has meant to the American Negro! Everywhere a terrible and terrifying mind is eating in, like acid, to the land, and making the stained and scarred and bleak landscape of a Harlem in New York or a Watts in Los Angeles. Segregation *is* the scene. The mental split has been entrenched in a physical abyss. From coast to coast it is the same. Few really seem to be able to rise above it. The dimensions are too great. A people of 24 million - or as large as the population of Canada - have been and are kept apart. Each race is being brought up on the far side of a gulf from the other.

Anger is, of course, nothing new. But the cry goes up, 'How long, O Lord, how long?' How long do black Americans have to wait to get their due? After all, they *are* Americans. William Tucker, the first negro child to be born in America, was baptized in Jamestown in 1624 - one year before the Plymouth Fathers landed in New England. Blacks were American before any New Englander. Why should they not be accepted as such? It is over 300 years since in 1661 they first petitioned to be free - free to be like their fellow Americans. Meeting no response, they organized the first slave conspiracy in 1663, in Gloucester County, Virginia, over 300 years ago.

In 1961, CORE (the Congress of Racial Equality) organized the first of the 'freedom rides' into the South, where convoys of buses and cars carried freedom demonstrators into the still essentially segregationist South. Meeting little response, the 'negro revolution' burst on Washington in 1963, in which 210,000 people marched to the statue of Lincoln, the Great Emancipator.

It is pathetic that these hundreds of years have passed with still so little change in the American mind. It is the mental climate, indeed, that has been responsible for black deprivation: *this* is behind the geography of inequality, not isotherm or isohyet, not relief or soil, nothing in the nature of the country, but only in the country of the mind.

That is why the 1960s formed the bloodiest decade in white–black relations in America; because over 300 years had passed since the first cry was made, and still the cry was not being heard. It is no wonder that the decade opened with the call by the black nationalist leader, Elijah Muhammed, for a separate black Republic in America. To step out from the Whites and set up a Black homeland, seemed the only effective step. 'Black power' organized itself for the threat.

Consider the situation. *First* (US Govt, 1967), black numbers seemed to be dropping. In 1900 they amounted to 8.8 out of 76 millions, or 12 per cent; in the mid-1960s they came to 21.5 out of 194 millions, or 11 per cent. Yet the Whites were urging birth-control on them. Rap Brown, head of the Student Non-violent Coordinating Committee set up in 1960, in his *Die, Nigger, Die* viewed birth-control as an attempt at genocide. Black nationalist, Daniel Watts, urged that, 'Our safety, our survival literally, depends on our ever increasing numbers.' The 'strength through numbers' movement called on 'the revenge of the cradle' to redress the balance between the white and black nations.

Secondly, the blacks had come to have the worst part of the American environment – the central city. The contrasts between central slums and suburban Edens were horrendous. *Negroes were the race of graceless space*: of the utilitarian, the ugly, the crowded, the airless, the shadowed, where no birds sang; of places put up with the least outlay for the greatest take. And the situation was getting worse as the 1960s progressed, as shown by the percentage of Negroes in the central cities of the great metropolitan areas (Table 3.1).

Table 3.1   Changing urban location of Negro and White population, 1950–66

	Negro			White		
	1950	*1960*	*1966*	*1950*	*1960*	*1966*
United States	100	100	100	100	100	100
Metro cities	56	65	69	59	63	64
Centre city	43	51	56	34	30	27
Urban fringe	13	13	13	26	33	37

Third, black income was at least 46 per cent lower than that of the Whites, with a far greater proportion under the poverty level. In fact, with 11 per cent of the nation's population, Blacks made up 39 per cent of the poor of America – and this was in one of the biggest and longest 'booms' that America had known. The boom went to the White, most Blacks were still bust. The Census report remarks, ' . . . the dollar gap between the nonwhite and the white family has increased. In 1960, only 15 per cent of all whites were under the then poverty line ($3,300 a year for a family of four), while 49 per cent of all blacks were.'

Fourth, tied in with this, unemployment rates among Blacks were twice what they were among Whites – in 1960 12.4 per cent of blacks were out of work, but only 6.0 per cent white. As the boom of the 1960s grew, unemployment did go down, but in the mid-1960s the rates were 7.3 per cent for the Blacks and 3.3 per cent for the Whites or a ratio of 2.2 Blacks unemployed for every White. In terms of occupation 27 per cent of the white working (male) population were in the professional or technical group and only 9 per cent of the Blacks, but only 6 per cent of the Whites were 'workers' compared with 20 per cent Black.

Fifth, partly explaining the above, education kept the gap gaping. In the great cities, where educational facilities ought to have been better and more enticing than elsewhere, while 72 per cent of the Blacks went to Grade 1, only 35 per cent were reported in Grade 12. This compared with the general average of 87 per cent in Grade 1 and 66 per cent in Grade 12. It was at the secondary-school level that the greatest disparities existed with, in 1960, only 36 per cent of the Blacks having completed 4 years of high school or more, compared with 63 per cent of the Whites. Again in 1960, only 3.9 per cent of male Negroes had completed college, contrasted with 15.7 per cent of Whites.

Sixth, housing conditions were still much worse for Blacks than Whites. In the South 75 per cent of black homes were dilapidated and lacked one or more of the basic plumbing facilities (hot water, toilet, fixed bath) compared with 19 per cent of the white homes. Though conditions were better in the cities (in Southern cities the figures were 46 per cent black, 11 per cent white; in the cities of the North and West, 15 per cent black, 6 per cent white) the imbalance was there.

All this greatly depressed and angered the black American. After all, had he not fought for his country in the recent war? Had his labour not helped to develop it? Was he not an important segment of the market? Had his talents not played a disproportionately high part in the sport, music, art, and literature of the land?

The mental depression grew so deep it exploded in the worst series of city riots America has ever witnessed, in which Blacks set fire to whole quarters of cities, even burning themselves out as a gesture of rage and despair. Nothing like this had ever happened in the other North American countries – Canada or Mexico; it was a uniquely American problem. It looked as if the American dream had collapsed.

The nation was shocked, especially when Martin Luther King, the great black leader, was assassinated. Lyndon Johnson helped Americans to pull themselves together. In 1964 he passed the most effective of the many Civil Rights bills since the first one was promulgated, in 1875, by General Grant. It was followed in 1965 by the Council on Equal Opportunity – a watchdog against discrimination. An immense effort was made by Whites to pay off the debt of ill-will and oppression suffered by the Blacks. The tide turned. The riots ceased. A sort of numb calm came upon the nation. The laws that had already been passed against discrimination were applied more stringently. Of particular importance were: the Supreme Court ruling of 1948 that federal and state courts should not enforce restrictive covenants (thus the practice by which in real-estate development Whites signed a convenant not to sell their homes to Negroes became ineffective); the Supreme Court ban in 1953 against segregation in restaurants and also in playgrounds and sports associations; and, finally, most important of all, the Supreme Court decision of 1954 making segregation unconstitutional in all state schools.

Here again, socially oriented decisions began to reorientate geography. After the violent revolts of the 1960s one began to see negro houses in formerly white areas. The federal housing subsidies paid to states and municipalities led to multiracial housing schemes. Multiracial playgrounds started to appear. New cafés and bars sprang up to serve both Black and White. Blacks were bussed to white schools, and school integration began in earnest.

This did not happen quickly or evenly. It met with frequent opposition. In Boston, for example, the 1970s saw repeated white riots against bussing. This occurred in the South End, an area that had come down in the world from a promising middle-class area lived in by native-born Anglo-Saxon Protestant Whites in the mid-nineteenth century, to a lower class district occupied mainly by foreign-born or families of foreign-born parents, largely of Italian extraction. They were not going to see their status lowered still further by a daily invasion of negro children into their schools. It was not until the state court ruled that they had to do so that the Whites complied. All over America school districts were either being reorganized so that their hinterlands took in both white and black communities or, if that could not be done, were opened up by bussing to children of the opposite race. This had a huge impact on American geography: every day one could see the buses pass, laden with white or black children, or see the mixed school lines form outside the school gates.

Black nativism

Many blacks were not content with this mix. It smacked of black assimilation in the white nation. Assimilation means extermination in such circumstances; it means the loss of black culture and black identity. Black nationalists began to turn against integration and demand separation – but under black governance. The black teacher movement, for example, wanted to remove all white teachers from schools with a black majority and replace them with Blacks. There were similar demands for black policemen in black precincts and black social workers in black ghettos. Voluntary apartheid became the order of the day. This soon started to be physically evident in the landscape where black capitalism replaced the white shopkeeper, or warehouseman, or office owner (and, of course, office worker) in the larger negro quarters. Like the revival of nativism among the Red Indians, a new nativism swept the Blacks. Slogans could be seen on the walls in all major cities, *Black is beautiful*. This movement literally printed itself on the landscape in billboards advertising brand-name products through black models and film stars. Lux soap was not to make a white skin whiter, but to bring out the loveliness of black skin, as seen in the glowing cheeks of a black beauty. Similarly, posters, or other images, of the black Christ could be not infrequently seen.

Indeed, the black religion movement went into full swing. A lot of Blacks objected to Sunday-school cards showing a white Christ with long blond hair and bright blue eyes gathering the children of the world to him – most of whom were coloured; they objected to Christmas cards of a white Madonna, with white angels in the background, bending down over a white infant, or giving him suck at a white breast. This white take-over of Jesus, Mary and Joseph, angels and cherubim, even God himself, is of course surprising in that, as Palestinians, the 'holy family' must almost certainly have been black-haired, black-eyed, and with an olive skin. They were, if anything, part of the coloured race. The famous pictures of the Madonna and babe ignored this. Francesca's *Nativity* shows a gold-haired Virgin with an ivory white skin looking down on a white Christ: Leonardo da Vinci's *Virgin of the Rocks* paints a Madonna with light-brown hair and pale silvery skin playing with a young auburn-haired Christ of glistening whiteness: Robert Campin's *Virgin and Child Before a Fire Screen* exhibits a woman with red-old hair, a pink-white skin and greenish-blue eyes nursing a white Christ with blue eyes and wheat-gold hair.

However, the Madonna of reality must have been very different. She must have had sloe-black eyes, and instead of red-gold hair, long wavy jet-black locks. Many modern black Americans find this image much more desirable. Cullen, the negro poet, revolted at the idea of a white Christ. He longed to be able to think of Him as black, like the black gods of Africa, the original gods of his race. Baldwin, the negro novelist, pointed out that if the white god went on in the way that the Whites behaved, it was time for a change. Not a few broke from Christianity altogether and set up the Black Mohammedan Church, because they felt that Muslims stressed equality and brotherhood. This change in *thought* has changed the *scene* with Black Muslim churches in many communities.

Black Americans today are thus creating a new geography, largely through their own efforts. But they still have far to go to raise their standard of living to that of the country as a whole. The following contrasts point to a yawning gap between White and Black, as late as 1975-76. (US Bureau of the Census, 1976). A black person still cannot expect to live as long as a white: only 7.1 per cent of the Blacks are over 65 years compared with 10.8 per cent whites – the toll of bad housing and ill-health reduces the black chance to live. Are there black St Petersburgs like the lovely town of that name in Florida for white retirement? Black age has made little impact on geography except in the cemetery: a point that Zelinsky might take up! Black youth is not too well served either. Although blacks have 40.6 per cent of their population under

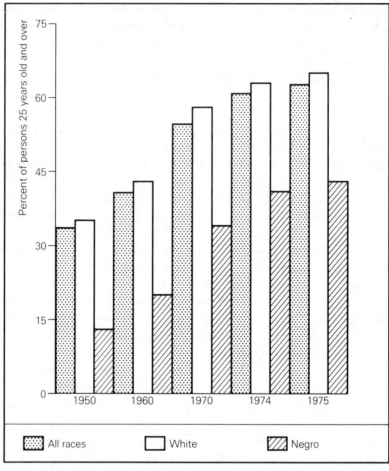

Fig. 3.3 *Percentage of population with four or more years of High School education,
1950–1975.* The negro lag behind white development in the USA is
nowhere more evident than in education. Although the absolute position
of the Negro has improved quite dramatically since the Second World
War, his relative status compared with the Whites has not greatly
changed: only about two-fifths of negroes as compared with three-fifths of
whites have had a reasonable school education.

18, compared with 31.3 per cent for whites, only 27 per cent of these ever get
on to college, as against 43 per cent whites. Only 43.5 per cent of adult Blacks
have completed 4 years of high school, compared to 65.7 per cent of Whites
(see Fig. 3.3). When Blacks grow to the age of marriage, fewer are able to set
up a husband-and-wife family. Only 61.8 per cent of their households are
headed by husband and wife together, contrasted with 87.7 per cent for
Whites. All kinds of pressures like poor housing, unemployment, the need to
look for jobs elsewhere, involvement in crime, or lack of continued good
health can break up a black family. Often the woman is left as the sole head

and immediate supporter of the children. Thirty-four per cent of black families, as compared with 9 per cent of white, are headed by the woman alone. This poses many a problem, not least of which is the care of her children when she goes out to work. Most Negroes have to pass this duty over to the grandparents. White mothers in the same situation are much more likely to use private day-care centres. Again, this difference shows up in the landscape: day-care centres are notable by their absence in most black districts.

While nearly as great a proportion of Blacks, 58 per cent, are in the labour force, compared with Whites (61 per cent) many more become unemployed – about 10 per cent compared with 4.8 per cent for Whites, and well above the national average of 5.3 per cent. Black communities thus see more people on street corners, with nothing to do but stand and stare, or drifting along aimlessly hoping to pick up a job, or queueing at labour exchanges, at social agencies, and other welfare offices, than white counterparts. Exploiting this substratum of humanity are saloons, pool halls, and cheap discothèques and cafes that become the haunt of those who have nothing to do. Here again, a different geography emerges with different social conditions.

Of those who do work only 28 per cent of Negroes find white-collar jobs compared with 51.2 per cent of Whites. Forty-two per cent are in blue-collar jobs, contrasted with 33 per cent Whites, and a much larger proportion, 27 per cent (against 11.8 per cent White) are confined to low-wage service work, as cleaners, lavatory attendants, doing the washing up, moving things round, and so on. The black life is without much grace or dignity or even interest and motivation. Many Blacks feel alienated and consequently do not participate: they show much less responsibility in voting, and often strike out against or offend society in vandalism and crime. The black crime rate is four to five times as high as the white.

Much of this is a reflection of poverty. While 6 per cent of all Americans were below the poverty line in 1975, no less than 16.5 per cent of blacks suffered that condition. Another 9.4 per cent of the general population were subpoor, contrasted with 14.1 per cent of all Negroes. That is to say nearly one in three Blacks suffered from not having enough to live a reasonably stable, comfortable, and healthy life: many endured hardship, hunger, anxiety, and fear. The median earnings of the Black are still, after all these years, only 62 per cent of those of the white American (see Fig. 3.4). This, too, is seen in the landscape in the cheaper and older cars, the more graceless and crowded homes, the lower-quality shops, and the less socially responsible institutions they have.

Is this the New Adam in the New Eden that Lewis talks about as the great American dream?

Black Americans are, none the less, Americans; they have never returned to Africa in any number, they differ fundamentally from the black

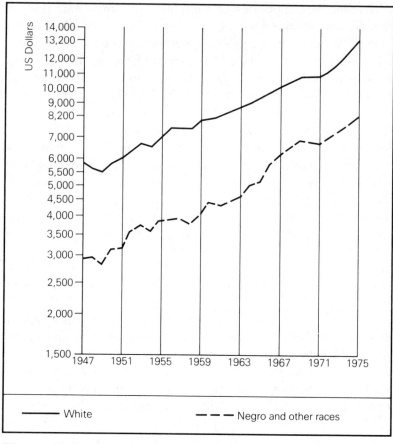

Fig. 3.4 *Median family income 1947–1975.* Black income is still well below white, though the ratio has increased from 51.72 per cent in 1947 at the end of the Second World War, to 62.12 per cent in 1975, at the third quarter of the century.

countries that gave them birth, or black Caribbeans, or Latin American blacks, or the Blacks that have become Gallicized or Anglicized in Europe. Their climb to freedom, slow though it may have been, is in an American style freedom, centred in individual competition and personal responsibility. As Frazier (1966) remarks most of them 'have become purely individuated'. Through their insistence on their own, individual liberty as part of the great libertarian tradition of the United States they have helped to make America what it is. As William Toll (1969) says, 'the long interdependence of white and black in America has created a unique civilization'.

Negroes have participated in general reform – from anti-trust movements to 'Women's Lib' – as well as in the reform of their own condition. They have played a big part in American writing, the arts, music, sport and athletics, in American college life, science, business, administration and the armed forces. In a sense it was because they might escape from a racist situation through individual contributions to the great 'universals' in life – as, for example, Baldwin has done – that their mark on American culture has become so significant. They were supremely to vindicate Bacon's conclusion about 'the blessings of adversity'.

Negro adversity has often come as a result of conflict between groups, and to overcome this, group organization and activity have been highly developed. Many black leaders have stressed group solidarity and group initiative, from Nat Turner, who proposed group revolt; to Marcus Garvey – black nationalism; and Elijah Muhammed – black separatism; Martin Luther King – black confrontation; to Stokely Carmichael – conflict revolution. But conflict between individuals, which is part of mainstream America, confers its blessings on Black and White alike. Booker T. Washington went after individual excellence, and W. E. Dubois urged the 'habits of thrift, industriousness' and 'push' on his people as the best way of making good. Negro successes have parallelled white ones where they have rested on individual enterprise, skill, perception and power. Negro élites have arisen along the same lines as white élites by contributions to American prowess. Indeed, communities of achievers have grown up, creating their own geography in élitist areas in their part of urban America – areas that attract outstanding talents from the country as a whole. The general level of negro life may leave much to be improved, but the freedom is there for improvement; and in the insistence on that freedom Negroes in America are making their mark on American society.

References

*Baldwin, J. (1963) *Another Country*, Dell Books, N.Y., pp. 17, 11, 29, 31, 51, 61, 77.

Bontemps, A. and **Conroy, J.** (1945) *They Seek a City*, Doubleday-Doran, N.Y., pp. x–xi.

Cash, W. J. (1941) *The Mind of the South*, Knopf, N.Y., 1960 edn p. vii., 1941, ibid., p. 143.

Chevalier, M. (1836) *Society, Manners and Politics in the United States;* Anchor edn, Doubleday, N.Y. (1961) p. 108.

Cooke, H. L. (1962) 'Early America as seen by her artists', *Natn. Geogr. Mag.*, Vol. 122, No. 3, Sept., p. 371.

Frazier, E. F. (1966) *The Negro Family in the United States*, Chicago, p. 220.

Jackson, J. B. (1972) *American Space*, Norton, N.Y., p. 151.

Jefferson, T. (1785:1964) *Notes on the State of Virginia* (1785) Harper edn. (1964), N.Y., p. 156.

McKitrick, E. L. (ed.) (1963) *Slavery Defended: Views of the Old South*, Prentice-Hall, N.J., pp. 86–98, 139–47.

Miller, P. and **Johnson, T. H.** (1963) *The Puritans*, Vol. 1, Harper, N.Y., p. 155.

Parkins, A. E. (1938) *The South*, Prentice Hall N.Y., pp. 2 ff.

Toll, W. (1969) 'The crisis of freedom: toward an interpretation of (American) negro life', *Amer. Studies*, **3,** No. 2 (Dec.), 265.

US Govt (1857) *Proceedings*, Supreme Court, US; Vol. 60, p. 393.

US Govt (1967) *The Status of American Negroes, a Statistical Review*, US Information Office, London.

US Bureau of the Census (1976) 'Population profile of the U.S.', *Current Population Reports*, Series P-20, No. 29, Mar. 1975.

Wish, H. (1950) *Society and Thought in Early America*, Longman, N.Y., p. 230.

---

*The sequence of page numbers at the end of the reference corresponds to the sequence of quotations in the text.

The clash of cultures

The foreign-born, and foreign minds

To replace the Indians and make use of the Negroes, Europeans came into America in great numbers. Indeed to an extent they *made* America, although native-born Americans grew in such numbers as to outstrip the foreign-born, and today far outnumber them. In 1975 nearly 400,000 foreigners migrated to America, but they formed only 0.18 per cent of the population. The American feels he can cope with this. It has become part of his tradition: indeed, if to be an American is to be something new, the United States finds at least part of its destiny in opening its doors to newcomers. Many of these could be new-doers.

Europeans from every section of that continent, together with Asians and Africans, Canadians and Mexicans, and others, have entered its gates and are still coming. Having sprung from Britain the country is still predominantly British, English-speaking, and Protestant, but people of German origin form a close second, followed by those from Italy. Latin Americans are next in order, with Canadians, including many French Canadians, not far behind. Poles and Ukrainians are also important. Currently, about 30 per cent of all immigrants are from the Western Hemisphere, and 40 per cent from elsewhere. This represents a big change, with Europe sinking back in the picture, and the Americas, Oceania, and Asia coming forward. The seven chief countries of origin in 1975 were Mexico, the Philippines, Korea, Cuba, Taiwan, Italy, and the Dominican Republic.

These have all brought with them their own cultures – their language, their food and clothing, their folklore and music, their literature, and their type of worship. This variety has enriched America enormously, yet at the same time it has tested American goodwill and understanding. Immigrants have enough of their own people that have settled in the United

States before them, to find among them a 'home from home'. Therefore many of them have been slow to adjust. A lot do not learn English for many years, or change their food or dress styles. In fact they tend to augment and reinforce the differences in America. Even if they make up barely 2 per cent of the population they top up the groups which they join, continually reminding them of their past, and keeping the old cultures alive. In this sense they have an importance out of all proportion to their numbers.

Among other things they bring in with them their Old-World prejudices and hatreds. A major problem has been the impatience of one group with another, for instance of the Protestant with the Catholic Irish, as if the old hatreds still mattered. Thus, cultures continue to clash with each other, dividing still more an already divided America. The fact is that, although many would-be Americans fled to the New World to escape intolerance in the Old, they often failed to be tolerant. Old habits and suspicions died hard – harder than they thought.

Perhaps one reason for this was that, to begin with, they did not *have to* put up with each other. An exceptional geography, full of emptiness, made room for exceptions. For those who came to America to pursue their own interests or work out their own ideals, come what may, the country was on their side. In Burnaby's (1775) travels (1759–60) he came on Germans who in their anxiety 'to live in perfect liberty' had got away to the Upper Shenandoah, in the heart of the Appalachians. They used the relief of the land to put them 'far from the bustle of the world'. They bought isolation with geography. They sought the land that would match their mind.

There was not the pressure, then, to give way – because there was a way to get out. One could close the front door to tolerance, because there was always a back door to dissent! Differences were frequent and often profound. Cushman once wrote, 'If we ever make a plantation, God works a miracle, especially considering how un-united amongst ourselves and devoid of good regiment we be.' Shortly after, Governor Bradford was complaining of 'controversie and discontente' – especially at the way Roger Williams was dividing the community with his views. Eventually Williams had to flee to Narragansett to be able to worship and live as he liked. Governor Winthrop describes whole towns that kept themselves apart and refused to have as citizens those who would not conform: but then, there was room for the non-conforming to set up new towns. Winthrop justified this self-centredness: 'Churches', he wrote, 'take liberty to receive or reject at their discretion.' Why should not 'towns make orders to the like effect'? Exclusiveness was accepted: differences in the mind made divisions on the ground.

Increasingly, however, there was less freedom to fly, and more fear of friction. The country as a whole, and its towns in particular, came to the situation where they had to make room for difference. In chapter 8, the efforts at such accommodation will be discussed. There never has been a lack of idealism in America: but then, there has never been a paucity of conceit. People who believed themselves right would not retreat. Unable to move on, they stood at bay. Ethnic and religious conflict resulted, that grew more intense as the population turned more dense. The city scene, especially, became scarred with communal conflict, not only as White contended with Black, but as native-born vied with foreign-born, people of one national origin with those of another, and one religious group strove with the next. These things have often acted in concert: for example, the native-born Anglo-Saxon Protestant Bostonian long contested the scene with foreign-born Irish Catholics, in a struggle that was frequently frustrating if not bitter. This was typical.

While these differences were at their greatest among uneducated minds, they did not stop there, but invaded the most lofty minds. Jefferson himself, as we have seen, was guilty of prejudice, if not intolerance, against the foreign-born. Living in Virginia, which was Anglo-Saxon and Anglican, he was disturbed at the dilution of this native-born stock by foreign-born settlers of very different origin. He wondered if America could come out of it, the America that he had fought for and led. There was the danger that it would be warped to foreign ways and its image become distorted.

A century went by, yet Henry James (James, 1907) felt the same anxiety, wondering what the aliens flooding into America would do with the country. This came out particularly in his return to New York, after his years in Europe. Here in the *American Scene* he remarked how 'the carful[i.e. the elevated railway] is a foreign carful; a row of faces, up and down, testifying without exception, to alienism unmistakable, alienism undisguised and unashamed'. It is true that the foreigners felt at home in America, because it was a land of foreigners! But 'what meaning', asks James in the presence of all the foreign habits, ideas, and ideals they brought with them, could one continue to attach to such a term as 'the American character'? There was of course, to begin with, 'a childlike rush of surrender' to America and a 'clutch at' being American. And thanks to the supremely gregarious nature of America this did help people get over their initial differences. But given time James asked, would not their separate traits come out? 'The doubt remains . . . whether the extinction of qualities ingrained in generations is to be taken for quite complete? Isn't it conceivable that, the business of slow comminglings and making-overs at last ended, they may rise again to the surface. . .?' James hoped of course that if they did so it would be in the *qualities* of their old traditions, qualities that would bring interest and colour and richness to American life. But the danger was that the ancient traditions would raise their heads as suspicion, prejudice, and hate.

Both things have happened. America has been both enriched and yet fragmented, both added to and yet divided by its foreign-born. Again, as with class, the powerful forces of competition and the intense struggle for success, have exploited the cultural differences. They have set one ethnic group or one religious sect against another until a scale of discrimination has been formed, making some lower and less worthy and others higher and more desirable in the land. And so, once again, the landscape itself takes on the divisions of the mind, and is everywhere divided into culture areas, making America a mosaic of strife.

Freedom is a mixed blessing and, as James says, there is such a thing in America as 'the freedom to grow up to be blighted'. This is certainly true where people use the great freedom America offers to blight the foreign-born, or the less-established immigrant, or the less-populous group, or the less acceptable cult, so as to create more room and prestige and power for themselves. Whole areas of blight have grown up in every large city. Indeed, blight has accumulated to alarming proportions. De Vise (1972, p. 50) has calculated that 'two thirds of Chicago's 4,900 industrial buildings are unsuitable or inadequate; half of the city's 575 miles of commercial streets are obsolete; a fourth of the commercial structures are vacant or unsuitable for commercial use; and a third of the city's 1,200,000 dwellings are substandard'. It is in this environment that many Americans are being brought up. Little wonder that they should revolt – or take it out on each other.

The ethnic conflict

Since the Anglo-Saxons were the first to come in and were in a ruling position when the Revolution occurred they continued to sway affairs. So often, both in city and countryside, they obtained the best sites. But they became increasingly challenged as Irish, Germans, Italians, and Slavs poured into the country. One of the oldest and most long-standing of struggles has been that between Anglo-Saxon Protestants and Roman Catholic Irish. This has scarred many a city in the United States from Boston, New York, and Philadelphia, across to Chicago, and eventually San Francisco.

Mention has already been made of the Bostonian situation. Here the Irish have been at a discount compared with the Anglo-Saxon for generations. The troubled history of misunderstanding and hostility between the two groups in the Old World reached across to the New. Since the Anglo-Saxons had come in to America first and set things up, they were dominant when the Irish started to arrive. The Anglo-Saxons held all the positions of power and they decided as to how, and how much, the Irish would be accepted. They welcomed the Irish as cheap labour, but did not greet them as social equals. They used their longing for a new start, but did not fulfil their hopes for a recognized place. As Thernstrom (1973) has pointed out 'the over-whelming majority of those in Boston who were in a position to hire, promote, fire, or lend money to others' were old-stock Yankees, many of whom were 'unfavourably disposed' to the Irish. He writes:

> *Back in the 1880's, Boston upper-class circles warmly applauded the tirades of Edward A. Freeman, whose ingenious solution to America's social problems was to hope that every Irishman would kill a Negro and then be hanged for it! As late as the 1920's Joseph P. Kennedy, the Irishman who was ultimately to become not only a millionaire but the U.S. Ambassador at the Court of St James, left Boston for New York because of his conviction that certain doors in the local business world would always remain closed to him..*

If a man as able as Kennedy felt frustrated, how much more *hoi polloi*? In their fight for freedom, the Irish felt the dice were weighted against them. They could go so far, but no further. Then they came up against the Anglo-Saxon élite. Most of the Irish started as workers, though a minority who were qualified before arrival obtained white-collar jobs. Relatively few of the workers climbed to middle-class positions; if they did so it was to humbler posts such as low-ranking civil servants, clerks, and shop assistants. What was more disconcerting, as Thernstrom shows, a great many of these ultimately skidded back into the working class. Not only that, but their sons did so as well; the fact that the father got to the lower-middle-class level did not mean that his son might reach the upper middle class. All too often the son fell back to where the father had started from. Of course there were brilliant exceptions, and Doyle, concentrating on these, has shown how certain Irish were able to push well up towards the top, but, until very recently, only a very few actually reached the top. This was left for the native-born Anglo-Saxon Yankee stock.

The stock, for example, represented in *The Late George Apley*, an heir to generations of Yankee sagacity, self-improvement, and success. A minor though significant and representative theme in Marquand's (1937) study is the Anglo-Saxon/Irish clash in Boston from the 1870s to the 1930s. In his quiet way, he presents the Apleys as well established, not only in property and finance but in the respect and goodwill of the community: they are leaders because they come of the stock of leaders, British by descent, Anglican, conservative, knowing the right people, and doing the right things.

The Anglo-Saxon élite

The novel starts with family antecedents, describing Great-Uncle William who 'if he wished, could live with the ostentation of the *nouveau riche*', but who, with a 'dislike for external show shared by those accustomed to money' lived a reasonably simple life in order to buy Rembrandts for the Art Museum, contribute anonymously to the South Boston playgrounds for underprivileged children, and support the 'family charity, the Apley Sailor's Home'. This did not in any way deny the right to get rich, which had for so many been for so long integral to the American dream, but it invoked the strong sense of trust which many of the American élite showed – and still show. The Apleys had come to America, not as poor immigrants driven by necessity, but as 'solid citizens, with substantial properties, who desired to take up a new abode because of conscience'. They were people who cared. And they continued to care about issues even when money put them beyond the need to care. For somehow, with their wealth, they developed a sense of *noblesse oblige*. Great-Aunt Jane once said to George Apley, 'You will never know how very close we come to being nobility. In a sense, indeed, we are nobility.' This was sheer Anglo-Saxon élitism!

The family certainly looked after its own social position. After several generations at Roxbury it moved into Boston where, in the early eighteenth century, it secured a place 'on the northend of Boston peninsula', then the chief centre of fashion. When this became invaded by poorer people, the Apleys moved away to the South End, since 'everyone was under the impression that this district would be one of the most solid residential sections of Boston instead of becoming, as it is today, a region of rooming houses, and worse'. When this area in turn was invaded by 'what is now our Business District', the Apleys tore down their house, and replaced it further west, on Beacon Hill. Later, they again shifted ground, to get as far away from the spread of the city as possible, 'on the water side of Beacon Street'. This *peregrination of prestige*, so typical of status-proving America, and of the American city, established the social distinction of the Apleys by making them geographically distinct. Thus, they obviously took care of themselves, but, in doing so, helped to build up and beautify the city as well – they were the leaven that leavened the growth of Boston.

Seeing that 'New England's future was essentially industrial' rather than commercial, the Apleys 'turned instinctively from the sea' and, just before the Civil War, founded the town of Apley Falls, on the Merrimac, where they built a fortune out of textiles. This gave them the power and put upon them the responsibility to shape the landscape as they liked. They tried nothing as Utopian as Robert Owen's *New Harmony*, yet they were obviously concerned to devise both a workable and a livable place. They provided what they thought were reasonable living and working conditions for their workers and helped families in difficulties through personal 'advice and assistance'. They seemed to like their role of shapers of the community. As a result 'they were not greatly in sympathy with the agitators of the time'.

Though not religious men, the Apleys believed in the Church. This was because, 'There is nothing like the discipline of Church.' George Apley grew alarmed when his son became irregular in attendance, and wrote, 'I cannot understand why you do not understand this.' But then discipline was the religion of the house. This was particularly so in matters of money. 'Try to think carefully,' George went on, 'exactly what you want. There is no satisfaction as great as spending wisely, and few annoyances as great as feeling that money has been wasted.' Here was the profound sense that wealth was a trust, which disciplined their whole lives. What the Apleys admired was 'a quiet world of mind and order', and what they strove for was 'a stability and a genuine society in a chaotic, nervous nation'. Consequently, it was 'by regular habits of life' that each new generation of Apleys was 'made to feel its own responsibility'. Here was the Boston of Henry James's heroic age – the age of 'plain living and high thinking'.

At the same time it was a Boston where you were expected to 'do the right things and know the right people'. When George Apley was up at Harvard he had had the indiscretion to attend a dance at Boston about which his people had not heard. His father, Thomas, wrote him, 'What worries me is that you are not meeting the right people.' His father kept hammering home the maxims of expected behaviour. 'It is our fondest hope', he wrote to George, 'that you will be taken into the Club which has had an Apley as a member for many generations. But your worthiness to become a member depends to a certain extent upon yourself. You must be sure to see the right people.. . .' George was in due course made a member of the Berkley Club, but disgraced himself, shortly after, by falling in love with an Irish girl from the South End (which had deteriorated by then into a lower-middle-class area).

The elder Apleys were shocked at this, and intervened at once. Romantic notions were swept aside; George had to remember who he was and where his duty lay!

The mental shock reflected the social gap. The girl was Irish and lower class. The social gap was at once stretched to a geographical gulf. George was packed off to Europe where he would forget the South End.

The emotions described here are not exaggerated; they reflect the profound sense of separation between Anglo-Saxon and Irish that had gone back to the days of Henry II, and were exacerbated by the native-born/foreign-born complex in America. The new American man could not strip himself of old European ghosts; they still haunted his path. Other old hatreds and prejudices were also carried over, as between the Germans and Slavs, and northern and southern Europeans, or Gentiles and Jews. The memory of national origins evoked all but instinctive biases that vitiated relationships. Native Americanism, allied with the Protestant élite, swept Boston, Philadelphia, and New York, as S. B. Warner (1972) has shown.

To return to Boston, it thus became very difficult for the Irish to move up or to move out. They were put in their place and hemmed in, and consequently, as Oscar Handlin (Handlin, 1941) said in his *Boston Immigrants*, the Irish 'felt obliged to erect a society within a society'. They made their own world. They came to a continent, but kept it a parish.

Religious conflict

Parochial institutions helped to create group solidarity. The church and the church school, the church societies, church newspapers, church suppers and other church activities focused life in on the community. Ethnic clubs, eating houses, games, cinemas left little need for the people to look outwards. They could satisfy most of their needs from among themselves: hence they grew more and more self-centred. The effects of what Raymond Breton calls 'institutional completeness', where all the major institutions of the larger society are rendered redundant by their duplication in the smaller community, maintained ethnic viability, and provided people not only with an awareness of, but a satisfaction in, being separate. Here was ethnic geography in the making!

Though Farrell (1932) probably never heard of this, nevertheless this is in a sense the theme of his novel on Chicago, where Studs Lonigan, the Catholic, grows up in a world so complete in itself that it leaves little incentive to adapt to others; on the contrary, it spurns others as though it not only had no need of them but would be better without them. The Catholic Church was largely responsible for this remarkable cohesiveness, self-sufficiency, and self-satisfaction of the group, although, since it was the Irish-Catholic Church it also depended on the Irishness of the community.

What Farrell *had* heard of were the theories of the then new school of social ecology worked out by Park, Burgess, and McKenzie (1925) which, simplified, stressed economic competition and social status. Economic rent dominated social structure and gave form to the city. Competition was reflected in status, and status was entrenched in location. Here was the urban geography of America. Farrell worked this out in terms of the struggle between Catholic, Jew, and Negro. Since Protestants by reason of history and ethos were on top, Catholics could not climb far; they took out their sense of frustration on Jews: both these white groups turned on the Negro. Prejudice was a combination here of religion, national origin, and race.

Farrell had a strong sense of the geographical positions these groups took up and held against each other. This was within the framework of the so-called Burgess zones, where the bid of finance and trade for the city centre and of high-class housing for the city margins left an *in-between belt* for that jostling of industries and working-class institutions which was the venue of the intensest religious and partisan struggles. The centre of Chicago was seen to have such high land-values as to be priced mainly for offices, hotels, the great metropolitan stores, and luxury apartments. Interdigitated with these was a zone in transition – which was a 'grey' zone, the zone of blight, or the shatter belt of the city, where offices and shops were expanding outwards, light industries and wholesale concerns were expanding inwards, and housing, caught in a giant squeeze, deteriorated to slum tenements. Beyond this, spread the working-class zone, made up of a mix of working men's homes and their work places – multistorey apartment blocks and triplexes in long rows ending up against factories or railway yards – interspersed with working-class institutions. Outside this grew the middle-class zone, with some row-houses, mostly of duplexes, but with many semidetached or detached houses, creating essentially residential neighbourhoods. There were few offices or works here since men went downtown for their employment. Finally, at the remote edge (in what has become America's golden fringe), where the competition by industry and business was not great, housing was given the maximum room, and commuter suburbs sprang up along radial routes, forming a disconnected outer ring of bits of city and bits of country where the upper-middle and upper classes lived.

In the intense struggle that went on for land, culture played its part as a counter or forfeit; the zone of blight where the poor, the foreign-born, and the coloured lived was marked by alienation and deprivation. Here the lack of social influence put these people at the mercy of all others, and particularly, of the Anglo-Saxon, Protestant American 'Establishment'. It was in writing for the disadvantaged that Dos Passos cried so passionately in his book *USA*, 'they have clubbed us off the streets they are stronger they are rich they hire and fire the politicians the newspaper editors the old judges the small men with reputations who make the college presidents . . . all right, we are two nations'. But though that is tragic enough, the real tragedy is that even in the 'nation' of the alienated, men still fly at each other's throats, White against Black, Anglo-Saxon against Irish, Catholic against Jew: here is the real edge to the bitterness that divides and keeps America divided.

The Catholic dilemma

Farrell saw this, and described it with a realism that was almost terrifying. What he set out to do was, in effect, to delimit 'the culture contours' of the shatter belt in Chicago, where the changing geography of the city had led to the rapid deterioration of a formerly stable working-class area. Here family homes lost out to the invasion of shops, offices, and tenements: those that were not abandoned to them, were squeezed out by them. More significantly, Irish Catholic homes became threatened by the influx of Jews and Negroes. In this instance, economics, the changing pressure on land; sociology, the changing composition of the population; and geography, the changing pattern of occupance – all went together to make an America at the front line of conflict. The area of stress lay roughly between the Union Stockyards on the west and Lake Michigan on the east, extending from the Chicago Ship Canal in the north to Chicago University in the south (see Fig. 4.1). The changes described followed upon a flight of a former Protestant

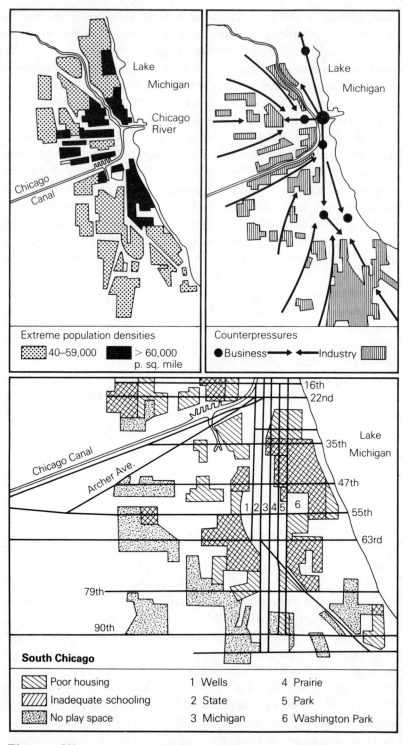

Fig. 4.1 *Chicago – aspects of social geography.* Areas of stress are where commercial invasion is rampant, housing is old, population is on the decline, white population is in flight, non-white – on the advance.

Anglo-Saxon group to metropolitan fringe areas, leaving positions that were infiltrated by Catholics. Rapid infilling by the Irish Catholics extended from Archer Avenue (in the industrial–wholesale complex reaching to the stockyards), lakewards along 31st and 35th to Wabash. Subsequently the families were traced southwards along Wabash to 58th, in a mixed industrial–shopping belt. A short while after, they seem to have moved east again, across State, Michigan, and Indiana to Prairie, that is, to better working-class and to middle-class areas nearer the lake. There was some movement along 61st, 63rd, and 67th to South Shore, a middle-class residential region below Chicago University.

The Jews came in on the heels of the Catholics, moving south along the main business and shopping streets, like State and Michigan, as far as 51st, buying up Irish property. Finally, the Negroes followed on, driving southwards along industrialized Archer and south down industrial and business streets like Halsted, Wabash, and State. They halted at temporary 'fronts' on 22nd, 35th, 51st and 58th. Today the whole area from the canal and stockyards to the university and the South Shore is predominantly Negro and Puerto Rican.

As Whites evacuated the areas of noise, smell, and dirt, of pressure and high tension, Blacks were sucked in. This was an economic matter to begin with – Whites could afford to avoid railways, stockyards, industry, and traffic, Blacks had to put up with them. Increasingly, however, social factors took over, and social prejudice, the social manipulation of status and creditability, and the social power of institutions, were used to block, deflect, guide, and control the flows of people and the geography of their ends.

The key to the Lonigan story is a Catholic-Irish sense of inferiority toward the Anglo-Saxon and Protestant majority which they got round by showing their superiority to Jews and Negroes. 'Hostility between Protestant and Catholic', as Warner (1971) has claimed 'had proved to be an enormously popular issue, to which thousands would respond' – as the riots in Boston and Philadelphia in the 1840s and the bloody Irish Draft Riots of New York in 1863 clearly indicated. Farrell took up the story in Chicago. The question is posed, 'Are the Irish 100 per cent American?' The Protestant answer was 'No' because the Pope was put first. This was the excuse for bitterness lasting right up to the 1920s.

Here we have then out in the open, both the violent prejudice against the Catholics, as not being good Americans, and the tough Irish reaction to it, taking on those whom they could better! This prejudice is behind a lot of Lonigan thinking. Studs Lonigan went to a Catholic school at St Patrick's on 61st Street, well in the Irish precinct, and was taught by the Sisters of Providence. Here he was given his firm sense of religious superiority for, although he was told 'all about Moses and Joseph and Daniel in the lion's den and Solomon who was wiser than any man that ever lived except Christ' yet he was assured that all this was nothing compared with 'the Popes who had the Holy Ghost to back up what they said'.

His father and mother had made many sacrifices to bring Studs up a good Catholic and were proud that he was not like the poor Irish who used the public (state) school. 'These poor Irish had fathers and mothers who didn't look after them and bring them up in the right atmosphere. Children should be sent to the Sisters' School even if it did take some sacrifice'. This indicated a division among the Irish themselves, between those, like the Lonigans who wanted to stay fully Catholic and others who were willing to identify themselves in many ways with the Anglo-Saxon Protestant majority by sending their children to the state schools. Such an internal division weakened the whole Irish position, but it nevertheless strengthened the assertiveness and aggregation of those who 'stuck by their guns'.

Patrick Lonigan, the father, had tried to face up to the prejudice against the Catholics by being as good as his superiors and climbing up the social ladder. Thus, he hoped to gain through class what he had lost by religion. He became his own boss, owned property, and boasted the status of a city landlord. He had come a long way, for *his* father had been nothing but a 'pauperized greenhorn'. They used to live in a very industrialized area around Blue Island and Archer Avenue and 'had stolen coal from the nearby railroad yards'. The changes in his life had been parallelled by changes in the city. 'Chicago was nothing like it used to be when over by St Ignatius Church and back of the yards were still white-men's neighbourhoods, and Prairie Avenue was a "tony" street where all the swells lived, like the Fields, who had a mansion at Nineteenth and Prairie, and the niggers and whores had not roosted around Twenty-second Street.'

But change had come swiftly. With growth at the periphery land values had increased at the centre. The high price of land in central Chicago had squeezed out most houses, both north and south. Tenements had to move out, along Wabash and State, and began to invade the inner margins of the working-class area, south of 22nd Street. Coloureds and poor Whites moved in among the Catholic Irish, who took flight further out, between 51st and 61st Streets. The Lonigan story is part of the Catholic struggle which, on the one hand, meant spearheading an attack on the established Anglo-Saxon Protestant area then still in the central-south zone, and, on the other, fighting a rearguard action against Jews and Negroes, who were snapping at their heels, in the inner south.

Cressey (1938) supports the account in his statistical study. The tremendous boom of the 1890s had brought five major railway lines into the city. These tried to get as near to the heart as possible, but of course could not compete for the hub itself, which was pre-empted by offices, stores, and hotels. For a time there was an extraordinary mix of housing, industry, and business. But by the early 1900s the central business district had begun to rise. It pushed outwards, that is, mainly to north and south. Streetcar lines enabled people to work in the centre and live further out. The famous Chicago El, or elevated railway, extended the process. The better-off people, mostly native Americans of Anglo-Saxon or German stock, moved to the fringe. Very fine residential areas sprang up towards Evanston to the north, the university to the south, and Oak Park in the southwest. As these were taken up by well-to-do, the poor immigrant flocked in and occupied the central areas: Irish, Poles, and later Italians came in, and took over the splintered areas between commerce and industry. In this, the Irish dominated. They were English-speaking and more used to American ways than others. But just before the First World War a big influx of people from Central Europe moved in, including many German and Polish Jews. Competition for space was severe. Those who got better jobs tended to move out; their homes were immediately snatched up by newcomers.

It is during this period of friction and change that the Lonigan story takes place. Near its opening, Pat Lonigan decides that, in spite of the success he had made in getting a good home, yet, for the sake of his sons,

> *the family would have to be moving soon. When he had bought their current building* [on Wabash, near 61st] *Wabash Avenue had been a nice decent respectable street for a self-respecting man to live with his family. But now, well, the niggers and the kikes* [Jews]*were getting in, and they were dirty. They'd have to get away from the eight-balls and tin-horn kikes. When these got into a neighbourhood property values went blooey. He'd sell, and get out.*

While he was waiting to do this, at a profit, young Studs Lonigan decided to make it tough on the newcomers who were invading his district. He responded to their challenge by hardening himself. This hardening became a major part of his life. A killer instinct in him was roused by his coach on the football field. Hugo Zip Malloy used to say to them, before the game:

> *You're going out there now . . . to play a man's game. There's only one way to play it. Play hard.hard! Get the other guy before he gets you. Knock him down! Let them drag him out. If you don't you might be the unlucky chump that's dragged out. And if any of you birds are carried off that grid-iron, cold, don't expect me to break down and weep. Play hard! It's the soft guys that get knocked silly in this game. And if there's any soft guys in this team, the sooner they get it in the neck, the better. You guys got to go in there and hit hard, hit often.. . .*

Malloy knew what he was doing. He had to train 'the fighting Irish' to fight or there would be none of them left.

In the meanwhile, Father Gilhooley toughened them in spirit! In his graduation address, he congratulated the parents at segregating themselves out and making themselves different from others. He praised those 'who had possessed the courage, the conscience, and the faith to give their children a good Catholic schooling'. The priest was supported by the parent. After the school graduation ceremony, in which the Lonigans had all dressed up in their best, the Old Man Lonigan said, 'Well, we did the right thing. I'm glad Father Gilhooley gave it to the people who send their children to the public schools, because the public schools ain't no place for Catholic children.'

Thus family, school, church, football club, saloon, and other institutions were visible signs and reminders in the geography of the precinct that the Catholics were different, and should keep themselves different, in spite of the many temptations to give up the struggle and merge with the rest. And yet, although their world was in strong contrast to that of the upper-class, Protestant, Anglo-Saxon universe typified by George Apley, it knew the same pressure to be true to itself. The Lonigans also strove to do the right thing and keep with the right people, only the right things and the right people were Catholic for them. After all, was not the American image that of each man 'doing his own thing'?

Although this made each a different American, in a sense it made an American of them each. They believed in themselves, even if it meant pitting themselves against each other. And they had the freedom both to believe in themselves and to show it. The showing of it divided them, but that they could show it made them, in a strange way, one; this is part of the American genius. Though Chicago warred in its many parts this helped to make Chicago. It tested out within itself that point which could then test fortune; certainly Studs must have thought of himself not only as a good Catholic but as a good American in standing up for his way.

The Jewish scapegoat

Unfortunately, this meant strife in contesting with others, particularly the Jews, *their* way. Religion was a sword as well as a balm. Although Studs Lonigan had no illusions about how the Catholics were regarded he did not want to get out of the conflict. His mother wished her son to go to college and have a chance to move up in the world. She saw that he could get out of the situation (in which he was becoming increasingly harder and more aggressive) by moving up. Then he would have a chance to mix with others and be the successful American. But Studs hated study and, unable to face up to the problem of bettering his prospects by improving himself, he tried to show that he was still the better of Jews and Negroes, and thus, in his own world, a superior being. It was the lazy way out. Instead of conquering himself, so as to move up the scale, he played conqueror to others, lower down the scale.

This is why conflict is so often the American way out. It saves the American from the real conflict, which is with himself. It was easier, in Lonigan's case, to push the Jews down, than to pull the Catholics up – hence the Jews were blamed and attacked to save the Catholics. One day Old Man O'Brien, a neighbour, was telling Studs about the great times in sport he once knew. He finished:

> But I ain't interested as I used to be. Baseball's the only clean game
> left. The Jews killed all the other games. The Kikes dirty up
> everything. There never was a white Jew, and there'll never be one. And
> now I'll be damned if they ain't coming in and spoiling our
> neighbourhood [Wabash]. Pretty soon a man will be afraid to wear a
> shamrock on St Patrick's day because there are so many noodle-soup
> drinkers around. I even got one next door to me. I'd never have bought
> my property if I'd knew I'd have to live next door to a Jew. But I don't
> speak to him, anyway.

Thus, prejudice was passed down from the older generation. Studs grew up in an atmosphere of hate, envy, fear, contempt, and violence.

A few days later he and his gang had scouted down from 58th to 53rd where, sure enough, they saw some Jews. 'Two hook-noses did come along. Andy and Johnny O'Brien stopped the shonickers. "Sock one of 'em", Studs said, "Say, christ-killer!" Johnny said to his man, "We ain't done nothin!" the guy pleaded. "Where are you from?" asked Red Kelly. "Fifty-first and Prairie." "That's a Jew neighbourhood", said Red, and said that all Jew neighbourhoods were a disgrace.' The Catholics were filled with anger that the Jews had advanced out of their neighbourhood into the Catholic one. They started a fight. '"Take that for killin' Christ", said Benny. "Hit him again, he's only a shoniker", said Davey. They gave the guy the clouts and left him moaning in the alley. The other Jew ran off.'

In this brutal but effective way the Catholics kept up their superiority and their separateness.

Even the lowest of the Catholics could put Jews in their place. In the low-class part of 58th, near the railway yards, lived a girl, Iris, 'the sweetheart of the pig-Irish' who showed herself off to the boys, and lay with those she liked. One night she let the gang see her. It happened that a fringe member of the group was Davey Cohen, a Jew by name, but living in the Catholic area, and tolerated because the Cohens were well off. The Cohens had tried to make good by leaving the main body of Jewry behind, to move among the Christians. But to show that even a 'well-off Jew' was below the contempt of the lowest of the Catholics, the girl Iris would not expose herself to Davey when his turn came up to look on her.

We are told:

> After leaving Iris, Davey Cohen walked around the neighbourhood
> brooding . . . It hurt, and made a guy pretty goddam sore, being cut cold

by Iris when she didn't bar even punks. She had told him, 'No soap,
Jew.' She had let him stay there [in the rendezvous] *while she undressed*
and showed herself off to the other guys. She had let him get anxious
like all the rest. Then Jew! She wouldn't let him touch her. If he didn't
leave she'd threatened to get Studs to sock him.

Davey was sick with indignation. He thought he'd really got in
with the gang. He'd even joined them on their raids against the jew-boys!
He'd cried out, in the last scrap, urging Benny to demolish a Jew, 'Hit him,
he's only a shonicker.' But it had availed him nothing. The meanest of the
Catholics could still look down on him. 'They had all shot craps for turns with
Iris. Studs had been first, then it was Davey's turn. When Studs came out,
"MMMMMM", he cried, and Davey had jumped up anxious and gone in –
and she had covered herself and called him a dirty Jew.'

Thus, humiliation was heaped upon the Jew even when he had
come into the Catholic neighbourhood and had property there and in
mundane ways was part of it; but one could never be integrated with it. The
Jews were never accepted. The Catholics could turn on them and make them
an outcast, in an instant. Davey Cohen was filled with mortification and, at
once, wished the worst for Iris: this was, that she would be taken by a nigger!
'Iris made him sore as hell. He hoped to hell she'd have a baby. She was so low
she wouldn't even bar a nigger!'

Thus Catholic mortified Jew, and Jew took it out on the Negro: this
was the American order of things. The Catholic (the whore of Babylon) who
was made to feel inferior to the Protestant, could be superior to the Jew (the
killer of God); the Jew (the son of Shem) could in turn look down on the Negro
(the son of Ham). Differences were rife: they were exacerbated, as David
Ward (Ward, 1968) has shown, by commercial invasion, making living
conditions worse and worse. Chicago had become a major wholesale, retail,
industrial, and transportation centre by the First World War, outstripping its
chief rival, St Louis. The railway lines were thickening up as industrial zones;
the Chicago river and canal were the sites of great lumber and coal yards,
markets, and wholesaling emporiums. These were all centripetal forces which
in their inward drive were crushing up against, and in many instances
crushing out, housing. At the same time they demanded a bigger work force.
More people had to live in less space: triplexes replaced duplexes, and the
working-man's multistorey tenement blocked out the sky. Meanwhile the
business boom had started a strong centripetal movement, impelling shops
and offices up Michigan and State, again at the cost of housing. The struggle
for a home was intense. This was partly put to a straightforward economic test
– those who could pay got their choice – but also to a social one, those who had
status got the first option. The force of petty snobbism, the power of social
pull, the strength of social stonewalling gave some people the 'lead in' and

pushed others back. This was what really made the geography of changing Chicago – and still does.

As Henry James feared, long-established social traits and symbols – the racial pecking order in Europe, for example – did reassert themselves. They came to the surface like huge iron-teethed rocks to endanger the ship of America. They always do in wars and depressions when the tide of humanity is low. This often means, whenever the tide of Americanism is high. For then the super-American is like a lion in the streets seeking whom he may devour. Everyone must conform or be subject to attack. The First World War was a high tide for Americanism, but a low tide for humanity. Tolerance was at an ebb. The killer instinct in the American had been roused to fever pitch. Studs 'remembered his history from the grammar school. We had, America had, the most glorious war record in all history. Old glory had never kissed the dust in defeat. . . . He was going to be a soldier of his country.' He tried to enlist, but was turned down as being too young. This filled him with disgust and anger. Nevertheless, he and the gang trained harder than ever, they made themselves still more tough. To be a true American was, in fact, to show *how* tough you could be. The war was a godsend. It invited all kinds of reprisals against anyone thought to be un-American, such as German Jews for example.

A young Jew came along the street just after the papers had announced 'Congress Declares War!' The 58th Street gang were moping along, excited but disconsolate. 'Hey there's that Jew punk, Stein. His old man speaks German. I'll bet he's a German spy', Red said. Studs grabbed Stein, a neatly dressed, 12-year-old sissy. Bawling, Stein asked what he had done. He shrieked to be let alone. Kenny said they would have a court-martial, and appointed himself judge. He went off and got a small American flag which he had stolen from a nearby five-and-ten-cent store.

> Stein was sentenced to kneel down and kiss the flag. He demurred, but rough handling made him change his mind. He knelt down and pressed his lips to the flag which had been placed on the sidewalk. He was hurtled forward by three swift kicks. Kenny grabbed his feet and Studs and Red nabbed him under the arms. They gave him the royal bumps, slamming his can against the sidewalk.

It was a savage hour: all the ancient and irrepressible, worse, irremediable savagery of the American against Pequot and Narragansett, against the pigeon of the air and the buffalo on the range, the hate which had carried Ahab across the seven seas after Moby Dick, was gathered up again in an America as hard as iron, an America that tolerated no difference, and made room for no exception.

This author was aware of it in the Second World War when he had occasion once to visit the great city of Detroit shortly after America had entered the fight. Like other countries, it had been sorely divided in pre-war days and had had those who favoured Fascism and those who supported Communism. But all that was swept aside. On every hand was the call to be one and undivided. Going into the bar of a hotel, the author saw in great gilt letters right across the canopy, 'We tolerate no other -ism than Americanism.' But of course this became the worst intolerance of all, as was seen in the *Young Manhood of Studs Lonigan*. The Catholics joined in the savagery of the hour to savage up their hated rivals, the Jews, who were, in a way, 'at war' with them by invading their neighbourhood. War was in everyone's mind. It left deep scars in the landscape.

The negro flogging-horse

Prejudice became stronger and conflict more cruel with the big influx of Southern Negroes into Chicago, as the First World War went on. The fighting in Europe completely blocked off immigration. There were no more poor Irish, Poles, Jews, and so on to do the common tasks. Poor-Whites from the South were enticed in to take their place. Meantime, American soldiers were pouring overseas. They had to be supported by armaments and supplies. Negroes from the South were also tempted north. Indeed, a huge influx of them took place, especially to St Louis, Chicago, and Detroit that had booming armaments industries and could be easily reached up the Mississippi. Half a million Negroes migrated to the North. They were needed – but little provision was made for them. Nothing like enough houses, schools, stores, street-cars, and other essential services could be provided. They went into abandoned homes and homes in poor repair, and pushed into subdivided houses and even sub-subdivided ones. Not unnaturally this pressed hard on those already there – the Jews, the Poles, the Irish, and so on. Tension mounted. It exploded in riots. There were twenty-six black riots in 1919, the worst in American history. The most severe of these took place in Washington, DC and in Chicago. Farrell could not help but bring them into his story, they were a shattering event in Chicago's life. Bitterness was extremely great. Blacks were accused of taking the jobs of white men, especially of those who had enlisted to fight at the front. Many Blacks secured the new jobs that sprang up as a result of the war, in competition with those Whites who still remained. On both counts they were hated, and this hatred burst out in July 1919 in the race riots that rocked Chicago.

The Irish gang at 58th Street, hearing that a shite boy, Clackey Merton, from only three blocks up, on 61st Street, had been murdered in the 'Black Belt', a negro salient south along State, decided to march down there and 'knock off the niggers. Young Horn appeared and breathlessly said there was a gang of niggers on Wabash.' This was intolerable! Wabash used to be

Irish; indeed some still lived there. Studs, who lived only a few blocks south, felt called on to defend it.

> *Studs led the gang along 58th over to Wabash. For two hours they prowled the disputed area between White and Black along Wabash and State, between Garfield and 59th, searching for niggers. They sang, shouted, yelled defiance at those houses and threw bricks into their windows where they thought niggers lived. They were joined by other groups, men as well as kids. They only caught a ten-year-old Negro boy. They took his clothes off. They burned his tail with lighted matches, urinated on him, and sent him running off naked.*

Violence took over the land. In this, geography very much mattered. Men fought over the changing fronts of their neighbourhoods just as much as they did over the swinging fronts of the battlefield. The loss of a block to Jew or to Negro was as bad, on the home front, as the loss of a line of trenches in Flanders, or a hill in Italy. Oddly enough, though a great deal has been written about the geography of world-front wars, little has been done on the geography of the urban-front war! Yet this has been as bitter, if not as devastating, as any foreign conflict. Certainly it was in the story of the Lonigans.

Flight as a way out

Old Man Lonigan saw that Wabash was a lost cause, even while his son was fighting so fiercely to ward off the Jew or the Negro. Consequently, he bought a new building on Michigan, near Carter School, and the Lonigans moved over there, living on the third floor. This was both further south, away from the canal, railway belt, and stockyards, and further east near the park. He thought he had done well in getting away from the gang-ridden 58th, but Studs resented the move – possibly he felt it was a sign of weakness rather than success – and he still kept up with the old gang.

The outer conflict led to conflict within. Division invaded the family. The father was anxious to maintain their position by moving further out, like the rest of the Catholics, not by staying put and holding back the tide of Jew and Black. He saw that that could only mean more fighting. He now threw his weight behind the mother in urging Studs 'to get on in life'. He grew angry at their son for always being on the streets, beating up Jews and Negroes, and coming in late at night. 'The neighbours will be thinking things, wonderin' if we, the landlords here, set a good example, and live decently ... I'm the *owner* of this here building, and I got to have a family that sets the right kind of example.' Patrick Lonigan's method of showing the difference between himself and the Jews was to widen the social distance between them, to improve his status and climb up into the middle class where he could become part of the Anglo-Saxon majority and thus be a distinct cut above any minority. Catholics on the way up, were on the move out; they sought a better venue. The father's answer to the climbing Jew was to climb higher, not to club him down. However, this positive approach of separation by progression was not followed by Studs who took the negative approach of separation by regression – 'keep the Jew down, don't let the nigger out of the gutter.'

In the meantime, the daughter, Frances Lonigan, did not think her father had been ambitious enough. He had not moved out sufficiently far. 'But father', she cried, when she heard they were to move to Michigan Avenue, 'even this neighbourhood is deteriorating. The best people in it are already moving over to Hyde Park or out to the south shore [both middle-class areas on the lake shore, bracketing Chicago University]. Soon I'll be ashamed to admit I live around here.' She felt her father had left it too late to move, and they had not moved far enough. In other words, he had not made the most of what geography could offer, to keep the Jew and the Negro at their distance. 'Young lady', the Old Man assured her, 'you're wrong. The niggers will be run-raggedy if they ever try to get past Wabash. This is a good decent neighbourhood full of respectable people, and it always will be so.'

Thus, a three-cornered struggle started up in the Lonigan family: (1) with Studs still loyal to 58th Street – even though it was becoming more Jewish, that was a reason to stay by it, and by those Catholics who were still left there to stem the invasion; (2) with the father having decided at last to move, but willing to move only to a middle position, not too far from their old haunts; and (3) with the ambitious young daughter, anxious to make a clean break in a flight well away from a Jewish or a negro take-over. These were the sorts of tensions that now afflicted the Catholics, hit by internal strains as well as external stresses. The geography of conflict had far-reaching effects.

A concentrated effort was made to stabilize the new battle lines by consolidating the Catholic hold on Michigan. The Catholic community there were made an extension of St Patrick's parish and at once began to centralize their power and position in a new church. Even the young Catholics, who hardly ever went to church, got behind this. 'Come on', said Red Kelly to Studs, urging him to go to a fund-raising meeting. 'The new church . . . is going to stop all this talk about the jiggs [Negroes] moving around here and ruining the neighbourhood. A new church will clinch the matter.'

In this way the Catholics made a strong effort to resist the tide of invasion by investing in a central institution as a rallying point. By developing a new social and educational life centred in such a concrete and dominating thing as a new parish church, they hoped to achieve that solidarity which would patch up the disintegration of their people. Men were asked to forget their individual interests and conform to the group. Separation was still the cry, and it led to a new focus of segregation. The American dream of being able to do their own thing created a landscape of going their own way in areas of separate development.

However, more and more Irish felt that they had not fled far enough. The O'Briens moved well on beyond Michigan. One day O'Brien met Lonigan and asked him what he had done.

> *I got a new building now on Michigan. It's going to be worth plenty, particularly since Father Gilhooley is going to build the new church.'* 'Pat I don't want to sound discouraging, but the whole neighbourhood [from Wabash through Prairie to Michigan] is being ruined, and quicker than you think. It's going to be so full of black clouds that a white man won't belong in it. Soon 58th and Prairie is going to look like 35th and State with them, now.' 'Golly, I hope not, but if it does, I'll be out. I'll turn a neat profit when I sell the building. But if that happens, it'll be a crime.' 'Crime or no crime, those kike [Jewish] real-estate bastards are getting in, and what for? To sell to niggers, that's what for. Mark my words.'*

Movement became a flight; after swithering as to whether they would stay (only to see their property go down) Catholics fled (even at the cost of leaving the places they had grown up in and loved). The Jews, so long despised and ill-treated by the Catholics, were getting their own back by buying property from the Catholic-in-flight, to sell it to Negroes-on-the-advance, thus causing more Catholics to flee than ever. If the flight became a panic, the Catholic would sell out cheap to the Jew, and the Jew would then sell dear to the Negro, making money from both enemy camps!

The struggle went on. Father Gilhooley's campaign for a new church on Michigan succeeded. In 1926 it was opened by the Cardinal Archbishop of the Irish, himself, who 'described the occasion as the greatest day in the history of St Patrick's parish'. It was a supreme sign that the Catholics had faith in themselves and meant to stand together.

However, the power of the Church could not prevail against the tide of change. As Kiang (1968) has shown, while in 1898, 46 per cent of Irish Catholics lived within three miles of the city centre, by 1920 only 19 per cent did. This was a reflection of their rising economic level but also of their greater social acceptance. They were in supervisory and managerial posts and also in positions of political influence. They were no longer satisfied with the conditions of life close to industry and commerce; they had pushed out to the suburbs along street-car and suburban railway lines. Their move was quickened by the fact that blacks were close on their heels. The riots of 1919 had forced the pace of change. The city knew it had to provide better facilities; and citizens realized that they had to make a place for the Southern Black. Geography altered. By the end of 1920 De Vise (1972, p. 64) claims that, 'Black residential areas had become well anchored . . . with concentrations in the near North, near West, and near South sides [within the central area]. State Street on the South Side, and Lake Street and Roosevelt Road on the West Side became the mainstream of Chicago's rapidly expanding black population.'

The centre-city Irish resisted as much as they could. They put their trust in their institutions which gave them a physical and social anchorage to their quarters. But these institutions – church, school, hall, club – merely stayed the speed of change, not its thrust. After a while the Lonigans felt that even Michigan Avenue was not safe. They had not moved out far enough. (Movement was such a feature of American life that it put stability at risk. A neighbourhood saw a trooping out as well as a drift into it; a decreasing number of its initial members stayed with it, and so it changed in character. As Thernstrom points out, though there might be 'distinct clusterings of particular groups at different points in time, not very many of the *same individuals* comprised the group over time'.) In this case, more fled than sought a refuge in the area. The Lonigans left their second home for a third. Flight had become a panic.

The Old Man was very regretful.

> '*Studs*', *he said*, '*I'd rather let the money I made on this building go to hell, and not be moving.*' *At his age it was only trouble and distress to uproot himself and make another change.* '*Hell, there's scarcely a white man left in the neighbourhood*', *Studs remarked*, '*I never thought that once they* [the Jews and the Negroes] *started coming, they'd come so fast.*' '*Yeah, it used to be a good neighbourhood.*'

The mother joined in, even more full of regrets than the father, but trying to make the best of it. '"Well, we're to have a *new* home", she said. "Yes, Mary", her husband, with evident sorrow, answered, "but no home will be like this one. Sunday in Church I watched Father Gilhooley. He's heart-broken poor man. Here he's built this beautiful new church and two year after it's built, all his parishioners are gone."'

So the last-ditch stand had not worked. The church which was to have been the last redoubt, had failed; it had not held people together. Yet another centre had to be built as the landmark for yet another stand; the mentality of flight led to a landscape of fluidity.

The irony, if not the tragedy, of the story is that those who fought the hardest against the Jews and the Negroes were themselves among the ones most completely to succumb. Studs Lonigan had dedicated himself to attack the Jews and beat back the Negroes; yet in the end it was a Jew who processed the sale of the Lonigan building, and it was a Negro who bought it. This showed the barrenness of the conflict. The years of persecution came back to roost in the house of the persecutors, like birds of unhappy prey. Conflict fed upon conflict.

The negro implosion

It is a pity that there is not a modern sequel to the Lonigan Story. It would show some interesting contrasts. One of these is the almost complete take-over of the centre city of the Chicago complex by the American Black. But what is more important, it would indicate the virtual replacement of the economic model, on which Farrell had based his book, by an ethnic model, brought into being by social forces. Farrell had followed Burgess – the leading urban sociologist of his day. Park and Burgess had worked out their urban scheme on the understanding: (1) that economic forces were paramount; (2) that they had free play; and (3) they controlled the social contour. With the discovery of a central place, people moved into it so as to exploit it. To capture centrality was to dominate accessibility and hence gain the hinterland. As people did move in, they bid against each other for space, and land values went up – highest at the centre and lowest at the margin. Only business could afford the highest land values, hence it took over the centre and formed the central business district. Industry demanded too much space to be at the very centre, yet it needed a fairly central position and so it created a series of subcentres on the edge of the central area. Here most of the work force lived. People who could afford it moved to the urban fringe where there was little competition from factory or office. Those who could not, crowded into the cheapest accommodation which lay in a zone in transition between the central business district and the industrial subcentres. If the city continued to grow, then each inner zone invaded each outer one, business succeeding to the transition zone, this being pushed back to the industrial area, industries expanding into the residential fringe, and this gobbling up the countryside. Thus poor, lower-middle, upper-middle, and upper classes formed geographical zones based upon the economic gradient; society was given shape by the economy. And if a man climbed up the economic slope he was free to move through the geographical zones: when poor, he would be in the transitional area; getting a stable job he would progress to the main working-class zone; moving into a white-collar job he would move out to a middle-class district; and if he became a manager he could command an outer suburb.

Not so in the de Visian city. This is one where social status dominates the geographical pattern, and cost is subordinate to caste. The de Vise (1972) zones (see Fig. 4.2) are essentially ethnic and rise from superordinate and subordinate relationships within a caste system: they are based on the premise of a fundamental status division between white and black castes, within which social class, tied to economic level, then operates. If the Burgess model worked, the rich Negro would be out in suburbia along with a Gatsby, along with a Carnegie, where social freedom permitted economic power. But economic power can only go so far in the de Visian

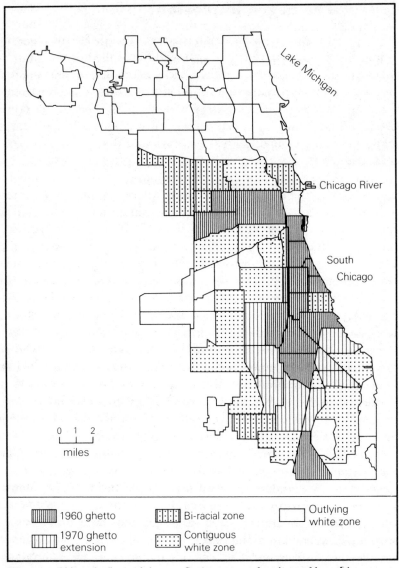

Fig. 4.2 *Chicago's five racial zones.* Status areas, dominated by white-negro caste differences, have come to control the social geography of the American city.

system and then it is stonewalled by caste divisions. The Negro does not move out as he moves up, for him there is no explosion out to the fringe, but an implosion in the centre, where he becomes ever more and more concentrated. Consequently the de Visian zones consist of: (1) a central black-saturated low-class ghetto: (2) a subcentral black-dominated but mixed lower-middle-class ghetto; (3) an inner-outer bi-racial middle-middle-class zone; (4) the main outer contiguous white upper-middle-class zone; and (5) finally an outer-

outer white upper-class zone. The so-called 'Black Belt' in central Chicago which had begun to take shape in the 1930s got progressively more black. The flight of the Whites to the margins made for a white ring that got increasingly white. The white ring then strangled any significant attempt at a breakout from the black core: the caste system took over from free enterprise. 'The percent of the city's Blacks living in tracts of over 50 per cent black population increased from 60 per cent in 1920 to 90 per cent in 1930. The proportion of Chicago city tracts with concentrations of 90 per cent or more black population climbed from 67 per cent in 1950, to 78 per cent in 1970.' In other words black gets more black. 'At the other end of the scale, the proportion of Blacks living in predominantly white areas has gone down every decade since 1920.' Whites keep themselves increasingly more white.

The clash of cultures is thus seen to be a major maker of American geography.

Conclusion

The American dream that Crèvecoeur once had of 'all people becoming as one' simply has not worked out. In Lonigan geography, the city had become a veritable battle-ground in which the different groups held on to their differences, and expressed their deep, and open, and avowed divisions by invading each other's spheres, or by making last-ditch stands to save beleaguered situations. Conflict marked every case. Stephen Crane began his novel *Maggie* with a fight on a waste lot. Scott Fitzgerald ended *The Great Gatsby* with death in the valley of ashes. Farrell's was a continuous struggle within one no-man's-land after another. These wastelands in the low parts of the central slums, the valley of ashes at every suburban fringe, the no-man's-land that divides and counterdivides the heart of each great city, exist in the American landscape, because they are there in the American mind. Wasteland thinking, ash-heap imagination, the no-man's-land of American sentiment have impregnated and scarred the American scene with widespread division and conflict.

Value-geography of this kind – social values splitting the geographical scene – has been to the fore too long. Fortunately, as we shall see, new values are gripping the American mind to create a counterbalance in the American landscape. The key is in the state of mind. Geography is simply the state of mind made concrete in the land.

Culture can be a most enriching thing. Given the mind to make the most of cultural differences by organizing them into a social mix may make a most stimulating society such as exists, for example, in Hawaii, a happy climax to the American experiment. Here bits of White, Polynesian, Japanese and other geographies have come together to make a marvellous and enviable mosaic in the living landscape.

References

Burnaby, A. (1775) *Travels Through the Middle Settlements of N. America, 1759–60.* Cornell Press edn (1960) Ithaca, N.Y. p. 40.

Cressey, P. F. (1938) 'Population succession in Chicago, 1898–1930', *Am. J. Soc.*, Vol. xliv, July, pp. 59–69.

De Vise, P. (1972) 'Chicago, 1931: ready for another fire?', in Peet, R. (ed.) *Geographical Perspectives on American Poverty*, Antipode Monographs, Worcester, Mass., pp. 50, 64.

*Farrell, J. T. (1932) *The Young Manhood of Studs Lonigan*, Forum Bks edn. (1948) N.Y., pp. 4, 12–19, 100, 111, 20, 45, 173–5, 180–8, 210, 235, 320–1.

Handlin, O. (1941) *Boston's Immigrants, 1790–1865*, Harvard U.P. Cambridge, Mass., p. 50.

James, H. (1907) *The American Scene*, Hart-Davis edn, London, pp. 125–9.

Kiang, Ying-Cheng (1968) 'The distribution of ethnic groups in Chicago', *Am. J. Soc.*, Vol. lxxiv, Nov., pp. 292–5.

*Marquand, J. P. (1937) *The Late George Apley*, Collins edn. pp. 17–18, 21, 30, 20, 25, 11, 28, 40–1, 71–2.

Park, R. E., Burgess, E. W. and **McKenzie, R. D.** (1925) (eds) *The City*, Univ. of Chicago Press, Chicago, pp. 47–62.

Thernstrom, S. A. (1973) *The Other Bostonians, Poverty and Progress in the American Metropolis*, Harvard U.P. Cambridge, Mass.

Ward, D. (1968) 'The emergence of central immigrant ghettos in American cities, 1840–1920', *Ann. Ass. Am. Geogr.*, Vol. 58, No. 2, pp. 291–9.

---

*The sequence of page numbers at the end of the reference corresponds to the sequence of quotations in the text.

5

The conflict of class

The classifying mind

The clash with Indian and Negro, and tensions between cultures, by no means exhausted conflict in America: class divisions also strained the myth of the new American man. As we have seen, internal strains existed from the first: before the American forebears came to America, they had been at odds. Bred of conflict in the Old World, conflict became their bread in the New. 'It is almost as if the initial experiencing of violence', Schlesinger (1968) claims 'fixed a primal curse on the nation – a curse which still shadows our day'. America is as much a country under a curse as the people of a promise.

Actually in a strange way, the promise is the curse. Being so free is to take freedoms with each other. Hence the clefts of class. According to American figures (US Bureau of the Census 1975), about a third of the population is in the lower class. Nearly one out of five of all children under 18 have grown up in this class. They grow up in a world peculiarly theirs. More of their parents get divorced, more are low-paid workers, more are out of work, more live in homes with less than a room per person, more suffer from ill-health, more are liable to have a criminal record than any other group in society. This is not just a matter of low income, *it is a life-style*, it is the way in which these young Americans are brought up and have their being. It is litter in the streets and ash yards to play in, ill-heated houses with ill-fitting doors and windows, saloons to offer forgetfulness, missions to fortify flagging faith, social agencies with long queues outside them, homes abandoned here, cars junked there: it is the geography at the end of one's tether. It is in fact the geography of the back spaces, where, as Harrington (1963) says, the poor have become lost; America is not aware of them, they are *invisible*. But they are none the less real.

The problem is almost beyond solution because it is a spin-off from the American dream itself. Basic to this dream has been individual freedom. The fruit of that freedom is individual competition. And the seed of that is conflict. It is not only that each man is out for himself, but that everyone 'gets on' by showing others 'where to get off'. Progress involves displacement. People's freedom to do something new for themselves, and shape their own destiny, often creates distinctions between them that grow into fixed, impassable gulfs.

Mental gulfs become gaps in the landscape, areas where the continuum of settlement is interrupted, where men place themselves apart. Each class, sect, and faction tries to get geography on its side; each seeks to win by capturing a base of operation; each uses corridors of advance; each hopes to extend its sphere of influence; each marks off its own territory. Whites segregate themselves from Blacks; the upper class put a chasm between themselves and the poor; Protestants, Catholics and Jews contest different quarters; mental divisions work themselves out in geographical divides.

Every American grows up in an area dominated by the divisions of race, cult, or class. Of these, class divisions are the most widespread, since every racial or cultural or religious group is also split by class. The new thing that men came to do in America did not prevent their being divided about it! Though division was part of the colonial system, it did not wither away with the Revolution: far from that, it continued. Stephen Crane's slum creation, Maggie, is as different and cut off from Fitzgerald's self-made tycoon, Gatsby, as though they lived in separate planets.

This disparity is undoubtedly of concern to the American. Equality has always been part of the American dream. But equality is conditioned by freedom. Although there is an equal chance for all, it is the chance given by freedom to rise like Gatsby or, like Maggie, fall. What the American dream, in fact, amounted to was the equal freedom for all men to make or break themselves. But if this were so, it only aggravated, and did not do away with, distinctions, ensuring merely that distinctions were not institutionalized. That America could give rise to a slum child like Maggie with all her tribulations and miseries and, in the same city, produce a Gatsby of extravagant opulence made its freedom a two-edged sword. 'Our society', writes Dollard (1937), in *Caste and Class* ' . . . is built on the opportunity to achieve the highest social distinction, highest class position, and highest financial rewards which every man beginning at the bottom and working to the top . . . can get for himself.' But that is only one side of the coin. True, the freedom to achieve is everyone's right, but then, so is the liability to be pulled down. That is the other side.

Here is a real dilemma.

Most Americans try to meet it by saying that, though their society is not equal, it can at least be equalizing. Division there may be, but it is constantly cancelling itself out. That is why, though classes occur, Americans believe themselves classless. As Lloyd Warner (Warner, 1965) in his *American Life* writes:

> *The most important thing about the American social system is that it is composed of two basic, but antithetical principles: the first, the principle of equality; the second, the principle of unequal status and of superior and inferior rank. The first declares that all men are equal and must have equal opportunity . . . The second makes it evident that . . . many of the values they treasure can exist only as long as they have a status system.*

The key to this paradox is of course social mobility – the ability to rise from log cabin to the White House, as President Lincoln did.

Americans accept being low as long as there is a hope of rising, and they tolerate the high because they know the fear of falling. This author was once astonished to hear a girl from San Francisco claim, 'But we don't have any classes. Everyone's free to find his own place.' This is a prevailing view. What it means is that no one need be tagged as *belonging* to a class because anyone can pull himself out of it. Class exists; but, ideally, no one needs to exist according to class.

Cooley (1966) once said, it was to prevent having a system of status by birth that America instituted class by competition. 'Precisely in the measure that a society departs from the condition [in which] the social function of the individual is determined by parentage [to one where] individual traits are recognized . . . in that measure must there be competition.' This created class differences, but it avoided caste divisions. 'The function of personal competition, considered as part of the social system, is to assign to each individual his place in that system.' Obviously, people who found the same place came to form a common class, but if through their efforts they could achieve a new place, they climbed to a higher class, and to that extent escaped the bonds of class.

While competition might help the American to step out from one class, conformism kept him in step in another. Once again a strange duality has come to exist. Going up or falling down the social scale the American is very much an individual, but at the level of achievement at which he comes to rest, he is just as much a conformist, having stuck his colours to the mast, as it were, of his new-found class. This conforming attitude is perhaps the main force in maintaining class distinctions, and is the main stumbling block to moving out of class. As a result of having conformed to a class pattern for most of their lives, the greater number of Americans, according to Packard, 'have difficulty adjusting to swift upward mobility, or . . . to the assumed humiliation of downward mobility'.

This may be because most Americans, even if they believe in the freedom to be different are none the less afraid of the responsibility of being unlike. When Henry James came back to America after many years spent in Europe, he discovered among other things that 'the American hated difference'. This is hard to credit in view of America's belief in personal competition and individual enterprise. Yet in fact, competition between individuals forces a person to identify himself as much as possible with his own group, otherwise that group may not support his enterprise. Consequently, though America is very individualistic, it is far from idiosyncratic in the sense of each man standing out on his own. 'I have seen many persons – but no personages', claimed Henry James (James, 1907) in *The American Scene*. He recalled a reply he had heard made, 'to a generous lady offering entertainment to a guest whose good impression she had had at heart. The guest said: "What kind of people should I like to meet? you ask. Why, my dear madam, do you have more than *one* kind?"' America seemed to James to be masses and masses of people, all herding together, all centring themselves in the one kind, as if no one really dared to be his simple, single self. He found 'the old discrimination in favour of the private (really, "privy") life' giving way everywhere 'to the expression of the gregarious state'. The highest common factor in America was the lowest common denominator!

Hence, powerful forces kept people acting in and for their group, and so divided one group from another. Class distinction flourished, even though it was distinctively American to move across class.

Class images and social areas

Once a class-riddled mind had developed, it created a class-ridden land. The two things, the mental image and the geographical reality, were intimately connected. In fact, class is one of the chief elements of American geography. People express identification with class through spatial identity. They belong to a class through claiming an area, or they choose an area in terms of class. And as Vance Packard (Packard, 1959) says, with their vastly increased ability to move from one area to another – about 100,000 United States families move and face new neighbours every day – 'millions of Americans judge not only homes but neighbourhoods much more carefully than before . . . in terms of status attached to them.' In this way *status areas* emerge. These 'heighten an awareness of status differences', according to Reissman (1961) in his study of *Class in American Society*, 'by bringing social peers together into a socially homogeneous environment' and thus giving them a hearth or home cut off from the hearths of higher or lower classes. In trying to protect the class with which they have identified themselves, Americans must mark out and defend an area that adequately expresses their status. They must find a district that 'reinforces the status image they wish to project of themselves. Home builders have happily helped the trend by emphasizing status appeals. Salesmen in their selling pitches stress such phrases as "upper brackets", "exclusive neighbourhood" and "executive-type buyers".' In this way, they make their customers feel that buying a home in their higher-priced development 'means they have arrived!'

People ensure social distinction by geographical division. Segregation is a fundamental American reality. Bourne's (1971) *Internal Structure of the City* brings that out in almost every term – economic, cultural, or political. The American class system 'maintains cultural, economic and social barriers which prevent intimate social inter-mixture between the slums, the middle class and the upper class. We know that human beings can learn their culture only from other human beings who already know and exhibit that culture.' Therefore, as Warner (1962) shows, 'by setting up barriers to social participation, the American social-class system prevents the vast majority of the children of the slums from learning any way of life except that of their own group. Thus the pivotal meaning of class . . . is that it defines and systematizes different learning-environments for children of different levels.' They grow up as though on different continents. In Warner's (1941) *Yankee City* the lower working class live down by the once-marshy and still damp riverside, behind the docks, with all their noise and smells. They have little to help them in the American struggle for existence. Eighty-five per cent of them have never finished high school, and 89 per cent end up in unskilled or semiskilled jobs. Ninety-four per cent of them live in rented apartments, badly in need of repair. Only 6 per cent of them own their own homes. This is an industrial, not a residential, area; home owning is at a discount. Houses are slap up against warehouses and factories, thick with pollution. Over half the people of this area are of foreign extraction, indeed nearly two-fifths are foreign-born. The district embraces all the Negroes in the city. Only 22 per cent belong to any kind of social club or association. They get most of their social life at home, or in the crowd, at bingo halls and in baseball stadiums. They are Catholic or fundamentalists by faith, with a highly ceremonial or else emotional religion, which no doubt helps them to put up with their conditions.

By contrast, the uppermost class lives on Hill Street, a name which speaks for itself, denoting not only superior height, but inaccessibility, and freedom from traffic, noise, and environmental hazard. Small families dwell in large houses, surrounded by trees and gardens. Eighty per cent of these are in the best condition, always kept well decorated. They are set in lots so spacious as to reduce the population density four or five times below that of the rest of the city. All this class are White and native-born, most of them are Anglo-Saxon and Episcopalian. They have been to university themselves and send their children there in turn, as a matter of course. A significantly high number of them belong to ten clubs or more, most of which are social and recreational; they spend their money on the house, decoration, entertainment, sport, and travel. Many have seaside or country cottages to which they go for long holidays. Their life is one of comfort and amenity.

These two groups are surely so distinct as hardly to belong to the same city, let alone the same country; yet they live at no great distance from each other. It was the same in the New York of *Maggie*, where the differences were if anything much greater. Here, an ever-increasing concentration of people, activities, and goods sharpened the competition for land. More and more of these wanted to be at the city centre. Specialization grew up as firms bidding for a position at the centre had to stress central functions. Like functions linked up with each other; for example, finance with administration and communications, until business districts emerged. Offices, department stores, and hotels got hold of the key junctions and the axial lines in Manhattan: they seized the crown of the island, forming New York's central business district (CBD), to push housing down-slope towards the sea. Meanwhile, industry, wholesaling, and transportation linked themselves at the waterfront and pushed housing back, up-slope. Those that lived between the two advancing fronts were caught in a veritable *shatter belt*. Their homes deteriorated into New York's 'lower-side' slums (see Fig. 5.1).

It is often difficult to make such conditions real through the conventional methods of geographical study, such as the statistical model. Realizing this, a number of geographers have been using the regional novel in the teaching of geography. Indeed at the 1972 convention of the International Geographical Union a special section was set up towards this end. Many geographers recognize in the novelist that sense of place which puts flesh on the statistical bones, as it were, making the connection between people and place more alive and more meaningful. Of course, by no means all novelists are concerned with the spatial setting, or the linkages between that setting and the human story; yet some bring out the links in a vivid and vital way. In doing so, a lot have been aware of how much class entrenches itself in, and becomes part of, the environment. Here the contrast between the lower and the upper end of the social scale is brought out by novelists who may have been unaware that over two-thirds of the poor live in centre-city situations in our great metropolitan communities, or that the suburbs account for four-fifths of the well-to-do, but who none the less make such realities live.

Slumscape America

Lower class districts were at their worst in the late nineteenth century when social Darwinism prevailed and the 'struggle for existence', enthroned in the mind, dominated the scene. Stephen Crane (1892) describes the situation in *Maggie*, a girl whose home was caught up in the outward pressure of shops from central Manhattan and the inward thrust

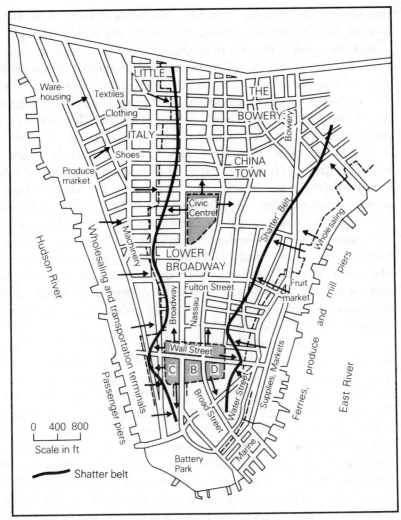

Fig. 5.1 *Lower Manhattan at the end of the nineteenth century.* The 'shatter belt' in American cities has long consisted of a zone of embattled housing, caught in the outward invasion of commerce from the central business district and the inward drive of transportation terminals and industry. 'Shattered' in this squeeze, housing deteriorates and is left to the poor – mainly foreign-born and non-whites.

of factories from the waterfront. The conflict between business and living quarters became more and more severe, commercial invasion leading to residential blight. In these circumstances, few residents made good: most went to the wall; such circumstances still prevail.

Maggie starts with fighting, as rival gangs of boys compete for 'a heap of gravel' in a vacant lot. In all the tight-packed area this was their only play space and was hotly contested. It lay next to a squalid 'apartment-house that arose from amid squat stables', in the heart of the Bowery. Maggie's brother, Jimmie, was in the thick of the fight, a habit which, while he was still 'a little boy, began to get him arrested. Before he'd reached a great age, he had a fair record', bringing disgrace upon the family. (One recalls that 66 per cent of the Riverside children in *Yankee City* had been had up for delinquency.) This fight was so furious it made some labourers look up, who had been 'unloading a scow at a dock in the [East] river'. Maggie's neighbourhood was just back of the waterfront, feeling the full impact of industrial expansion. Her father, also a labourer, returning home 'carrying his dinner-pail and smoking a pipe', put a stop to the fighting, and herded his family to their house. Maggie had been out on the street looking after her younger brother to get him out of the way of their mother, who was making the supper: she upbraided Jimmie, the older brother, for being so rough, but got slapped by him for the trouble. Fighting ran in the family! When they got home, their mother stormed at them, exasperated at Jimmie for fighting, and blaming it on the father. Mr Johnson walked out, without waiting for supper, and went to a nearby saloon where he drowned his sorrow in drink, complaining to all and sundry, 'Why do I come an' drin' whisk' here this way? 'Cause home reg'lar living hell!'

The whole atmosphere of the district bred conflict. The tenement was in a lane popularly known as Rum Alley. A tall, ungainly, begrimed 'careening building' it stood in a 'dark region' from which the sun was shut out by the high apartment blocks and by the factories and warehouses near the river. The tenement 'creaked from the weight of humanity stamping about its bowels'. It was made up of 'dark stairways and . . . gloomy halls' from which two-roomed flats were reached. One room was the kitchen where the family lived by day, and where the parents slept; the other was a bedroom for the children. The whole place was dirty, since the inmates had long ceased to care about appearances. Along the halls and stairs 'in all unhandy places there were buckets, brooms, rags and bottles', and outside 'long streamers of garments fluttered from the fire-escapes'. At the street side, 'a dozen gruesome doorways gave up loads of babies to the gutter'. Mothers in cramped and crowded conditions pushed out their young. Even 'infants played or fought in the street'. They had nothing else to do and nowhere else to go.

Working conditions were as harsh and unhappy as conditions in the home. Jimmie grew up to drive a horse-drawn truck and 'invaded the turmoil and tumble of the down-town streets' where his life consisted of cutting out and shouting down other truck drivers and raging at the police. Every day drew his aggressive instincts out, and made him more quarrelsome and tougher with the years. At home he continued to fight his mother, driving her to still more drink, and was hard on his sister, especially when she went out with Pete, the bar-keeper at a local saloon. He felt disgraced by her. 'Dis t'ing queers us!' he cried.

Maggie, meanwhile, had got a job as a seamstress in a neighbouring shirt factory, 'where they made collars and cuffs. She received a stool and a machine in a room where sat twenty girls of various shades of yellow discontent' straining their eyes in winter under the flickering gas lamps, and sweating in summer in the muggy heat by the river. 'Maggie perched on the stool and treadled at her machine all day, turning out collars.'

The factory 'began to appear to her mind as a dreary place of endless grinding. The air in the establishment strangled her. She knew she was gradually and surely shrivelling in the hot, stuffy room. The place was filled with a whirl of noises and odours. The fat foreigner who owned the factory . . . was a detestable character', always driving them on to the last minute of their time and the last ounce of their strength.

Maggie's way out was to dream herself into a different world. In the midst of 'the broken furniture, grimy walls, general disorder and dirt of her home' and to get her mind off 'the eternal moan of the proprietor' at work, 'her dim thoughts were often searching for far-away lands where the little hills sing together in the morning'.

She never came upon them, but she ran up against Pete who seemed exotic enough, and who in his smart clothes, with his shining patent-leather shoes, and plastered-down, pomade-smooth hair, was so different from her brothers and her father. She fell in love with him. 'Pete's elegant occupation [as a barman in a neighbourhood saloon] brought him, no doubt, into contact with people who had money and manners', such as theatre-goers who, late at night, finished off their festive evening in the Bowery by an exciting visit to an East Side bar. Then 'the restless doors of the saloons, clashing to and fro, disclosed animated rows of men . . . in an atmosphere of pleasure and prosperity'.

Although Maggie had been told she was doing wrong in going with Pete, she saw many others acting as she did. Most of the younger people were in revolt against their elders. They wanted new ways. The old standards were not enough. In any case one set of standards challenged another, as Jew and Armenian, Irish and Anglo-Saxon clashed almost daily. This could only have confused people. The Bowery thronged with different groups, at odds with each other. Most of the crowds met with at the Variety, or in the bars, were foreign-born. Jostling with each other, wherever they went, they jostled each other's ideas. Thus, ideas were thrown into what Henry James (James, 1907) called, the American cauldron. Out of this came the American character! It was no wonder, in that case, that the American character contained in it so much confusion and conflict. This was especially so with the working class, with Maggie's class, besieged and battered, as they were, by so many conflicting traditions.

Pete enjoyed the crowds that milled through the Bowery. He took Maggie to music halls and variety theatres, where she got away from an 'earth composed of hardships and insults', and even let herself 'wonder if the culture of refinement she had seen imitated by the heroine on the stage could be acquired by a girl who lived in a tenement and worked in a shirt factory', The hero's march in the play, from poverty, in the first act, to wealth and triumph in the final one, 'might not be altogether beyond the bounds of hope'. It was after all, the great American dream.

Her dreaming, however, came up abruptly against her mother, who railed at her for despising her own home and going out with Pete. The mother 'who was often drunk and always raving', all but 'dared' the young girl to leave and go off with her lover. 'Yeh've gone to d'devil, Mag Johnson. Yer a disgrace t'yer people. Go wid him, curse ye, and good riddance.' When Maggie, in despair at how to resolve the situation, *does* leave home, the drunken mother cries, 'Ah, who would t'ink such a bad girl could grow up in our family!' Drink was a protest against poverty; immorality an admission of it.

The saloon was the best sited and most imposing building in the street, and it gave Maggie some *cachet* that Pete worked here. 'On a corner this glass-fronted building shed a yellow glare upon the pavements. Its open mouth called seductively to passengers to enter and annihilate rage.' It was highly decorated and warm, full of music and of company. 'The elementary senses of it all seemed to be opulence.. . .' Pete was earning good money and he often took Maggie out. In the Variety Theatre 'the sound of the music drifted to Maggie's ears . . . and made her dream. She thought of her former Rum Alley environment and of her collar-and-cuff manufactory, and . . . imagined [for herself] a future rosy-tinted because of its distance from all that she had experienced before'. Like other young Americans she and Pete would rise. He had energy and initiative enough. Perhaps they would climb to the top!

Things went on in this hazy state of dreamy illusion, until one day Pete met a former lover of his, Nell, who had left him for better prospects in Buffalo but, disappointed there, had come back to the Bowery. Nell was much more experienced than Maggie, more worldly, flashing fine clothes and stilted manners at her men, and she recaptured Pete.

Maggie had to leave his apartment. At first she did not dare go home, but finally, in complete desperation, returned to her mother – only to be met with the full 'torrent of her mother's wrath'. The mother heaped on Maggie all the bitterness and frustration with which life at the fag-end of New York, at the sewer's spout of America, had filled her. 'She screamed at Maggie', catching Jimmie up into her flood of condemnation. '"Look at her! Der's yer sister. Ain' she a dandy! She's her mudder's purty darling yet, ain' she? Ain' she sweet – deh *beast*!"' The flailing terrible sarcasm was too much for Maggie, especially as her brother, too, 'expressed horror' at being contaminated by her.

'Maggie turned and went.' She became a girl of the streets. She plied her wretched trade, and must have felt more crushed than ever since, day by day, she saw Pete rise to wealth and ease. He became so well off that he sported 'half a dozen women including Nell gleefully laughing and hovering about him. "I'm good f'ler, girls! An'body trea's me right, I allus trea's zem right!" "To be sure", they cried in hearty chorus. "You're the kind of man we like.. . ."'

Perhaps the knowledge of Pete's success, and of what she might have had if only she had played him right, became gall and poison to Maggie. In any case, on the night in which he was glorying in his bevy of admirers, she took her life, where the Bowery came down to the docks, in the East Side river.

This happened on a depressing, raw, chill evening, such as made men run to the Elevated stations or call cabs rather than fight the weather. Maggie had been in one of the few down-town parks. One likes to think that, in this, she was getting as near as she could to her 'far-away lands'; enjoying, perhaps, the last relic of that green, open, and bird-sweet world which graced Manhattan before business took over. But actually she was searching for anyone who 'among the wet wanderers, in attitudes of chronic dejection' might feel enough for her to buy her a meal. Then she drifted out into the streets where she saw others, like herself, 'of the painted cohorts of the city', seeking their men. Maggie crossed avenues glittering with the downtown shine of shops and restaurants, offices, and hotels, where 'electric lights, whirring softly, shed a blurred radiance'. She passed on to lower New York's night-life area, at the back of the respectable businesses, and beside the multifarious traffic of the ill-lit river.

Here 'she went into the throng emerging from [the theatres and clubs and other] places of forgetfulness'. Men turned up the collars of their coats and women, no doubt looking as rosy-tinted under the theatre lights as once she thought her future would be, pulled their warm evening cloaks about them, waiting for cabs to take them to fabulous uptown residences. These people were 'intent upon reaching a distant home' and so did not see her; she was part of the invisible poor.

Maggie dragged her feet into the dark regions of factory and of tenement known all too well to her. Perhaps she thought of 'the dust-stained walls and scant and crude furniture of her home' and of the mother always centred in 'the sound of a storm of crashes and curses'. In any event, she came to the point of despair, where she would not even return the stare of 'a tall young man, smoking a cigarette with a sublime air' though he 'strolled near the girl' full of a look of utter *ennui*. He, for his part, when he saw how soiled she was, turned abruptly away.

'The girl walked on out of the realm of restaurants and saloons.' She made some last despondent passes at the few men hurrying by, but they avoided her, or answered her pleas with '"Not this eve – some other eve."'

The wretchedness and chill of those 'gloomy districts near the river' to which she at last descended, took hold of Maggie. Here 'tall black factories shut in the street and only occasional beams of light fell across the side-walks from the saloons'. This was the dead-end of the town, where the slum tenements were squeezed into smoke-filled nooks and noisy crannies between towering factories and squat, squalid warehouses.

Maggie must have realized she had come to the end of her tether as 'she went into the blackness of the final block. The shutters of the tall buildings were closed like grim lips. Afar off the lights of the avenues glittered as if from an impossible distance.' At the feet of the tall buildings, as though from the edge of a cliff, appeared the 'deathly hue of the river'.

Maggie let herself fall, and ended the bleakness of her days.

This story of conflict, bitterness, illusion, and disillusionment was redolent of the fierce freedom which in America's effort to be different could end in tragedy. The scene of Stephen Crane's story, where business and industry squeeze out the home, reflects a mind in which individual competition and conflict dominate. The American city is a balance of tensions – tipped against the ill-favoured. Maggie's walk to death was downslope, from the high crown of Manhattan to its lowest edge: it was a cross-section of the geography of urban tension in the great American city. Her personal decline showed her failure to maintain *social* status. This was measured by her inability to climb the *economic* ladder. Hence, she ended her days in the *geographical* sump. She could not equal the freedom that might have given her equality: her choice was to fly, but the flight ended in failure.

Fringescape America

Flight could, of course, be a sign of success. The flight to the suburban fringe is America's No. 1 success story (see Fig. 5.2). Class separates itself out with distance; to climb up is to fly out. At first well-to-do New York fled to Murray Hill and Greenwich Village; then, as these became invaded by commerce, they moved to Central Park; still later they escaped the throng of the city in Morningside. This choice region itself became pre-empted by shops, apartment blocks, and institutions so those that could afford it fled off Manhattan altogether, to the fringes of settlement along the north shore of Long Island or up the heights bordering the Hudson. Of course, it cost them a lot in time and money to commute back to town, but the possession of these things was the very asset that set them off from the middle and lower classes: they bought prestige at the expense of time, and exploited distance to show how distant they were from the ordinary man. This was exactly what Gatsby (Fitzgerald, 1925) did in showing how far he had gone.

When he chose a site on Long Island Sound he was helping to extend

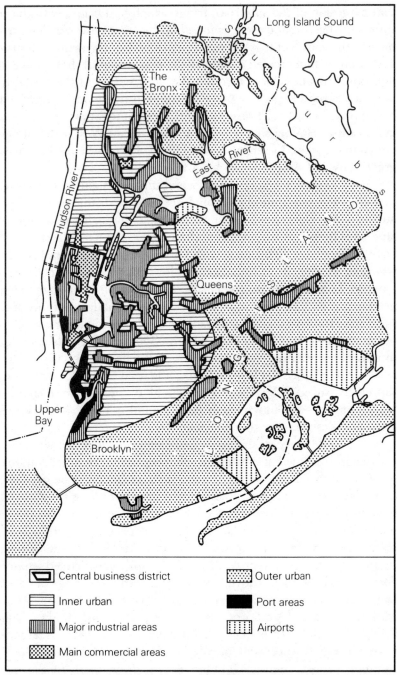

Fig. 5.2 *New York: major urban zones.* The flight to the suburbs is an escape by affluent Americans from the main commercial areas of the downtown and the industrial areas of the inner city. As pressures from shops, offices, and factories thin off, the value of housing increases and attracts the well-to-do and, in particular, the *nouveau riche*.

that explosion of the suburban fringe which had begun with the commuter train and been made more compelling by the motor car. The tremendous push to the centre of the American city by offices, departmental stores, hotels, and theatres had created a flight to the margins of all those who could afford light and air and space, through the 'affirmation of their wealth'. Gatsby bought the most expensive place he could, using it for a magnificent show of hospitality, but all in a brash, boastful, strident way that revealed his essential lack of taste. Having succeeded in the American West he felt it necessary to crown that success by setting up the House of Gatsby in the East, where all the great houses of America had been founded.

Gatsby's mansion had been built by a wealthy brewer whose plan in doing so was to 'Found a Family'. It showed a distinctly 'feudal silhouette', and to Nick Carraway, Gatsby's friend, it had all the appearance of an 'ancestral home'. It was meant to show that Gatsby had 'arrived', and was to have impressed a girl, Daisy, with whom Gatsby had once been in love but who had turned from him because he had then been too poor. She had married Tom Buchanan, a very successful western business man who felt the need to crown his career in New York. Gatsby made a fortune, and followed suit. The House of Gatsby stood opposite the Buchanan residence across one of the yacht-flecked bays of Long Island Sound. Here Gatsby put on a lavish display of his wealth to outshine his rival, Buchanan, and to win back Daisy if he could. He hoped her love for him would revive and that, when she saw how supremely successful he was, she would divorce Tom Buchanan, marry Gatsby, and, who knows, help him 'Found a Family' in the great house originally designed for that purpose.

The story deals, then, with men on the make who are trying to become part of the Establishment. They represent that freedom to climb the social scale which allows the lowest (such as Gatsby once was) to equal the best. They were 'the new races of men' of whom long ago Crèvecoeur had spoken. In part of Fitzgerald's story he gives a long list of all the new-made men who used to come to Gatsby's famous parties, including stockbrokers, manufacturers who had made their fortune in the new industries, film promoters, promoters of jazz, theatrical people, new-fledged senators, society doctors, and the like, drawn from an extraordinary range of nationalities – Ismays and Chrysties, Bulls and Dewars, with O'Donovans, O'Brians and McCarties, with Voltaires, Schraeders, Abrams, Finks, Cohens and Schwartzes, and with Belugas, de Jongs, da Fontanoes and Palmettoes. Here were the newly successful of all the European stocks in America whose common possession of new-found power drew them to the new-formed suburb. They made a whole new class, that of the new-doers, which gave their area its character. Here *class* had become pre-eminent, knitting together Gentile and Jew, Protestant and Catholic, Anglo-Saxon, German, French, Italian, what have you.

As a result, the suburb that Gatsby helped to make, called West Egg, was a community of its own, which could perhaps only have developed on the fringe of New York: a group of people who, like Gatsby, had risen from rags to riches in their own lifetime, and who did not know how to adjust except to people like themselves. They could conform to no one else, so they made 'a world complete in itself, with its own standards and its own figures'. But though they constituted an upper class, they did not belong to the uppermost level: this is an important point in Fitzgerald. Gatsby and his friends did not have time and tradition, as well as money, on their side like the really established families.

And this is where the tragedy of Gatsby begins. Culture does not only come of money, it comes of – generations of money! It comes of the knowledge across those generations of how to make use of money. As was said of the House of Sartoris, 'quality ain't only what you *is*, but what you *does*'. And it was in his doing, that the undoing of Gatsby lay. He may have moved in with what he thought were the right people, but he did not know how to do the right things. This was, of course, typical of what Henry James called the 'aspect of the new rich' in the New-World landscape, that 'chain of villas' thrusting themselves out from their suburban woods and lawns with 'an air of unmitigated publicity – loud, and assertive . . .'.

The fact is, of course, that money does not make the élite. Although the rise from rags to riches may set a stamp upon a man and make him part of what people call Society, unless he has the Jeffersonian touch – the aristocracy of taste, he is not really 'Society'. This is well brought out in Birmingham's (1968) fascinating study, *The Right People*. He begins:

> In America there is Society. Then there is Real *Society*. Real Society is part of Society – the upper part. Everybody who is in Society knows who the people in Real Society are. But the people in Real Society do not necessarily know who the other Society people are. The two groups seldom mix. Real Society is composed of older [*i.e. more established*] families. Old Families are better people. Better people are nicer people. Newer people may be richer than older people. That doesn't matter. Ordinary Society people may get to be Real Society people one day only if they work at it. It sounds confusing, but is really very simple. Cream rises to the top.

Gatsby got into Society by his wealth, but failed to become Real Society through his lack of breeding. He showed no taste, no discrimination. Compared with Maggie and her world he had 'made it'. But not knowing what to do with it, he fell into tragedy almost as great as hers. In the first place he made a tragic mistake in buying a house which, in terms of taste, was an absolute freak. Its builder, the rich brewer who wanted to 'Found a Family' had made it 'a period piece', we are told, but in fact it was an extraordinary hotch-potch of different periods. 'Gatsby's mansion was a collosal affair by any standard – it was a factual imitation [in the French baronial style] of some Hotel de Ville in Normandie, with a tower on one side.. . .' Yet, quite incongruously, it had 'a marble swimming pool' on the other side, together with great verandahs on which, in summer evenings, jazz bands played to dancing flappers, and 'a bar with a real brass rail . . . dispensed gins and liquors and cordials'. However, it was not this clash of feudal with modern which was so disconcerting as the conflict of styles collected together within the house. These included a 'Merton College high Gothic library, panelled with carved English oak, and probably transported complete from some ruin overseas'; a beautifully decorated 'Marie Antoinette music room'; the neo-classic revival of 'Restoration salons', for indoor dancing, with their mirrors and Corinthian pillars; and, in Gatsby's own quarters in the mansion, 'an Adam study' of the Scottish Renaissance.

Only a person with pots of cash but no soul could have built – or bought – such a place. Its existence shows us again the power of those crude monetary standards that could push Maggie and her people downslope to the dark and waste interstices between factory and warehouse, yet could give a man like Gatsby, out on the suburban fringe, all or anything that wealth could buy.

Here was an American, a member of the New World, who through his freedom to compete, had won far more than most of his fellows, and could indulge in all that struck him as most imposing from the Old World. Personal competition which had pushed Maggie into .the river, gave the earth to Gatsby. And this is brought out vividly, in the *scene*. Stephen Crane used adjectives for the Bowery such as a *dark* region, a *squalid* area, full of *gloomy* tenements, with *gruesome* doorways, and workshops that were *dreary* places of endless *grinding*. Fitzgerald's story is diffused with light and air and music.

> *There was music from Gatsby's house all through the summer nights. In his blue gardens men and girls came and went like moths among the whisperings and the champagne and the stars. At high tide in the afternoon, his guests dived from the tower of his raft, or took the sun on the hot sand of his beach while his two motor-boats slit the waters of the sound. On week-ends his Rolls Royce became an omnibus, bearing parties to and from the city, while his station-wagon scampered like a brisk yellow bug to meet all trains. And on Mondays eight servants . . . toiled all day with mops and scrubbing brushes and hammers and garden-shears, repairing the ravages of the night before.*

In this contrast is the key. The American image holds both light and dark; the dark side of freedom is the cost of the bright. But in the brightness itself is the dice of dark. A false throw can lose all. Gatsby may have risen like a star, but he fell like a meteor.

It was showing off his *class* to Daisy that really lost Gatsby the love he had striven to renew. Through his friend, Nick Carraway, who was Daisy's cousin, he managed to get Daisy over to his mansion, on her own. Here he tried to impress her with all that he had done and all that he had got, as if to assure her that at last he was one of her class – only more rich, and more successful. He had more than made up the gap that once existed between their stations. Surely she would change her mind, impressed by all he had achieved. He took Daisy throughout his house, made her admire the library and music room, had her look in on powder rooms, showed her bathrooms with rich, deeply sunken baths, and, leading her to his bedroom, 'opened two hulking patent cabinets which held his massed suits and dressing-gowns and ties, and his shirts, piled like bricks in stacks a dozen high. "I've got a man in England who buys me clothes", Gatsby told her. "He sends over a selection of things at the beginning of each season – spring and fall."' (The implication was plain! Had *she* ever had as much? Had *Tom*, her husband? Wouldn't it have been better if she'd waited until Gatsby had succeeded rather than married Tom Buchanan? What could her marriage give her, compared with all that Gatsby might have offered?) Gatsby thereupon 'took out a pile of shirts and began throwing them, one by one, before her, shirts of sheer linen and thick silk and fine flannel which . . . fell and covered the table in many-coloured disarray. He brought more, and the soft rich heap mounted higher, shirts with stripes and scrolls and plaids, in coral and apple-green and lavender and faint orange, with monograms of Indian blue.'

Daisy at first seems to have been moved by all Gatsby's efforts. Aware of her husband's flirtation, if not infidelity, she was almost prepared to break up her marriage and go back to her first love, when the brashness of Gatsby came over her, and forced her to have her doubts. She became appalled at the ostentation and bad taste and vulgarity of a huge party to which he invited both Daisy and Tom, especially as Tom found it all so cheap and tawdry. Gatsby realized the mistake he made, fired most of his servants, and no longer startled the neighbourhood with his garish grandiloquence. But it was too late; the tide had set against him.

It brought him to his ruin. One day he and his friend Nick and the two Buchanans drove up to New York. They hired a suite of rooms in the Plaza. They were about to beat the heat with ice-cold drinks when they fell into a quarrel. With the extraordinary ineptitude of a man who 'pushed his class' Gatsby challenged Tom Buchanan for Daisy's love. Although Daisy confessed that she had loved Gatsby she would not go so far as to say she had never loved Tom. At this, Tom let the advantage of his better breeding show up the spuriousness of Gatsby's position. Seeing that he had begun to shake her resolve and as a 'dare' to Gatsby, Tom told the pair to drive home in Gatsby's car while he followed in his own. He was convinced that, by the end of the drive, Daisy would have come to her senses and have given Gatsby up.

Daisy took the wheel. She drove at a furious speed. Her despair and anger made her so reckless she had a dreadful accident, running over a woman. Gatsby was horrified and his instinctive reaction was to take over the wheel and speed on. They drove home without stopping to see what had happened to the woman.

But Tom stopped. Seeing a crowd outside Wilson's garage he was at once gripped with fear. He pushed through the circle of people and saw the woman, Mrs Wilson, on a bench, a blanket pulled over her. She was dead! Outraged and appalled, he told Wilson that the car which had done the deed was Gatsby's. Wilson went that afternoon and shot Gatsby dead, after which he took his own life. Thus in the end the Great Gatsby's greatness did not save him, he went down like every other mortal, and with him perished that House of Gatsby which he had so obviously hoped to establish.

Symbolic of America, perhaps, the tragedy occurred in what Fitzgerald called 'the valley of ashes'. This was a regular no-man's-land, a zone of separation, between the city itself and its suburbs where, beyond the railway tracks fringing New York and at the end of the bridge leaving Long Island, was a belt of wasteland, made up of ash dumps and trash dumps, garbage piles and piles of old cars. It represented that least accessible and lowest, and therefore least-valued and lowest-priced, part of the central community before access was made to the higher and healthier land of the island, with villas half-buried in vernal woods. Here in this price-saddle, this value-hollow, the waste product, the burnt-out ash of men's endeavour, was dumped. This is surely significant. Between the world of wealth and the world of poverty is a valley of separation which has become for America a valley of ashes.

> About half way between *West Egg* [the suburb] *and New York* [the central city] *the motor road hastily joins the railroad and runs beside it for a quarter of a mile, so as to shrink away from a certain desolate area of land. This is a valley of ashes – a fantastic farm where ashes grow like wheat into ridges; where ashes take the form of houses and chimneys and rising smoke.... Occasionally a line of gray cars crawls along an invisible track, gives out a ghastly creek, and comes to rest; and immediately, ash-gray men swarm up with leaden spades and stir up an impenetrable cloud....*

Once this is behind, both car and train can speed on to New York, where they soon lose themselves in the signs, on every hand, of its dynamic, fantastic growth.

It was here in this waste land of America that tragedy finally struck – land made desolate by those same forces of unbridled competition, unlimited freedom and untutored power which had created the lower and the upper worlds of Crane's *Maggie* and the *Gatsby* of Fitzgerald. The American dream in putting freedom first, put itself at risk, and opened for itself a valley of ashes, where dreaming came to grief.

It was no wonder that, when Gatsby's friend, Nick Carraway, left Long Island to go back to his home, he looked with sadness at those summer-crowned trees and rich lawns which were the relics of the world of sweet green grace that New York·had once been before the Americans took over. 'As the moon rose, the inessential houses began to melt away until gradually I became aware of the old island here that flowered once for Dutch sailors' eyes – a fresh, green breast of the new world.' Fitzgerald challenges men to think out what has happened since. Here 'for a transitory enchanted moment man must have held his breath in the presence of this continent . . . face to face for the last time in history with something commensurate to his capacity for wonder'.

Was it all to end up in a valley of ashes or could America still make the initial wonder, the Great American dream, work itself out in the landscape?

Geographical implications

The American myth that he is free to cross class boundaries and therefore live in a classless society is a myth indeed. In reality most are born into a class and are subject to a class-cut society. This is partly economic and partly geographical. In an economy that glorifies free enterprise and puts profit first, power is given into the hands of those who have capital and know-how, and this power is used to entrench their own position. Even corporation and income tax do not enable enough redistribution of power to alter that. The richest nation in the world still has one in eight people in poverty, and one in three people in near-poverty. Moreover, part of the entrenchment of economic power is through geographical protection. Those who can afford it capture the areas of comparative advantage, and not merely leave the disadvantaged in, but in fact push them out, to the geographical limbo. Geography comes to seal up the well-to-do in well-off regions, and seal away the rest in less auspicious areas. Furthermore, it is within the power of the well-to-do to decide which are the areas to use and how to use them. It is their choice that the central areas of cities should be mainly for business – which therefore ruins them for living. They make the suburbs the choice sites for living, and segregate themselves off from down-town conflict.

The American will not get rid of class until he alters his dream, until for example he puts *we* and *ours* before *me* and *mine*, the general good before private gain. It is not enough to say that private gain is for the general good, because in the meantime the inequalities created at the individual level become entrenched on a group basis. That is where the geographer comes in –

to show the territorial impact of inequality and how it builds up whole regions of injustice. We need a new regional geography not concerned so much with the economic maximization of areas of comparative advantage, but with the equalization of territorial injustice. To do this means helping to create a new dream, in which perhaps the truly classless society might emerge, because spatial justice would be achieved. This could only be done if one emphasized the social value of land and, instead of an economic bid-rent curve, had a social equalization plane, as the basis of land-use.

But this would require a new mental geography. At present the pinnacle of personal competition decides the economic gradient which in turn controls the social contour: the community is structured, as much as it can be so, after the individual. But economic ends should flow from social needs. Individual freedom should work to free the group – free it from poverty and circumscription, and for well-being and content.

Of all America's divisions that of class should be the least easy to accept. It does not go with the image of the American as 'the new order of man'. It smacks very much of the Old Adam in us still – which was to have been left behind in the Old World! Yet it is, in fact, now in the Old World that the new concept of social space is growing, making the use of land a function of social not economic gain, of public and not private good.

References

Birmingham, S. (1968) *The Right People*, Little, Brown, Boston, p. 3.

Bourne, L. S. (ed.) (1971) *Internal Structure of the City*, Oxford Univ. Press, Toronto, pp. 97–103.

Cooley, C. H. (1966) 'The function of personal competition', in Ginger, R. (ed.) *American Social Thought*, Hill & Wang, N.Y., p. 123.

*Crane, S. (1892) *An Omnibus*, Stallman, R. W. (ed) Knopf (1952) N.Y., *Part 1, Bowery Tales, Maggie: A Girl of the Streets*, pp. 43–4, 58, 46–8, 62, 87, 69, 64, 101, 77, 79, 97, 103–4.

Dollard, J. (1937) *Caste and Class in a Southern Town*, Doubleday Anchor, 3rd edn. (1957) N.Y., p. 65.

*Fitzgerald, F. Scott (1925) *The Great Gatsby*, Scribner edn (1953) N.Y., 5–6, 62–3, 105, 5, 40, 45, 92, 39, 93–4.

Harrington, J. (1963) *The Other America*, Macmillan, N.Y. p. 10.

James, H. (1907) *The American Scene*, Hart Davis edn, London, p. 67.

Packard, V. (1959) *The Status Seekers*, McKay N.Y., pp. 78–92.

Reissman, L. (1961) *Class in American Society*, Free Press, Glencoe, p. 30.

Schlesinger, A. (Jr.), (1968) *Violence: America in the Sixties*, Signet, N.Y., pp. 31, 43.

US Bureau of the Census (1975) *Current Population Reports*, 'Population profile of the United States', Ser. P-20, No. 279.

Warner, W. L. (1965) *American Life, Dream and Reality*, U. of Chicago Pr, Chicago, p. 127.

---

*The sequence of page numbers at the end of the reference corresponds to the sequence of quotations in the text.

Poverty and crime

Poverty and America

It has always been part of the American dream that America would take in the poor and needy of the world and give them new hope in a new life: America was the world of the second chance. And to many it did indeed mean a new world and their at long last dream. But the freedom to achieve was also the freedom to fail. There are 26 million US citizens today below the poverty level. This is a large number never to have achieved their dream. On the contrary they have found themselves exploited: cleaned out by an America full of that sharpness where every man plays his own hand. The American system can give and give most generously, but it can also take away. Many an immigrant was simply made use of; Negroes were brought in to be exploited; and the Indian went to the wall. The liberty that America offered was not the liberty of each, qualified by the like liberty of all; it was the liberty to get away with as much as the rest would bear. It was the liberty to put oneself to the test and go as far as one could. This undoubtedly meant that men like Carnegie, who grew up a poor lad in a cottage, could end with a mansion, one of the richest men in the world. But not all were as aggressive and ruthless or able and sufficient as Carnegie. Many a poor immigrant, especially those without the language or education, remained poor. Indeed, many an American, born and bred in the country, never got out of poverty. Even now one in eight do not have adequate food and shelter, but live on a poor diet in substandard housing.

This poverty is, to an extent, involved in the American way itself. The individualism that America admires, in a system of open competition, puts a cruel edge to success. Of course, one dreams of the success. When Crèvecoeur (1782:1963) left France for Canada, and then left Canada for revolutionary America, it was for a society of 'individuals of all races . . . whose labour is founded on self interest. Nothing has stronger allurement', he went on, than when 'each man works for himself'. To him, America was the self-made man. He realized that this meant struggle. He did not object to that. Indeed he felt that America could only make good through struggle.

He himself had fought in the French War and had suffered in the American Revolution, losing his wife. He saw how immigrants strove with each other, the earlier ones exploiting the later ones. He says:

> *The pioneer remembers his former difficulties: no one assisted* him, *why should he assist* others? *He has had to struggle alone through difficult situations: he therefore deals hardly with his new neighbours. Fearful of all fraud in all his dealings and transactions, he arms himself with it! Each is on guard in his daily intercourse. If this is not 'bellum omnium contra omnes' 'tis a general mass of keenness and sagacity acting against another mass of sagacity!*

Yet this is a keenness that keeps America constantly honed, sharp-edged, and ready.

The ideal persisted. In Jefferson's Inaugural Address he referred to the right of each American to 'the use of our own faculties and the acquisition of our own industry'. If individuals worked sufficiently hard, the nation would take care of itself. Should enough individuals make use of their freedom to make enough money, the benefits would flow to the rest.

And there is a sense in which this has happened; no American is poor like the poor of, let us say, Bangladesh. The general affluence means that many of the American poor have their own car or TV set. They would be considered well-off by the dwellers in the *favella*, the shack-towns of Brazil. Yet they *are* poor by American standards – they are poorly housed and fed and trained, have poor jobs (if any jobs at all) and are poor in status and in power. They do not acquire an adequate return for their industry; many do not find the opportunity to use their own faculties. They are born into poverty and become locked into it for the rest of their lives.

A lot of Americans cannot believe that this is the case, and blame the individual concerned for his plight. As Peet (1972) points out:

> *Two basic stances on the causes of poverty may be recognized. Poverty can either be blamed on characteristics of individuals or groups – elements in personality, in family structure or in [group] subculture – or on economic and social circumstances which lie . . . well beyond the control of individuals. In its crudest form this dichotomy is stated in terms of a poor person being poor because 'he does not try hard enough' or because of 'circumstances beyond his control'.*

Peet goes on to describe a Gallup poll which showed that 'when those who could not make up their mind or could make no choice between the two positions were excluded, 54 per cent attributed poverty to lack of effort, and 46 per cent to circumstances'. O. Lewis is quoted as saying that the poverty subculture is itself a major cause. 'By the time slum children are age six or seven they have usually absorbed the basic values and attitudes of their subculture [of poverty] and are not psychologically geared to take full advantage of the increased opportunities which may occur in their life-time.' They are scared or sceptical, lack hope, have little faith and so show next to no initiative. They have lost – if they ever had – the 'belief in their own industry' and what any man could get if he only went out and 'worked for himself'. In 1975, 7.8 millions, in the employment ages, could not find work.

This is doubtless true, but though it may explain, it should not be allowed to explain away, poverty. That such a subculture should exist in America is itself a blight on the American dream. Surely America did not fight the Revolution so that 12 per cent of all its people should be below the poverty level. (1975, 12.21 per cent) If this is so, perhaps it should have another revolution and come up with another system. Far too many people are too poor, to blame the individual – although not to blame individualism! That many individuals may be presumed to have 'defects in mentality or behaviour' might be the case, but have these defects not been brought about – or at least been brought out and exacerbated – by an individualism that does, in effect, amount to *'bellum omium contra omnes'*?

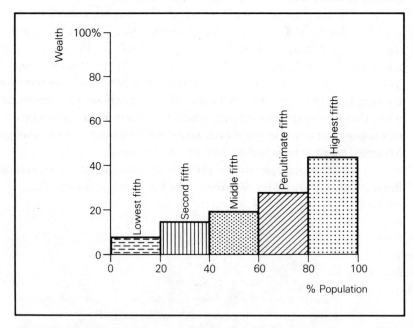

Fig. 6.1 *Family income, 1975.* Inequality is a marked feature of an American society long dedicated to individual enterprise and free competition. However, income redistribution through taxation does level up community conditions.

In 1975, the lowest 20 per cent of families, ranked by income, received only 5.5 per cent of the income of all families; the next lowest 20 per cent, had only 11.9 (see Fig. 6.1). Thus the 40 per cent making up the bulk of the workers of America, had 17.4 per cent of American family income; the next 40 per cent representing the middle class, had 41.5 per cent of the income – which about matched. But the top 20 per cent, America's upper class, had as much again, i.e. 41.1 per cent. Altogether 15.4 per cent of all families were classified as poor or subpoor (US Bureau of the Census, 'Population profile', *Current Population Reports*, Ser. P-20, July 1977).

Such poverty is not a random thing. It does not occur haphazardly here or there as it well might if it went back merely to the individual. It goes back to the situations in which individuals are put, and these situations repeat themselves so frequently and on such a mass scale as to create *poverty regions*.

This is where social geography comes in. There are social images that put values on the land, and its use, which offer some places to those who are advantaged and leave the rest to the disadvantaged. Poverty is left to areas of social denigration which then become regions of geographical deterioration. Such regions might show up physical disabilities like isolation, rugged relief, and an inclement or unproductive climate. But they might occur in the best of physical circumstances where for social reasons these had become undesirable, like Fitzgerald's valley of the ashes.

Poverty areas

There are two broad categories of poverty – urban and rural. Urban poverty occurs mainly in the cities of a million or over, and, in these, mainly in the older cities. It is especially prevalent in the central areas of these cities. It festers in the ethnic ghettos, particularly in the Negro, Puerto-Rican, Mexican and Indian quarters, which now make up 66 per cent of the urban poor, but also in the ghettos of the poorer Europeans – the Italian, Greek, Portuguese, and Polish communities, and in Asian precincts. Rural poverty is characteristic of isolated areas, hilly country, eroded farmland, cut-over districts, and mined-out regions. Many of these parts were settled by native-born Americans of Anglo-Saxon, Irish, and early migrant stocks from Western Europe. Included are extensive sections in the South farmed by negro tenants or sharecroppers. Few Asian or recent European groups have moved into and become derelict in rural America.

Social values in the city

These tend to be in inverse ratio to economic values. Where there is intense economic pressure for space, there is a social vacuum. Where economic values ease off, social values take over. The poor are sucked into the vacuum; the rich are part of the take-over zone. America centres its city in the business district, made up principally of offices, shops, hotels, and passenger terminals (except for space-consuming air terminals). There is little room here for home and hearth. Residents must be either very rich to vie for central access, or very poor to fill up the nooks and crannies of graceless space. Commerce pushes out along the great axial routes to the city hinterland. At the same time, industry – at least that industry which seeks a city market or uses city services – thrusts in. A zone of conflict emerges, shattered by this out – in invasion. Here social values are low; speculators are always hoping to make a profit by spearheading the commercial invasion *out* or the industrial invasion *in*. Household conditions within metropolitan areas are distinctly worse inside central-city areas (see Fig. 6.2).

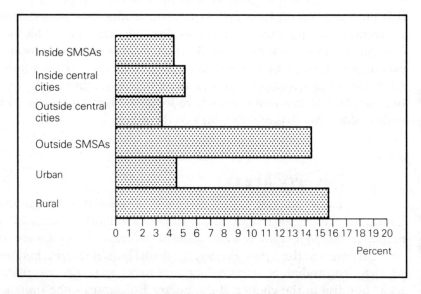

Fig. 6.2 *Urban and rural poverty, 1975 as indicated by percentage sub-standard households.* Urban poverty, though less than rural, is more concentrated. It dominates the inner city, especially in large metropolitan areas, where housing deteriorates at the invasion of commerce and industry.

Here, housing is at a discount. If it can be bought over and turned into business-making space it disappears. Nevertheless, in the interstices between the radial roads and railways, housing meets the need of the many families working in the shops and offices of the city centre or the industries and transport terminals of the surrounding subcentres. If this housing can be dense enough it can pack in a sufficient number of tenants to give landlords an income until they sell out to factory or office. This is the land left to the poor: land with very little light because the tenements are built too tall, with next to no play space because tenement crowds up to tenement, with no quiet since it is close to the axial invasion lines, and no cleanliness, choked with the smog of traffic, factory chimneys, and hotel boiler-houses.

Graceless space is here at its worst. It is filled with those who cannot expect grace in their days, the recent immigrant from poor countries abroad – the Caribbean, Mediterranean Europe, the Middle East, Negroes and poor-Whites from the South (and their progeny now sons of the slum), Indians, and others who, too, have little education and few skills. It is here that the Bowery, Chinatown, Little Sicily, and the East Side of New York are found. This has swallowed up Greenwich Village, and witnessed Harlem grow. This is Northside and Southside Boston and the fate of Roxbury. This, too, Southside Chicago; and Watts, LA. This is death city in Detroit and skid row in San Francisco. Railway routes and roads carrying truck traffic (both lined with industry) drag the inner city belt of poverty well out, often cutting swathes across the suburbs. Pockets of poverty occur around what were former towns (with commerce and industry) incorporated into the metropolis. Patches of rural land at the city fringe gone dead while awaiting urban development, often invite the poor in a scatter of shacks, among dirt roads and weeds.

What makes the matter worse is that many poor, including immigrants, seek the city out, in order to get relief. Indeed, as Gottmann claims, this is one of the factors that makes urban centrality still such a potent force in social geography. Yet many of those who live on relief live at a very low level. However affluent America is, many Americans go hungry. In the 1977 report of eighteen private social agencies in New York, called *Myths and Realities of Welfare* it was found that 56 per cent of welfare mothers were unable to provide their families with 'a nutritionally adequate diet'; in fact 41 per cent of these families 'experienced varying degrees of hunger *at all times*'. This made a considerable number, since in all there were 1.2 million on relief.

Yet as more of the poor come into the city they make matters worse. They compete with each other in having to pay higher rents for fewer services; they are subject to ever more crowding; schools and hospitals are also crowded and inadequate; there are few facilities for a social life, and even fewer for recreation. The percentage of centre-city people in metropolitan areas involved in the frequent change of home is distinctly higher (48.5/28.4 per cent) than elsewhere in the SMAs, (Standard Metropolitan Areas) and goes with higher divorce rates (112/63 per thousand), more single-head families (13.4/12.3 per cent) and higher unemployment (8.3/5.4 per cent). Downward movement in income and status may lead to eviction or the disheartening slump to the slum. The search for work is increasingly more difficult: individuals are having to go out further to get jobs, especially with the decentralization of offices and light industry to the suburbs. As Davies and Albaum (1972) show there is now a reverse commuter problem with 'increasing distance between low-income city centre dwellers and decentralized work-place location. Together with poor educational attainment, skill deficiencies, low motivation and discriminatory living practices, the reverse-commuter problem is yet another causal factor behind the high unemployment levels' of the urban poor. The city finds it more and more expensive to provide public transport for this and for inner city traffic, it gets less revenue and has to put out more money on policing, fire protection, social welfare, and general maintenance and repairs.

In fact many cities cannot meet the cost and have to draw heavily on their state or on the federal government (see Fig. 6.3). Slum-clearance and urban-renewal programmes are going ahead, but they fall far short of the need. America spends nothing like the European countries on low-cost public

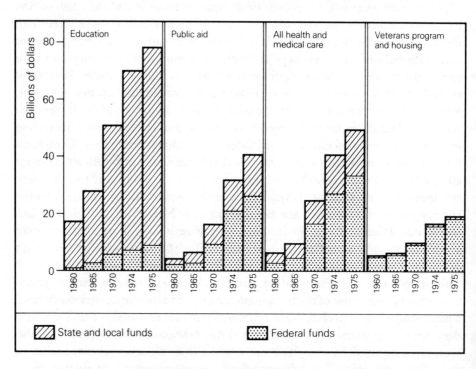

Fig. 6.3 *Social Welfare expenditures under selected public programmes 1960–1975.* Although welfare spending in the United States is all but monumental that on low cost public housing is surprisingly low.

housing. Less than 1 per cent of its revenues go into this compared with 13 per cent in Britain for example, or even more in Sweden. (Indeed only 1.047 per cent of the total federal welfare expenses, themselves only a part of all US outlay, goes into housing.) Of course, most countries have still far to go in what Harvey (1972) calls a 'just distribution (of wealth) justly arrived at'. To do this in the United States would require a basic reshaping of the American image to include 'the necessity for social cooperation in seeking individual advancement'. It was not until Roosevelt's 'New Deal' and Lyndon Johnson's 'War on Poverty' that much was done along these lines.

Massive rural poverty was what led Johnson to take action especially in Appalachia and the Ozarks. Here is the worst poverty in America. But all throughout the South, poor-Whites and even poorer Negroes pose a grave problem. Here, 15 per cent of all families, and 40 per cent of individuals outside the family are below the poverty level. Other bad areas are back-country New England, in cut-over areas, also in the cut-over barrens of the Upper Great Lakes and Pacific Northwest, and the mined-out districts of the Superior Upland, around Lake Superior, and of the old mining centres of the Rockies (see Fig. 6.4).

The poor-Whites of the southern Piedmont and the plateaux of the southern Appalachians and Ozarks have been disadvantaged for a longer period than any others in the United States, including even the Negro. For they date back to the indentured labourers brought over from England for the initial development and settlement of the South. When these finished their period of service, they left town or plantation and struck out for the bush, where they squatted on the land and lived their own life. As the tide of settlement came in behind them across the coastal plain they moved up to the Piedmont, and as this was invaded they pushed through the Blue Mountains into the maze of ridges and valleys in the Appalachian Mountains. Always they were independent and apart. Of all individualistic Americans they were the most individual – but this did not spur them on to riches and success, on the contrary it led them to eke out a living in the 'back country' where they could be by themselves. The South became divided between the highly sophisticated 'tidewater gentlemen' and the rough-and-ready 'back-country boys'. The latter grew in number until at the Civil War 5 million of the 8 million Whites were the poor-white element. They represented the largest community of the poor in the United States. Most of them lived on isolated farms, with a wooden shack on an earthen floor, a crib or two for the corn they produced from a small field, and a shed where they kept dried peas or beans, carrots, and potatoes. They lived mainly by hunting, especially for wild pig that roamed the forests in great droves. They were illiterate, could not count, never took part in public affairs, and paid no taxes. Their ruling passion was to remain free. It was a passion that made it increasingly difficult for them to adjust, particularly after Reconstruction when the freed slave could challenge their position. They despised the Blacks, yet were despised by better-off Whites. They therefore retreated into isolation. Here social isolation found support in geographical isolation and kept the poor-Whites apart. It is not true to say they were poor because of their rugged and difficult environment, rather they sought that environment out because of those values that made them poor. Here again the social factor was the most important in their geography. Naturally poor areas were sought out by socially poor settlers until poor-white 'belts' developed.

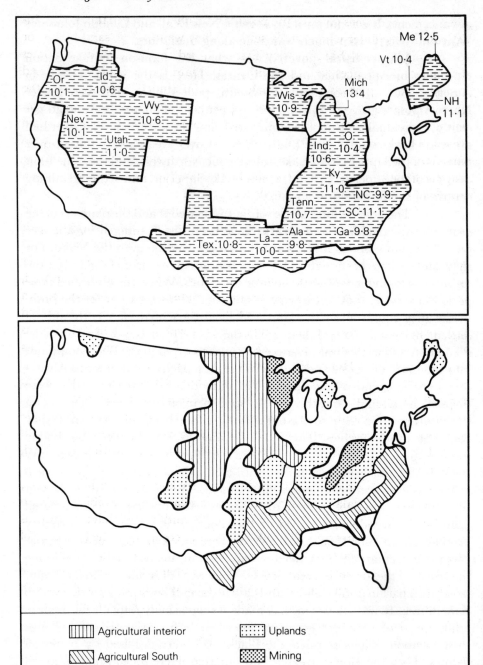

Fig. 6.4 *Regions of greatest personal income growth, (percent per annum) 1976 (top) and regions of poverty, 1960 (bottom).* Rural poverty is widespread, especially where natural resources, once thought plentiful, have been 'burned up' by wasteful exploitation. *However, anti-poverty programs have revolutionized the situation, producing rapid-growth regions.*

The names given to the poor-Whites often reflected the geographical conditions under whichd they settled. They were called 'sand-hillers' or 'pineywood tackies' because they first occupied the old stranded beaches forming sandy terraces on the Atlantic Coast Plain. These sandy terraces had a vegetation of pinewoods, with palmetto palm and thorn bush. Once the pines were cleared, the soil became rapidly eroded by gullying and sheet wash, and any plantations that had replaced the pinewoods soon deteriorated to the point of ruin. This became widely known and planters avoided such sand-hill areas. Hence, they were the very areas sought out by poor-Whites anxious to be on their own. They did not rely on the soil for a living, but on streams for fishing and relict woods for hunting.

Other names given to the poor-Whites were 'red necks' and 'crackers'. These were the inhabitants of the heavily eroded red lateritic soils of Georgia, Alabama, and Louisiana. The laterite, once the topsoil was removed, was found to be almost as hard as brick, and in the dry weather would split into numerous cracks. A man who was so uneducated, unenterprising, and inefficient as to content himself with cut-over scrub in washed-out, sun-cracked laterite was called a cracker. This sun-cracked laterite got extremely dusty in a long spell of dry weather and the red dust was driven by the wind into houses, clothes, skin – filming everything with its unmistakable tint. Hence 'red-neckers'.

Poor-Whites were also referred to as 'clay-eaters'. This was a general appellation throughout the South where malnutrition and debility, resulting from not only a poor diet but a very unbalanced one, made people feel perpetually hungry and gave them a craving to fill themselves even with clay. Eating clay satisfied the craving but left the eater with a stretched, sunken face and a pot-belly.

Finally, many of the poor-Whites were known as the 'hollow men', because, in the Appalachians, they sought out isolated, inaccessible hollows so that they could live completely by themselves and to themselves. This was especially the case in the larger sink-hole basins, common in the limestone of the Cumberland Plateau.

Over the centuries these poor-Whites have continued in the same way of living. In 1950 their life was much as Governor Hammond of South Carolina described it in 1850: 'Some cannot be said to work at all. They obtain a precarious subsistence by occasional jobs, by hunting and fishing.' Many now depend on welfare to eke out their corn or potato patch and the few chickens they raise. It was only in the 1960s under Lyndon Johnson, that things began to change.

Yet change is difficult to organize. Their desire to live by themselves scattered them over the land. They not only isolated themselves from the Negro and the rich White but also from each other. They are hardly ever to be found in hamlets or villages, but live in separated individual farmsteads, no nearer than within gunshot of each other. This means that their shops, schools, churches, and saloons are also single and separate, scattered among the little farmsteads, at bridging points or the meeting of rural trails. Few parts of America witness such a widely disseminated settlement of individual houses and institutions.

The latter are poorly developed. Schools are having to be amalgamated and children bussed to the new consolidated schools to get away from the small and ill-equipped places that were so common – and that still exist. The larger parish scheme which depends on the closure of some churches in favour of concentrating on others, has made little headway. The small church, usually of a fundamentalist, evangelical sort, is still supported. The poor-Whites are part of the 'bible belt' where highly emotional bible-based religion holds sway. This deep-grained conservatism makes it difficult for them to change.

Yet a remarkable programme of farm improvement, weed eradication, the checking of erosion, contour-ploughing, and reafforestation is beginning to take effect. Rural electrification is also allowing small industries to spring up. These, added to fine new high schools, training centres, and social halls, are building up little towns which are giving leadership and cohesion. Life is improving – there has been remarkable growth in some traditionally poor areas, like Appalachia.

The poor-Whites are by no means confined to the South. For one thing many Southern poor-Whites have moved up in the North, and now fill poor-White ghettos in the inner city areas of the great metropolis. Here they vie with Indian and black Americans for tenements close to freight terminals and factories. One wonders why they made the move because they have only exchanged the rural for the urban slum. Few have made good. Here is an example, perhaps, where the poverty subculture has them trapped.

Other poor-Whites include large numbers of French Canadians in northern New England, especially in parts of Maine that have been cut-over and burnt-over so often that they have become virtual barrens. Former lumber camps have disappeared, but a handful of families have been left here and there in the poor scrub that has sprung up. Toynbee, the English historian, expressed astonishment at seeing abandoned settlements, farms where the fields were going back into bush and where farmhouses, warped and with their paint peeling off, had become virtual shacks, all in the space of a day's drive from Boston. He obviously had not read Henry Adams (Adams, 1889:1965) who described the collapse of up-state New England when the rich plains of Ohio were discovered in the early nineteenth century. Adams had seen men wrestling the stumps of trees out of the ground, only to find the ground more full of stones than soil: broken hearted, but not broken, they moved on. Who would have stayed in the glacial waste?

Cut-over wastes soon came to characterize the West as well as the

East. The shores of the Great Lakes were ravaged between 1820 and 1890 where oak and pine were torn out of the rich lake-shore forests for the rapid building up of the great industrial cities from Buffalo through Cleveland and Detroit to Chicago – still great gulpers of wood for housing, newsprint, and wood-based chemicals. Many parts did, of course, stay in forest through natural regeneration, but on the rough rolling land of the great terminal moraines and the sweeps of sandy deltas, gully and sheet erosion made it difficult for good timber to come back. Here lumber camps became ghost towns, and the spread of waste left poor families to get poorer. Further west, in Washington and Oregon, clear-cutting of large areas led to swift and often savage erosion on the steep slopes of mountains facing the full sweep of the Pacific rains. Although the wet and mild climate and long growing season helped regeneration, and consequently, the forest came back more than it did in many eastern parts, nevertheless cut-over wastes often occurred. The lumber camps then moved on; but they left poor families that stayed because of inertia or local attachments.

In fact, the cycle of lumber camps generally resulted in this: first single men and a few married families (as for example, of the supervisors) would move in, and bunkhouses and family shacks go up. As cutting progressed, the settlement would attract more people: some of the young men brought newly wed wives in, and family life would take root. In time schools, churches, and stores would give the appearance of a settled life. But then the problem of getting work for school-leavers would appear; not all could hope for a job in the town, girls in particular left. The family might leave with them. If the region became cut out much quicker than the forest could come back, the lumber men would move on. The town could then find itself with no substantial base. Businesses would migrate, schools close. Yet a few families would continue, finding enough odd jobs to keep themselves alive, or living on relief. Such has often been the story of America's cut-over barrens.

Poor-Whites also typify mined-out areas, as for example around the southern and western uplands backing Lake Superior, or in the Ozarks, or in parts of the Appalachians or West Mountain States. Mining is by its very nature a robber economy: it is bound to consume the basis of its wealth. The mining boom attracts swift and widespread settlement, as for instance the iron-mining towns of Marquette, Gogebic, Mesabi, and Cuyuna around Lake Superior. As the boom gets under way it draws in speculators of all kinds. These push development still more. Americans enjoy the excitement of a great leap forward. To get wealth and to get it quickly the mines are creamed of their high-grade ore. When they reach low grades they close up, and mining moves on. The boom is bust. It swings to another venue – the Steep Rock or Labrador, Canada; or to Venezuela; or Mauretania. Money, machines, management, and skilled labour also switch, and the communities left behind have very little to offer. Poverty creeps in. The population drops away to where it cannot support high schools, hockey teams, or even bingo halls. A low-grade life is matched with the low-grade ore.

A big part of the problem is that these settlements are based on a single resource. There may be no alternative ways of earning a living. These one-resource towns have their difficulties at the best of times. Decisions are made from above – from the mine-owner or his manager. Very often they are made at a distance, in some remote board of directors in Chicago or New York. Many workers have a feeling of alienation: their views are not called for or taken into account. Consequently, they have little loyalty, as the town declines they move out: that movement itself hastens decline. Social life is very structured. The élite of the mine are the town élite, and yet this local élite is only part of an intermediate organization in a hierarchical set-up going back, not just to the mine-owner, but the financial interests on which he is dependent. In fact, the hierarchy of the mine or mill becomes the hierarchy of the town. Status in the town depends on status in the mine. One has to respect the supervisor on the street to keep his respect down the shaft. Yet one must not get too 'pally', because he might be moved on. These are irksome conditions to those who want more choice; if choice in the mine itself narrows, such people leave. The ones that stay soon have little option. Women have less opportunity than men, because men dominate the work force. The maleness of a mining town with its male clubs, male halls, male saloons, male sports, male recreation thrusts itself upon one in the daily scene. Should the town grow, auxiliary services are demanded that need women; as the town dwindles, these close up. Many women move even before that happens. A grave imbalance becomes still more grave. A kind of social malaise spreads through the town: poverty is part of this and increases as the town decreases.

Ill-being geography

It is obvious, then, that poverty has a very geographic connotation. Man has impoverished the land and poor land has been left with poor people. This is so whether we are dealing with the rural waste or the urban desert. The results show up in the distribution of malaise. David Smith's (Smith 1972) remarkable work on social well-being, or as it might be better called social ill-being, reveals how repeatedly some regions show up at the lower end of the social scale. The South, for one, Maine and other outback parts of New England, the southern tier of the Mountain States, and certain areas of the Great Lakes States and the western Plains. Even sectors that are very affluent like southern New England, the mid-Atlantic States and California suffer from pockets of distress and poverty. The Central Mountain and Pacific Northwest States are generally above average, but have significant areas of ill-being. The highest score (in terms of socio-economic well-being) are the

States of New York, Connecticut, Massachusetts and California, while the lowest (or most negative) are in Mississippi, followed by South Carolina, Alabama, and Arkansas.

The deep depression of the late 1970s made things worse for the better states and, of course, confirmed in their social and economic woes, the already 'bad' states. According to the Department of Labour (1976) the average number of US unemployed (those receiving unemployment benefits), as a percentage of the employed was 5.2: Maine and Vermont had 7.15, Michigan 8.3, and Washington State 7.7 – these are all areas with cut-over or mined-out wastes; the Lower Mississippi and South Atlantic States (excepting Florida) had averages ranging from 6.7 in Arkansas to 6.5 in South Carolina, much of this due to rural, and especially farm, poverty. Strangely, Smith's highest rating States, in terms of general affluence, had unemployment scores of 5.9 New York, 5.8 Connecticut, 7.0 Massachusetts, and 5.8 California. These obviously were plagued with the industrial poor. Even the richest regions are not free from ill-being.

The Negroes are a special case. Along with other non-white people (Indians, Puerto Ricans, Mexicans) they form the ground swell of poverty, both in the country-side and in the towns. When franchised after the Civil War they were too poor to buy land or businesses; they lived as tenants, sharecroppers or hired hands on the little plots into which the plantations were divided, in small wooden houses with no indoor plumbing, and with few tools and machines at their disposal. This is still very largely their condition. Their education and skills are not enough to get them out of their plight. In the mid-1970s only 40 per cent of all Blacks over 25 years had finished their schooling compared with 63 per cent of Whites. Younger Blacks were making the effort to complete high school, but only 27 per cent got as far as one year of college, contrasted with 43 per cent Whites.

There are twice as many unemployed Blacks (9.8 per cent) as there are Whites 4.8 per cent), while black poor are proportionally three and a half times as many as the white. Yet in these conditions far more negro women (31.6 per cent) find themselves with a family of five or more to look after than whites (20.7 per cent). And since there are far more families among Negroes dependent on the woman as the sole head and provider (30.0:9.9 per cent), her lot is a hard one indeed. As compared with Whites, even as late as 1975, Blacks were more prone to be cooped up in the centre cities of metropolitan areas, to be much less educated, to be confined mainly to blue-collar jobs or, indeed, to be jobless.

Thus, while poverty and America, taken as a whole, seem to be antonyms, for too many Americans they are all but synonymous. The fact that one can quote 2.5 per cent of Negroes as being in the top income bracket, because of their successful boxers and TV stars, or that 28.6 per cent have succeeded to white-collar occupations (but 51.2 per cent of Whites are so employed), or that more Blacks are moving to the suburbs than before, and now constitute 16 per cent of the outer metropolitan ring – while promising a better future, still cannot reverse the fact that 31.4 per cent are below the poverty line.

What is the manifest destiny of *these* Americans?

Crime in America

One night well be forgiven if one were to answer – 'Protest'. And certainly they do just that. And, as we have noted, this has contributed to the violence that has seemed to be part and parcel of American life. Indeed, a lot of the social geography of America is the geography of violence – of the struggle between White and Indian, Black and White, the lower and the upper classes, Gentile against Jew, Protestant against Catholic – the whole gamut.

How senseless, one is inclined to say; but in a sense it is part of the American way. Rap Brown, the black student leader, on being rebuked for negro violence retorted, 'Violence is as American as cherry pie?' America was born of revolution. It 'bloodied its spear' to come of age, and its course has been marked by blood ever since. As Schlesinger (1968) says in his report on US violence, Americans commit more acts of violence in a year than the United Kingdom, Germany, and Japan put together.

This is acknowledged in American statistics themselves which compare US crime rates with those of other leading countries. The American homicide rate, per 100,000 of the population, is currently 15.5 for men and 4.3 for women. Contrast these statistics with those for other countries shown in table 6.1.

Table 6.1 Contrasted national homicide rates (per 100,000 population)

	Men	Women
USA	15.5	4.3
Canada	3.2	1.7
Australia	2.4	1.5
Italy	1.7	0.6
Japan	1.6	1.0
West Germany	1.5	0.0
Sweden	1.2	0.9
France	1.1	0.5
England	1.0	0.8

It is surprising that when the comparatively law-abiding stocks of English, German, and Italian make up such a large proportion of Americans, America should be so lawless. Something happened to the Old-World man when he moved to the New. Even Australia and Canada show this, with twice and thrice the amount of killing ever known in their motherland. But the American experience is five to seven times more violent again!

Of course America came into being through violence. It had a bloody beginning. And the United States maintained its unitedness only through violence, through the bloodiest civil war. Somehow the use of violence continued in America, and continued on a personal basis. Perhaps it was the experience of individual Americans in killing Indians and lynching Negroes and shooting down gunmen before being shot themselves that kept up the bloodiness in their tradition. Tupper and Bailey (1967) make an interesting point when they say that Americans scorn Canadians because the latter chose evolution rather than revolution, 'Canadian independence being granted peacefully and gradually and without bloodshed'. In America, 'The break from the mother-country was clean, swift and complete.' This is how many Americans seem to like to solve their problems – to shoot out what they cannot argue out. James Baldwin claims in *Another Country*, that Americans take out on each other the conflict they cannot resolve in themselves. If this were true it would explain the ubiquitous nature of American violence, now part of the whole American scene. In any case, as Rose (1969, p. ix) says, quite blandly – indeed with indecent smugness, violence having become an all-but respected cult – 'American culture tolerates, approves, propagates, and rewards violence'. So there it is, though to the European such an acceptance is not only astonishing but devastating.

The extent of violence can hardly be believed. The author would not credit the warnings he received on first going to teach in New York. The Dean had kindly got him and his wife accommodation at a married students' residence. It could be approached down any one of three streets, 'but don't ever take these two. You could be mugged there. Only this way is safe, it is under the surveillance of our campus police.' One could not believe one's ears. After a while we grew careless. The Dean was being a fussy old man. But on taking one of the forbidden roads my wife was in fact attacked, and it was only her agility as a one-time international field-hockey star that saved her. Not long after, the two of us were walking the 'great white way' taking photographs of the brilliant display of theatre signs when a policeman touched us on the shoulder. 'You had better get in that bus and go home', he said. 'You're being followed. Twice when you've put your camera up to take a picture a man has almost snatched it away. He's off now, but he'll be back.' On exchanging these experiences with members of faculty we discovered that not one had failed to be attacked or suffer the threat of attack. And no wonder, New York has an incredible record. (US Department of Commerce, 1972). It has over half a million serious crimes a year. These include murder, rape, robbery with violence, and assault. There are about 220 murders each year, and over 500 cases of rape. But New York is by no means exceptional.

Washington, DC, Los Angeles, Baltimore, Detroit, Cleveland, Chicago, and San Francisco all have high crime rates.

In terms of total crimes, other than minor offences, cities rank as shown in Table 6.2.

Table 6.2.   Total serious crimes in major U.S. cities

New York	517,716	San Francisco	57,136
Los Angeles	175,719	Dallas	50,501
Chicago	128,017	St Louis	45,915
Detroit	127,630	Philadelphia	45,734
Baltimore	62,150	Cleveland	44,564
Houston	59,883	Boston	38,294
Washington	59,311	New Orleans	35,150

It might be more meaningful to look at this in terms of crime per 100,000 of the population and, more significantly still, of the number of crimes of violence per 100,000 (US Dept Commerce, 1976a). In the latter case cities would have the order (1976) shown in Table 6.3.

Table 6.3.   Crimes of violence per 100,000 population, U.S. cities

Detroit	2,121	San Francisco	1,364
Baltimore	1,862	Chicago	1,180
New York	1,781	Los Angeles	1,114
Washington	1,774	Indianapolis	925
Cleveland	1,576	Philadelphia	867

Narrowing the view still further, the murder rate would come up with the score, (1976) as in Table 6.4:

Table 6.4.   Murder rates in US cities per 100,000 people

Detroit	44.2	Houston	25.3
Cleveland	43.6	Philadelphia	23.0
Washington	32.8	New York	22.2
Baltimore	30.0	San Francisco	20.6
Dallas	27.4	Los Angeles	20.3
Chicago	26.0	Indianapolis	18.9

These all have much higher rates than prevail in any European or Japanese city. They reflect the conflicts already discussed that have ravaged and indeed still cleave American society, between White and Indian, White and Black, foreign- and native-born, Protestant and Catholic, Gentile and Jew, the upper and the lower classes, the 'establishment' and youth, and the outer suburban and inner 'ghetto-ized' city.

The rate of crime is increasing. Both the national and the metropolitan averages are going up, and in the 1970s have been climbing at a

steeper gradient than before (see Fig. 6.5). Violent though America has been
in the past it shows little sign of being able to get on top of this: America is

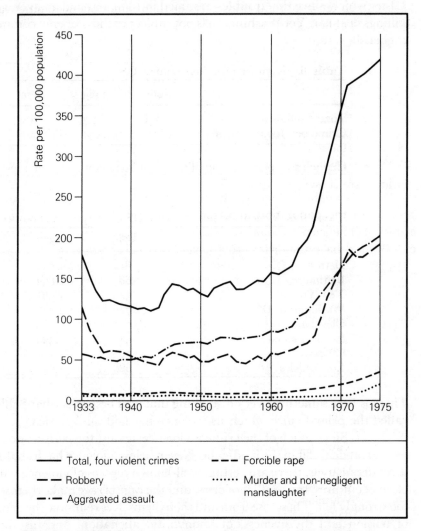

Fig. 6.5 *Violent Crime, 1933–1975.* Crime in America, reflecting the
conflicts of race and class and the economic inequalities of a highly
competitive society, is extensive and on the increase. The right of citizens
to carry guns adds an element of violence.

becoming more violent still. Table 6.5 shows that there are really quite
startling differences between 1965 and 1975 *(US Statistical Abstract, 1976, Sect.*
5, p. 153).

Most cities have gone ahead of the national average in their rate of
increase in the crime rate, with the notable exception of the national capital,
Washington (though its rate is still high). Washington announced with some

pride and relief that it had only had 208 killings in 1977, compared with former average of 212 per year. But this is about the average for embattled Ulster which, since the 'troubles' resumed in 1969, has had an average of 210 killings per year. Yet Washington is not subject to those openly committed to a guerilla war!

Table 6.5 Number of serious crimes (USA)

	1960	1965	1970	1975
Total (millions)	3.4	4.7	8.2	11.3
Crime per 100,000 popn	1,876	2,434	3,961	5,282

Crime rates per 100,000 of the population for *violent* crimes – major cities – are shown in Table 6.6:

Table 6.6. Violent crimes in major US cities, per 100,000 people

	1965	1970	1975
Detroit	614	1,934	2,121
Baltimore	687	1,862	2,088
New York	345	1,381	1,781
Washington, DC	723	2,227	1,774
Cleveland	393	1,060	1,576
San Francisco	541	1,339	1,346
Chicago	760	1,101	1,180
Los Angeles	686	1,062	1,114

There is here something very disturbing that well bespeaks what Schlesinger called the primal curse which its violence has laid on America.

Since much of the crime is violence against the person one does not see a great deal of it in the landscape. Nevertheless, violence has its habitation, it resides in areas, there are certain well-known regions of violence where the clash of cultures, the conflict of class, and the rage of race make themselves all too strongly felt. These rise from and then themselves reinforce the geography of tension and divisiveness, of anonymity, alienation, and instability, of unemployment, broken homes, dilapidated houses, low education, and uncertain health.

The South has the highest rate of crime, followed by the industrialized states of the mid-Atlantic coast and the Great Lakes. California is also crime-ridden. The poverty in the South would make us expect this distribution, but not the affluence of the Far West. However, the crimes of today are the crimes of affluence almost as much as of poverty. Look at David Smith's maps of ill-being and well-being in the United States; contrast particularly the maps of wealth and pathology. The wealthiest states have some of the worst social pathology in the United States; they are the homes of drug-taking, serious crimes, and riots, in them Gatsby and Maggie are side by side – the upper fifth of society having 41 per cent of the wealth and the lowest fifth with 5.5 per cent (*US Com. Popn. Profile* 1974, published 1975, Series P-20, No. 279). When one sees a cartogram where a whole state is given a common level, one misses the profound differences that may exist there, as for instance between white fruit-owners in California and Mexican fruit-pickers, or the white ship-owners of New York and the negro stevedores.

Greater than regional divergences are the contrasts between rural and urban America, or small-town and metropolitan America. (US Dept Commerce, 1976b). Cities excite crime, and crime exploits the city. The city adds to the tensions and deepens the divisions out of which conflict springs, it also supplies the anonymity and fluidity that assist the criminal operator. This is especially true of the American city where economic values dominate and give rise to a competition that can be both fierce and cruel. Criminals as much as business men compete for central places, where they have their own CBD – the criminal business district. Table 6.7 shows area and type of crime (1975) per 100,000 of the population.

Table 6.7 Crimes by area and type, 1975. Rate per 100,000 of population

	SMSAs		Other cities		Rural areas	
	Total	Rate	Total	Rate	Total	Rate
All crimes	9,551,000	–	1,051,000	–	665,000	–
All violent crimes	907,000	–	64,000	–	56,000	–
Murder	16,000	11	11,000	6	3,000	8
Rape	49,000	31	3,000	13	4,000	12
Robbery	443,000	284	14,000	58	8,000	23
Assault (with bodily harm)	398,000	255	46,000	192	41,000	124

The conditions in the American metropolis have reached saturation point, there are just not enough police, and courts, and court officials, gaols and centres of detention to cope. In New York and other big cities the courts are going 24 hours a day. The author recalls going to a downtown court in New York where the magistrate did not finish the afternoon's cases until well after midnight. In one instance a group of men were paraded before him for having been drunk and disorderly: they were too poor to pay a fine, and the gaol was too full to take them, so he simply admonished them severely. They smiled, saluted, and shuffled away. They would be back for a repeat performance.

What is serious has been the way juveniles have entered crime. Juvenile delinquency is going through America like a fever. The young are sorely tried: there is often no work for them. Bad as Britain's economic plight may be, its unemployment rate is only about a half that of America. American

Blacks, Indians, Mexicans, and Puerto Ricans have a rate of unemployment (13.9 per cent) far higher than the rest of the country (5.2 per cent). There are many to a family (33 per cent come from homes with five or more members), they live in poor houses in crowded districts, many drop out of school early: what is there for them? Forty-one per cent of the whole black population are under 18 years. But of course they are not the only ones to revolt. In the America of today perhaps the most rebellious youth are those of the middle class, whose standards, even if they have been brought up in them, they detest. They scorn 'law and order' as being a keystone of the bourgeois system. Hence they have joined the vandals and delinquents.

According to the 1976 *Statistical Abstract* (US Dept Commerce, 1976c) the Juvenile Courts handled 33⅓ million cases of juvenile delinquency – an increase of over 3 million from 1960. There were 45,694 juveniles in public custody, of which no less than 10,637 were girls. Over 26,000 were in training schools, and 11,000 in detention centres. A great number of these were up for drug offences, including the use of so-called hard drugs. In fact, the use of hard drugs compared with marijuana was as 5:3.

The most alarming situation is that juveniles are now into serious crime and that the incidence of young people in such crime is increasing far more than that of adults. The details shown in Table 6.8 was a considered estimate of the position by *US News* (1974).

Table 6.8 Juvenile crime compared with adult, per cent increase in arrests, 1960–74

Nature of crime	Juvenile (under 18) % increase	Adult (over 18) % increase
Murder	201	86
Rape	132	95
Robbery	299	125
Assault	206	101
Burglary	104	59
Prostitution	282	62
Drug abuse	4,673	74
Drunken driving	401	188

America's 'death city', Detroit

Detroit city stands out as a leader in violence by any count. It is, of course, a big city with 4,343,000 people. Size of that order exerts a great deal of pressure on space and helps to create tension in those competing for it. But New York with about 10 million (not counting the contiguous built-up areas in New Jersey), Los Angeles with nearly 7 million, and Chicago with about 7 million do not have such high rates of crime. Detroit has earned its name as death city because, for its size, it has more murders than any other place. In fact there are such a lot of deaths they no longer make news.

In Detroit four times more people are killed every year than in Northern Ireland.

The world press and television constantly focus on Ulster, as though it were a terrible place: well, so it is, but it is no worse than Detroit – why should the media not turn on Detroit? Because they have come to accept it as a fact of existence. Violence is America, and Detroit is America's most violent city: somehow, that's that! However, the situation was so bad in 1974, that *US News*, 6 May, had an article 'And in Detroit, three murders a day!' (compare Ulster, with three killings every five days at that time). Meanwhile, Detroit's record of rape, robbery, assault, burglary, and theft is far worse. The *US Statistical Abstracts* (1976) brings this out forcibly. Crimes against the person and property (rate per 100,000 of the population) metropolitan Detroit, 1975, compared with New York, Chicago, and Los Angeles are as shown in Table 6.9.

Table 6.9. Crimes by principal categories in major U.S. cities. Rates per 100,000 population.

	Detroit	**New York**	**Chicago**	**Los Angeles**
Total population (million)	4.34	9.63	6.97	6.93
All crimes, rate	10,870	7,831	7,487	8,184
Crimes of violence				
Total crimes of violence, rate	2,121	1,781	1,180	1,114
Individual crimes, rate				
Murder	44.2	22.2	26.0	20.3
Rape	99.4	52.1	52.6	64.8
Robbery	1,488	1,121	704	534
Assault	490	586	397	494
Crimes of property				
Total crimes of property, rate	8,748	6,050	6,308	7,070
Individual crimes, rate				
Burglary	3,228	2,835	1,502	2,530
Theft	2,526	2,544	3,743	3,415
Cars (theft)	1,994	1,121	1,063	1,124

It will be seen from Table 6.9 that the situation in Detroit has become very critical. The figures for crime must be put against other social and economic statistics if the position is to be understood. (Unfortunately the only general breakdown available (see Table 6.10) is that based on the last census – 1970; further, it is based on Detroit itself, and not the metropolitan region. Nevertheless, it is very revealing. See US Dept Commerce, 1972).

Table 6.10.   Detroit, urban social geography

Population	
Total	1,511,336
Female (%)	52.1
White (%)	55.6
Black (%)	43.7
Foreign born (%)	22.6
Birth rate	19.0
Death rate	12.4
Median age	30.1
Education	
Persons <25 with 4 yr. high school (%)	41.8
Persons <25 with 4 yr. college (%)	6.2
Negroes <25 with elementary schooling (%)	53.1
Labour force	
Total labour force (thousands)	604.7
Female labour force (%)	39.2
Unemployed (%)	7.2
Labour force in manufacturing (%)	35.9
Labour force in trade (%)	18.7
Labour force, professional/managerial (%)	16.0
Labour force, business services (%)	8.3
Labour force, sale and clerical (%)	25.1
Labour force, crafts and foremen (%)	12.4
Income	
Income average per family	$10,038
Poor family $3,000–7,000 (%)	29.7
Near-poor family $7,000–10,000 (%)	19.9
Above average family $10,000–25,000 (%)	46.6
Well-to-do family <$25,000 (%)	3.7
Median white income	$11,051
Median negro income	$8,639
Housing	
Housing, median no. rooms	5.1
Housing in one-unit structures (%)	54.4
New housing, one-unit structures (%)	24.1
New housing, multiple-unit structures (%)	73.7
Housing more than 20 yr old (%)	84.3
Housing with more than one person per room (%)	11
Houses owner occupied (%)	60
Negroes owning house (%)	51.1
Household and Family	
One-person households (%)	11.3
Residence in same household for 5 yr (%)	54.7
Female head household (%)	18.0

Families with children under 6 yr (%)	24.8
Families with persons < 18 yr (%)	41.7
Families with persons > 65 yr (%)	17.7

Transport

Own one or more car per family (%)	72.0
Use public transport to work (%)	18.4

Looking at the figures in Table 6.10 one wonders how they end up as 'death city'. There is a strong female element in the population which ought to be stabilizing. More than half the homes are not subdivided, and the majority are owner occupied. A reasonable proportion of the city have gone to high school. Most families have lived in their neighbourhood for at least 5 years. The median income is in excess of the national average, and the vast majority run their own car.

As against this, the high proportion of Negroes might suggest Black–White tension. How can this go with a thing like crime?

Here is one of America's dilemmas – an essentially middle-of-the-road, middle-class, respectable and stable society, it nevertheless provokes conflict, frustration and violence. It is the Peyton Place of peoples, its beauty marred by cruelty, its kindness by ugliness: only to a worse degree – to a degree beyond the usual human expectation.

In Detroit's case, tension might be expected from the Black/White balance. Also, there is a far higher share of foreign-born: if these are White and poor, as most of them could be, they would resent the increase in Negroes, and, at the same time, might be pecked at by native-born Whites. Here is certainly cause for conflict. The city is young, and the young are often impatient and aggressive. The poor and the near-poor, amounting to 49.6 per cent of the population, are more numerous than the middle class (46.6 per cent), so class conflict could be an issue. A very much higher proportion of the people than in most cities, or in America as a whole, work in factories. The stock of professional people is low. This may mean a lack of balance, again with aggressive traits given weight. The poor support of public transportation suggests a distinct preference for privatism – and all that *that* involves. The higher than national rate of unemployment must be frustrating, especially for so many young and forceful persons, if they are indeed anxious to do things on their own.

One is not sure whether even all this would add up to violence. It makes it possible, but does not necessarily imply it. Yet as Bunge has pointed out in his magnificent analysis of the situation, the elements are so juxtaposed that they must strike fire from each other. There has been such an implosion of Blacks cooped up, cabined, and confined between the high towers of town-centred big business and the rimming stacks of polluting factories, followed by an explosion of Whites into the outer suburbs, that geography provides little basis for mingling, far less merging. The poor-Whites are caught between the two conditions and are ground between them, with no escape. These trends once started, have got progressively worse. Geography has become so identified with different life styles that bionic communities have emerged each testing out its own life-genius and power. This, one takes it, is what lies behind the concept of the three biological cities into which Detroit is divided and which are presented to us in Abler et al. (1975).

This is *real* human geography. With boldness and imagination, insight and flair, we are shown a city in terms of its real images and the live problems they have created. At the centre is the 'city of death' perceived as violence and despair, impoverishment and decline (see Fig. 6a). Around it is the 'city of need', imaged as inadequate, alienated, and torn. It acts as a buffer between the struggling and angry heart and the peripheral limbs, visioned as the 'city of superfluity'. The Negroes and other Non-Whites are cramped tight in their ghettos, unable to get beyond the bulwarks of heavy industry which act as barriers to a social mix (see Fig. 6b). The white minority groups sink into a pathetic nonentity, either in at the centre or out on the margins, an impasse that has filled their youth with disillusionment. Delinquency is high among these. The affluence of the middle class, locked in the homogeneous suburbs of their own separation, puts them into a different universe.

Between 1950 and 1970 the population of Detroit proper fell from 1,850,000 to 1,511,000 – mostly by the white flight out. In that time the number of young Blacks multiplied almost three times from 180,000 to 449,000. They grew up to fierce competition for work, or no work at all. They were bred in strain and stress. Conflict was their climate. Of the 30,260 males arrested for serious crimes in Detroit, in 1974, 80 per cent were Black.

Adding to all these problems, as Mazzarolo points out, '500,000 handguns are believed to be in Detroit – one for every three citizens'!

This is certainly not the New Eden. And as for the New Adam he had better rethink his dream: he has a long way to go yet before seeding the 'new race of man'.

In the meanwhile, crime gets ingrained into an area. It develops its own subculture, with the police and the city fathers as the enemy, and leaders of crime as its heroes. These leaders entrench the system by exploiting their lieutenants and the rank and file in a *crime ring*, in the organized business of crime. As this flourishes they move into the big crime industry, including the systematic invasion of legitimate business and the corruption of government. It is here that New York, Chicago, and Los Angeles come into their own, with really big business to infiltrate and with whole orders of government to suborn.

This is why the federal government is becoming increasingly

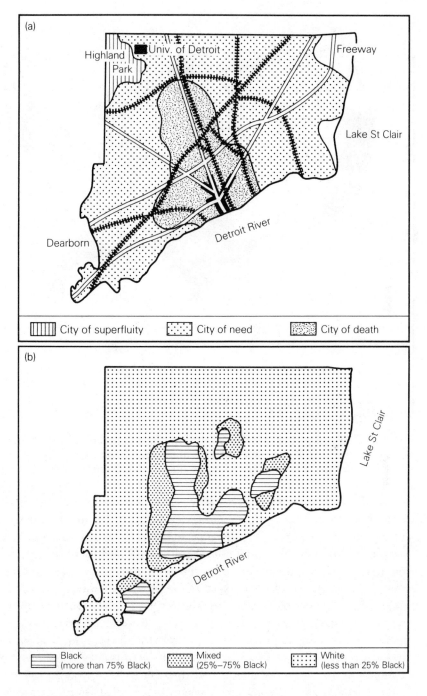

Fig. 6.6a and 6.6b *Economic status areas and racial regions in Detroit.* Detroit, America's death city, shows the relation of crime to urban pressures, social deprivation, race conflict, and economic inequalities. All major cities share these conditions and suffer from violent crime.

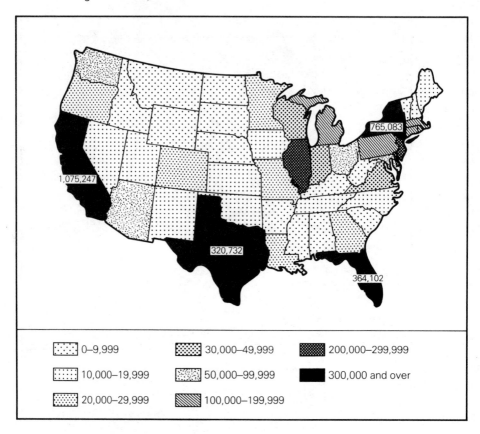

Fig. 6.7 *Alien population, 1970's.* Aliens bulk large in the north-eastern and south-western states, but those recognised are only a proportion of the total since there are so many illegal immigrants.

involved, because the large crime rings are nation-wide, their business indeed may be multinational, as for example in the trade in drugs. They organize corruption not just at the city or even state level but within the federal services themselves, on federal construction projects, the supply of the armed forces, the federal mail, illegal immigration into the USA, and so forth. The smuggling of aliens and the exploitation of aliens without papers are now major issues. Crimes of violence become petty stuff, they are mere by-products, the main crimes are against the substance of the state. This is why it is such a grave matter when one hears that violence is integral to American culture and that crimes are simply a way of getting at the affluence which the political-economic system does not adequately distribute (Rose, 1969, p xxi ff). Do the affluent leaders of the great crime organizations distribute their gains more equitably?

It is the insidious way in which the massive exploitation and corruption of the American people has been carried out by the crime business that is so disturbing. The Annual Report of the US Attorney-General (US Dept Justice, 1975) is alarming reading, not because of the crimes of violence, which are in fact small potatoes, but the sapping, if not poisoning, of the life-blood of the nation. The major number of defendants on trial in the federal courts are those dealing in: banking offences, shipping regulations, smuggling contraband, illegal immigration, falsification of citizenship documents, mail and wire fraud, illegal trafficking in controlled substances (such as drugs), counterfeiting money and stamps, organizing prison escapes, attempted bribery of prison officials, interference with other government officers, extortion of 'protection money', fraud against the US government, income tax evasion, offences against the integrity of federal programmes (ranging from food-stamp programmes for the poor to wildlife conservation), subvention of jurisdictional statues, liquor-law violations, obstruction of justice, dealing in stolen property, passport falsification, and – a major item – gun-running and other evasions of weapon control. The list goes on, including a great range of crimes some of which though small in number, like spying for an enemy state, may be none the less dangerous to the country.

Here again one asks, is this geography? It would not be, had it not its location. But most of these crimes are highly organized and directed from criminal headquarters in New York, Boston, Chicago, Los Angeles – the nerve centres of the nation. Even in these great central places it is centralized, it has its locus. For instance, in Upton Sinclair's (Sinclair, 1929) novel *Boston*, which was really a tirade against 'the lying, chicanery and corruption of which the financial and commercial interests in the city were capable in their defence of property, in contrast to their indifference to the defence of justice' (symbolized in the infamous trial and victimization of two actual-life figures, Sacco and Vanzetti) he has Ponzi, a crooked Italian business man, locate himself in the heart of the CBD. Ponzi, we read, 'opened a dingy little office in School Street, quite in the correct Boston tradition – for many of the big New England corporations had dingy little offices in some of those two-hundred-year-old houses in dark and narrow streets at the town centre'.

Crime like most other aspects of society is eminently geographical, in this case looking for a site that combined maximum centrality with maximum anonymity – a perfect geographic set-up. When it comes to the principles of industrial location the crime industry knows all about central place theory, the maximization of comparative advantage, and the advantages of agglomerization! It accepts the implications of the bid-rent curve in the structure of the city, and bids as much as any other big corporation for the point of maximum accessibility. Here in what appear to be unimpeachable operations it carries on the rape and murder of society.

References

Abler, R., Janelle, D., Philbrick, A., and **Sommer, J.** *Human Geography in a Shrinking World*, Duxbury Press, Belmont, Cal., p. 150.

Adams, H. (1889:1965) *History of the United States of America*, Cornell Paperback, *The United States in 1800*, Ithaca, N.Y. (1965), p 41.

Crèvecoeur, J. H. St. J. de (1782:1963) *Letters from an American Farmer* (1782) Signet edn, N.Y. (1963) Letter 111, 'What is an American?', pp. 60–99.

Davies, S. and **Albaum, M.,** (1972) 'Work-residence disparities', in Peet (ed.), *Geographical Perspectives on American Poverty*, Antipode Press, Worcester, Mass., pp. 72, 76.

Harvey, D. (1972) 'Social justice and spatial systems', in Peet, op. cit., p. 103.

Peet, R. (1972) 'Some issues in the social geography of Poverty', in Peet, op. cit., pp. 6–7.

Rose, T. (ed.) (1969) *Violence in America*, Random House, N.Y., pp. ix, xxi ff.

Schlesinger, A., Jr. (1968) *Violence: America in the Sixties*, Signet, N.Y., p. 43.

Sinclair, U. (1929) *Boston*, Werner Laurie, London, p. 270.

Smith, D. (1972) 'Towards a geography of well-being: inter-state variations in the U.S.', in Peet, op. cit., p. 29.

Tupper, S. and **Bailey, D.** (1967) *Canada and the United States*, Hawthorne Press, N.Y., p. 40.

US Commerce (1972) *City and Country Data Book*, Bureau of the Census, pp. 629 ff.

US Dept Commerce (1976a) 'Crime rates by major cities', *US Statistical Abstracts*, Sect. 5, *Law Enforcement*, p. 155.

US Dept Commerce (1976b) Op cit., 'Crimes by type and area', p. 153.

US Dept Commerce (1976c) Op. cit., 'Juvenile Courts – cases handled', p. 170.

US Dept Justice (1975) 'Criminal cases and defendants in the US District Court by offense', *Annual Report*, Office of the Attorney-General, pp. 12–3.

US Dept Labor (1976) 'Number receiving unemployment benefit as per cent of those in covered employment', *Annual Report*, Table iii.

US News (1974) 'All kinds of crime – growing, growing, growing', No. 77, 16 Dec., p. 33.

The urban duality

The city dominates American life. All the main characteristics and problems of the nation – race, religion, class, sex, age, occupation, standard of living, ideology, and power – have their focus here. It is a social geography of America in itself.

Three out of four Americans live in cities. Two out of three, or 143 millions, are in metropolitan areas. These huge urbanized regions are made up of central cities, surrounded by a ring of suburbs or satellite communities. Forty-three per cent are centre-city dwellers; 57 per cent live in the suburban ring. Centre cities are old, crowded, polluted, with low-income recent immigrants and coloured people (77 per cent of urban Blacks live here): yet they contain the main businesses and metropolitan institutions. To keep them dynamic, both business and government are spending a lot on urban renewal. The outer ring is expanding rapidly with middle/upper-class housing, suburban shops, schools, churches and colleges, recreation, and decentralized business. Of 214 million Americans, 122 million live in the suburban fringe. Most of these are white. Private land speculation pushes development out to the rural edge, often called exurbia. Recent government loans for new homes have also added to suburban growth, though on a highly planned basis. There is great and constant movement within the different parts of the urban area. Of the US population, 35 million or 16.6 per cent change address every year, mostly in or between cities. Much of this is due to the displacement of residential by commercial areas, much to the competition for better jobs, or the contest for status and the shift of ethnic and class groups. Throughout the last 150 years cities have grown more rapidly than the country: since 1970, metropolitan areas have slowed down to 3.8 per cent per annum in favour of the explosion of the city into countryside districts, now growing at 5 per cent per annum. Private speculation is largely responsible for this burst out.

Since cities are the culture of their people in concrete expression,

American cities reflect that essential dualism in American life between the freedom to be different and the right to be equal. Privatism has been the main force, but concern for the community has none the less persisted. The fact that America broke away from Britain gave it a breakaway mind, but although this meant for many a breakaway *from* control, stressing freedom, for others it was a breakaway *to* design, emphasizing responsibility. Both trends are present. During colonial days both vied with each other: Boston, New York, New Jersey, and Baltimore were fine and private places, where even institutions behaved as competing entities; New Haven, Philadelphia, and Savannah were set up as planned communities. Increasingly, however, the private sector came to the fore. The American Revolution broke out in the same year, 1776, that the *Wealth of Nations* was published. The growth of America went with the rise of capitalism. Even in Philadelphia, as S. B. Warner (Warner, 1971, p. 3) shows 'the Quakers were unable to sustain the primacy of religion against . . . cheap land and private opportunity. Privatism had become the American tradition. Its essence lay in its concentration upon the individual and the individual's search for wealth.' But individual competition so weakened and endangered community control that a strong reaction began in the late nineteenth century which, by the mid-twentieth century, had roused a new concern for social design: freedom was matched by equality. The New York regional plan of 1969, called for 'policies and goals . . . in terms of people'. It was a *social* plan. Today, both equal rights and individual freedoms are being balanced one with the other in American development.

The individualistic breakaway

America early broke away from feudalistic controls as Crèvecoeur (1782: 1963) claimed, to a new order where there were 'no kings, no courts, no great lords who possess everything, no ecclesiastical dominion, no invisible power giving to a few a very visible one'. Towns were not centred in palace, mansion, and cathedral, however much they might have had their courthouses and churches. Institutional life, though strong, was not overpowering. Individual interests became paramount. The central business district replaced the cultural institutional centre as the symbol of urban America.

European towns grew up by the fusion of a series of complexes, each budding from a great institution; the palace complex saw the royal house and park linked with the town houses of nobility at court, with goldsmiths, and jewellers, fashion shops and wine merchants, together with guardhouses and barracks – which, in their turn, induced taverns, bawdy houses, and chapels to cater to the vices or stiffen the virtues of the soldiery. A cathedral complex of schools, hospitals, almshouses, printeries, and booksellers, and the houses of doctors and lawyers, would make up another quarter. The whole became knit together by city regulations that jealously supported the powers of the community over the individual.

The European tradition was centred in the institution: each institution was the centre of a cell; even if one institution, like the palace or the cathedral, dominated, other institutions were important in their own set of linkages. The system consisted of a system within a cell in a system of cells (see Fig. 7.1). Thus, each cell had its businesses, mills or workshops, cultural or social centres, recreation and housing.

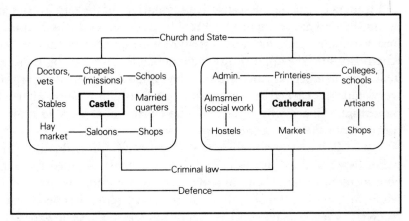

Fig. 7.1 *Model of the mediaeval European city.* The American city broke away from the mediaeval model. The city was made up of a series of cells each focused on a major feudal institution. Each cell replicated most of the features of the others: hence there was no central business district as in the American city, but many separate markets. Cultural–institutional centres were dominant.

It was American to break away from all this, to achieve on a new continent, as Crèvecoeur claimed, something 'different from what men had hitherto seen'. As Powell (1970) has shown, 'to emigrate from accustomed social institutions and relationships . . . meant a startling transformation. Townsmen had to change or abandon almost every formal institution which they had taken for granted.'

Institutions there were, of course, but the chief of these were business and professional, they were set up by individuals exercising individual choice, following individual interest, by individual initiative in a system of individual competition. If cell-like districts were to grow up in the city they consisted of the central business district, industrial districts, and residential districts, established on the basis of individual decision.

However, it should be said that the breakaway mind had already begun to unsettle Britain before it helped to settle America. American origins included in them the breakup of these origins. Many settlers came from a London thick in the throes of change. This was seen in an explosion of suburbs, so noted even in Shakespeare's day that he could make Portia say, 'Dwell I but in the suburbs of your good pleasure? If no more, Portia is Brutus' harlot, not his wife.' (*Julius Caesar*, Act I, Sc. II, l. 280–82).

That suburb was to city as harlot to wife, was no figment. The greater degree of licence in the suburbs was an Elizabethan scandal. In 1592, suburbs seemed to Henry Chettle (Chettle, 1592: 1916), 'no other but dark dens for adulterers, thieves, murderers and every mischief worker'. However, they nursed other kinds of liberties as well, including: the freedom of craftsmen and traders to escape the restrictive regulations of the city liveries and to set up on their own; the chance for French, German, and Dutch immigrants to find a refuge; scope for land speculators to make a fortune in jerry-built tenements; and the opportunity for independents to start up their own sects. This last was especially important. 'The suburbs', Valerie Pearl (1961) writes, 'very quickly earned a reputation for Puritanism and, after 1640, for radicalism.' One might argue that the culture of at least Puritan America sprang from the cult of the suburb.

Self-assertion, self-reliance, initiative, individualism, and innovation were all part of this cult. In 1612, Helwys founded the first Baptist church in England, at Spitalfields, a suburb outside the walls of London, where he 'gave to religious toleration the finest and fullest defence it had ever received' when he claimed, 'Let them be heretics, Turks, Jews or whatsoever, it appertains not to the earthly power to punish them [for their belief] in the least measure.' Underwood (1947) remarks, 'clearly the authorities could not ignore such a challenge. Helwys was thrown into prison.' Reaction grew strong. King James threatened to 'make the Puritans conform, or else harry them out of the land'. Harried, they came to America, where individual 'cussedness' was at least as important as group coaction in the American landscape.

Take the 'new light' movement in Boston, by which Mrs Hutchinson and her brother Mr Wheelwright believed that people should be led by their own inner light – it so divided the town that, according to Governor Winthrop, 'there was great danger of a tumult'. Consequently, the two stubborn dissidents were 'disenfranchised and banished'. But this was only a spur to them to set up another settlement, at Providence. Colonization by separation became an American tradition.

This sort of separateness, based on individual choice, made even institutions behave in an individualistic way, competing with each other on the basis of their individual interests and attractions. Early British travellers in America were struck by this trait. When the Rev. Andrew Burnaby (Burnaby, 1760: 1960) visited Boston in 1759 he commented on 'the great number of people of different persuasions': there were beside 'three churches, some thirteen or fourteen meeting houses'. When in New York, Burnaby counted 'two churches, the old, or Trinity Church, and the new one, or St. George's besides . . . several other places of worship, namely two Low Dutch Calvinist churches, one High Dutch ditto, one French ditto, one German Lutheran church, one Presbyterian meeting house, one Quaker ditto, one anabaptist ditto, one Moravian ditto, and a Jewish synagogue'. Obviously, self-assertion and self-distinction had become built-in features. The American city was a patchwork quilt of contrarieties, based on distinct creeds, languages, national origins, and customs.

Increasingly, these characteristics were to become focused on secular interests rather than religious institutions – on business rather than the Church. This marks an important change in the American city, with the economic forces becoming more central than social and cultural ones. Indeed, the cultural core soon became swamped, and started to disintegrate, its place being taken by the business base. This was to distinguish the American from the European city. In London, even though business did grow to such great importance that, we are told 'the desire of profit greatly increased building', nevertheless, respect was still paid to palaces, the Tower, cathedrals, the Guildhall, and other social institutions. Yet in New York similar institutions were diminished, crowded out, downgraded, and even forced to flee to the outskirts – and often, at that, in the span of a lifetime. Meanwhile, offices and hotels took over the skyline in their place.

This was made the easier by the adoption of that 'perfect liberty' for which Adam Smith (Smith, 1776: 1843) argued so strongly in his *Wealth of Nations*, the liberty 'to leave open every channel into which by its own tendencies industry may be carried. . . .' Economic liberty was boosted by the new political liberty, and increasingly took over the city, especially in New England and the mid-Atlantic States. After the Civil War, it seized the heart of the Southern city, and dominated the city of the West, to make the central business district central to the American city. As Jackson (1972) remarks, when Atlanta rose from the ashes in 1865 it replaced the old, all-but 'countrified diversity of its downtown section with the uniformity of buildings entirely devoted to commerce'. In burnt-out Richmond, too, 'the emergence of the new-style downtown district took place, exclusively devoted to offices. . . .'

New York – the economic breakaway

Supremely, business took over the skyline of New York. A hundred years after Burnaby had singled out 'old Trinity Church with its spire' as one of the landmarks of New York, Henry James (James, 1908: 1946) described it as made all but invisible in the downtown scene, shadowed by Wall Street skyscrapers. Though 'beauty was the aim of the creator of the spire of Trinity Church', averred Henry James, this had been 'mercilessly deprived of its visibility, so cruelly overtopped [by an office block], though once . . . the pride of the town'. Business looking down on the Church – this was the new America.

Not that churches were lacking; but they had given up their dominance: they were no longer characterized by that conspicuous consumption of space now associated with offices, departmental stores, and hotels. Actually, another observer, Von Hübner wrote, 'what struck me most in New York is the enormous number of buildings consecrated to public worship'. Yet none of these hit the eye. 'I speak not of the great Gothic cathedral', Von Hübner (1871:1949) went on, 'which belongs to *another order of ideas*, but of the innumerable little churches.' These are often parts of larger buildings used for tenements or shops. 'In Europe, the massive pile of the cathedral, and the belfries, spires, towers and high roofs of the other churches, stand out against the sky . . . and, seen from a distance, give to each town a particular character. In New York it is quite the reverse.' The character of the American town is set by business.

This change in the landscape was due to a change in mind. *Mindscape America is behind American geography*. To turn Crèvecoeur around, secular dominion gave to the few a visible power that made the rest invisible. For, as James insisted, the 'very first care' of business was to 'make the churches inconspicuous', indeed unnoticeable in New York. The new dominants of the sky, 'crowned not only with no history but no credible possibility of time for history, and consecrated by no uses save the commercial at any cost are the expression of things lately and currently *done*, done on a large impersonal stage and on the basis of inordinate gain'. *These* were becoming the symbols of that America 'the whole theory of whose life is active pecuniary gain and active pecuniary gain alone'. The skyscrapers 'never even begin to speak to you', James continues, 'in the manner of the builded majesties of the world as we have heretofore known such – towers or temples or fortresses or palaces – with the authority of things permanent. Skyscrapers are the last word of economic ingenuity – until another word be written.' These 'monsters of the mere market . . . are a conspiracy against the very idea of the ancient graces'. America is what is new, what is brash, what is powerful, and what is efficient. The American city is shaped by the forces of the 'mere market'.

In this, the hotel becomes the very epitome of America. James wrote, 'verily, one is tempted to ask if the hotel spirit may not just be the American spirit . . . most finding itself'. The hotel is the supreme example of America's genius for organization – here are opulence and utility, comfort and hygiene, a complete gregariousness but absolute privacy, a place where 'everyone is in everything', as compared with Europe, 'where it is only certain people who are in anything'. The American hotel, James suggests, is 'a new order under the sun'.

The *hotel at the heart* of the American city, the *cathedral at the core* of the European one, here are the basic contrasts (see Fig. 7.2) The hotel is out for profit, though of course it provides services. It can only be profitable if it is at the town centre. Its profit is made from serving office blocks, departmental stores, railway or bus terminals, theatres and cinemas. It links up banking, insurance, shopping, eating, and recreation, with the incoming and outgoing tides of people that flow through the city centre. It towers into the sky, lifting men's eyes to *gain*, meanwhile making invisible the church whose spire serves only to show how God has been topped by mammon.

Business centrality has taken over the central institutions: hotel, shop, and office are at the apex of America. This is because they are at the peak of how America values the land. Values are *economic*; they allow little for the social worth of space, far less for an aesthetic quotation. The fight for space leaves small room for land that is not profit-making. Henry James brought this out in his visit to the Waldorf-Astoria. The hotel, in seeking centrality, had sacrificed amenity. It was cheek-by-jowl with other businesses, each struggling for a position of power. Each had to have access to the maximum amount of traffic, and hence was thronged with traffic and noise. Consequently 'the frontal majesty' of the hotel, exposed to the 'vulgar assault of the street' was affected by 'an absence of margin, by meagreness of site, the preclusion of court or garden' to such an extent that the builder had no other alternative than 'to seek his reward in the sky'. (Contrast it to the Metropolitan Museum of Art removed from the commercial competition for space.)

The competitive bid for space shaped the American city. Since space had to make a profit, and profits were highest at the centre (to which activities and people converged) the American city was forced into a cone-like structure, with an ever higher skyline over the point of highest price. Here, land-values shot up so high that, to meet them, buildings had to shoot up still higher.

It is no wonder that when academics came to study the American city they made land-value its shaping force (see Fig. 7.3). Park, Burgess, and McKenzie (1925:1947) in their now classical study of *The City* made land-values central. They offered seven propositions: first, that in a society of free and open competition, demand for space is reflected in the price-value put on land. Demand increases with population as more and more people compete for the advantages cities appear to offer. Secondly, land-values are highest at the point of greatest concentration. At such a point, space is at an absolute premium. Thirdly, further increases of population at the periphery push up land-values at the centre still more. Fourthly, as a corollary of this, pressure of land-values at the centre then radiates out and determines values over the

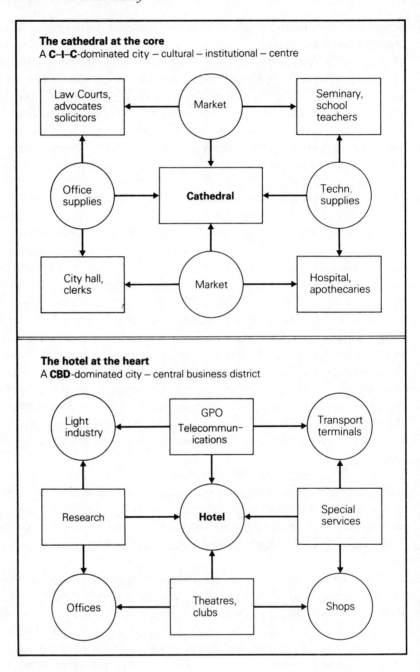

Fig. 7.2 *The cathedral at the core versus the hotel at the heart. European and American models contrasted.* The heart of the American city, dominated by business and by business linkages, is significantly different from at least the more established European cities still centred in great cultural and social institutions.

whole city. Fifthly, land-values thus give activities within a city 'an orderly distribution and a characteristic pattern'. Sixthly, this pattern tends 'to assume the form of a series of concentric circles each of which circumscribes an

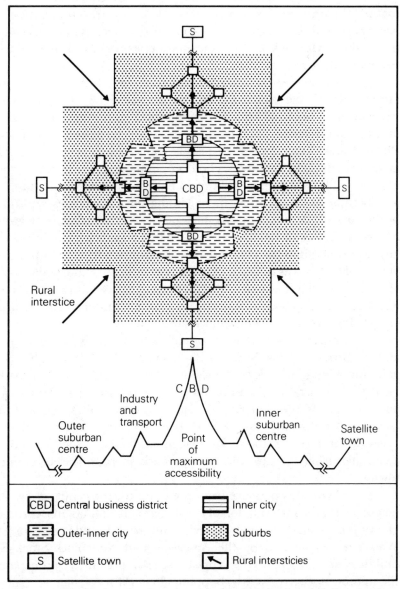

Fig. 7.3 *Model of an American city with typical land-value graph.* Land-values give shape to the American city. A model of that city would show the central business district commanding the highest values at the point of maximum access, with a general reduction of values towards the city margins, except for urban subcentres, suburban centres, and satellite towns where local land-value peaks occur.

area of decreasing mobility and density'. Seventhly, competition for land is
reflected in social status. Hence 'land values become an index to the social life
of a community'. They serve to delimit the cultural contour of the city.

Although Boston and Philadelphia had certain historic advantages
that put them ahead of New York, when 'free and open competition' obtained
New York with its magnificent sea-invaded waterways and its command of
the Hudson–Mohawk gap into the interior, leapt ahead and became the most
valued of all American sites.

Its success increased demand. The Hudson, the East River,
Harlem River, the North Sound, the Passaic River – all the connecting
waterways – became crowded with docks and warehouses, backed by
industry and housing. The population swiftly surpassed that of Boston and
Philadelphia. More and more people competed to take advantage of this
great growth point (see the section on population in Carey's 1976 study).

The widely peopled region had its focus in Manhattan. The focal
area became narrowed to southern Manhattan as the ferries, sea-tunnels, and
bridges from Brooklyn, Queens, Jersey City, Perth Amboy, and Staten Island
met near the ocean point. The great Battery Park which had taken up the
larger part of this in the Dutch regime, became whittled away to a mere ghost
of itself. The fort was pulled down: the port built out. And business sprang up.
Here space soon became at a premium. Space-wasters like recreation,
warehousing, large-scale industry, social institutions, and housing were
crowded out by retail stores and financial offices.

Further increase in the population, especially in Brooklyn, Queens,
and the Bronx, but also as far as Patterson and Hudson Heights, pushed up
values in Manhattan, particularly after the Pennsylvania Railroad and the
New York Central Railroad had terminals in the central part of the island,
and the rapid-transit underground railways were built, to connect with Long
Island and the mainland. Later still, the Washington Bridge and Hudson
Freeway and the Triborough Bridge and Roosevelt Freeway enabled
commuters from 35 to 40 miles away to work, shop, and be entertained downtown.

With this pressure from the margins, the centre grew. It grew in
height – with the introduction of the skyscrapers that fascinated yet appalled
Henry James – and also in complexity and size. The old business area around
Wall Street, anchored by the American and New York Stock Exchange
buildings and the great New York banks, still prevailed, but expansion into
the midtown occurred, with shopping along Fifth Avenue, recreation along
Broadway, and new offices, hotels, and luxury apartments on Park Avenue.
The pressure on space, translated into the highest land values in America, led
to the most specialized use of land, with tightly grouped, functionally linked
buildings that increased the centrality of Manhattan. Head offices once in
other cities moved there: the new World-port built the two highest office

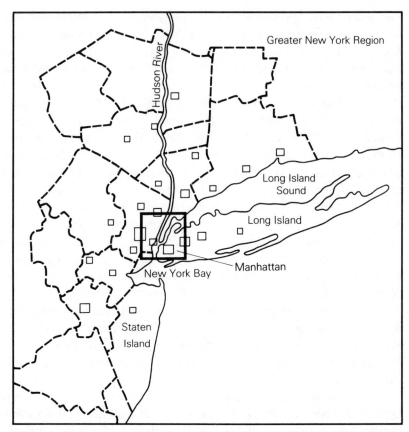

Fig. 7.4 *Projected office jobs, Greater New York, 2000.* The centrality of New York, on America's eastern seaboard, and the centrality of Lower Manhattan in the New York region, have produced an extraordinary concentration of finance, commerce, transport, and the 'media', giving New York economic controls over most of America. Squares indicate business centres; their size is in proportion to their business.

skyscrapers in the world at the edge of the old downtown. The linkage between offices, telecommunications, hotels, clubs, and transport not only served business, but city hall and the United Nations, also theatres and cafés, the great centres of the performing arts, galleries and museums: these in their turn were added attractions for stores, fashion shops, residential hotels, and luxury apartments. In the meantime, in the narrow but well-placed interstices, the tenements still drew their downtown dwellers in the Bowery, Chinatown, Greenwich Village, Stuyvesant, and the West Side.

The continuing success of centralizing forces in the business area, in spite of traffic problems and the critical shortage of building space, pushed land-values back towards Morningside Heights and also to Brooklyn and the Bronx, with commercial invasion replacing institutions and housing. Sectors of stepped values developed along axial lines, as for example Broadway with business passing through shopping, restaurants, and theatres, to apartment housing, educational institutions, parks, and the take-off for the suburbs. Land-values thus created an orderly stacking of land-uses from central Manhattan up to Washington Heights, or across to Long Island and Staten Island.

In the broadest way, land-values backed themselves up from peaks in downtown and midtown Manhattan, through huge concentric zones including: (1) the outer-inner industrial districts of East River and the Hackensack flats; (2) the inner-outer suburbs, mainly of middle-class families, in Long Island, the Bronx, and Jersey City; (3) the outer ring of middle- and upper-class suburbs up the Hudson, along Long Island Sound, and into the Piedmont fringe of Connecticut and New Jersey (here one passes into the exurbia of high-class developments and private estates).

Social geography has come to reflect this economic order with a ring of middle- and upper-class suburbs around a working-class centre: in ethnic terms this has increasingly meant a white periphery round a black core.

The American land ethic that 'the only function of land is to enable its owner to make money', has, in Berry's (1972) words, made 'the shape of every American city respond almost entirely to the operation of private market forces'. What is true of New York is characteristic of Boston or Philadelphia, Chicago or San Francisco.

Even where planned for aesthetic meaning or social significance, land developed an economic *cachet*; in Philadelphia, for example, land designed for pomp and circumstance, as the setting for great institutions, or platted for pleasure, its great square making space for grace, nevertheless passed to the speculator, and was split up and exploited for business. Street blocks were divided up into narrow alleys 'so that little houses might be crowded onto the back lots of the houses facing the main streets'. Business men took a street-front location, their workmen and other help had to crowd into the back alleys. As Warner (1975, p. 15) has pointed out, no less a person than Benjamin Franklin made use of the 'back alley process with his house lot off Market Street. He built a row of three houses . . . turning his home yard into an interior lot.' Here space was being used at the expense of grace.

Later, the 'old pattern of proprietors living on the front streets and the unskilled in the alleys and the back streets' turned to proprietors living at the outer fringe and the workers in the city's inner core. Thus, 'income, and hence class, segregation came to exist'. (Warner, 1971, pp. 171, 173).

In other words, as already noted, economic gradients worked themselves out in social contours. These were affirmed in the landscape. Distinct social areas came to mark the American city – and this in spite of the general belief in social equality. But the fact is, to earn social distance meant to buy geographical space; the further one went *up* the social scale the further *out* one moved in geographical location. A man's freedom to get ahead of others involved the necessity to go beyond them. The notion of equality did not produce a dead-level society. Far from it: great heights and depths prevailed, because American equality signified, in a marked degree, the chance to secure the maximum economic reward and the highest social recognition one could for oneself. That few got to the top, but many fell to the bottom, did not destroy the myth that each was equal to the other in being able to rise – or open to fall. As long as the system was open-ended it gave the illusion of being equitable; and this image in the mind then freed men for their unequal struggles.

Boston – the social breakaway

The bid for status led to a constant social breakaway in the American city. This differed from its European counterpart in that it was more general, more persistent, and more free. The surge to the suburb that characterized London continued in America on a still wider scale. As has been mentioned, in part, the Puritan sects were part of the suburban cult. They got on by getting out, and this tradition they carried over to and advanced in America. Where they stepped out of a district or town new immigrants came in, taking over the houses they had left behind them. As these immigrants then became accepted, it was a sign of being a good American to move out. Fresh immigrants divided up and filled the houses they had abandoned. Thus new-made men kept pushing out, and those who had still to make their way came after. The social scene in America became, in Howell's words, 'the self-guided search for self-improvement'. As he showed for Boston, each person was trying to pull himself up by his own bootlaces. In doing this each came to find his own level on the social scale. This was shown by his bid for geographical position.

Bidding for position is of two sorts: the bid to be in at the centre so far as business is concerned; and the bid to be out at the edge, when living is valued. The in-bid forces up the price of land used for profit; the out-bid land fit for pleasure. Not unnaturally the bid must be higher for high-profit land: plotted on a graph this makes for an overall bid-curve that rises in steepness towards the centre. Yet the bid for pleasant living constantly puts up the price of residential land, and as constantly forces it further and further out to the margins. The freedom to bid has become a speculator's fever in America, and ranks the various districts of the city according to their status.

That this was something unusually American, evolved in the general American breakaway, is not often realized, yet as Robson (1973) points out, 'studies of pre-industrial cities have repeatedly demonstrated a reversal of Park and Burgess's social gradient, since pre-industrial cities have the rich living at the core, and the poor at the periphery. Subsequent change to an American pattern, with the poor living at the centre and the rich at the margins' had to await the economic, social, and technological changes spearheaded by the Americans.

Change is of the essence. As Saul (1970) has shown it is *the* discriminating American feature. He is concerned with it at the technological level. He quotes a very telling remark made by a European visitor early in the nineteenth century who said, 'Everything new is quickly introduced here. There is no clinging to old ways.' This was equally true in social terms. Status areas were quickly tried out: if found wanting, they were as quickly changed. People did not cling to neighbourhoods for their own sakes, as in England where church, school, club, and pub so often anchor a family, even if that family is fit to change and go to a better district.

The Puritans, then, brought over and developed a status-conscious society. The early struggle for the 'dignity of the pews' in the New England church, such as at Deerfield, by which a town meeting had formally to recognize the status divisions within a congregation by designating 'ye fore seat in ye front Gallerie shall be equal in dignity to ye second seats in ye Body of ye meeting house, and ye fore seat in ye side Galleries shall be equal to ye 4th seats in ye Body of the house', this became translated on a city-wide scale to a *dignity of the districts*, with certain neighbourhoods being given distinctly higher status than others (see Fig. 7.5).

Nowhere has this been better described than in Howells's (1885:1963) study of nineteenth-century Boston presented in *The Rise of Silas Lapham*. The hero is a typical American business man who wanted to 'make the most of the unlimited opportunity' present in his country, and was determined to 'grasp all in his own hand'. He is first seen as a barefoot boy on a countryside farm. As he makes good in the paint business his father started, he moves into town, thus merging with that growing crowd of future-seekers which, coming in from the periphery, built up land-values at the centre. Subsequently, as he begins to make good, he moves out of the crowded purlieus of the inner city to spacious and gracious living at the city margin. This is the American myth personified, and gives a picture of the American city as it was shaped by the self-made man.

Boston grew up on a narrow-necked peninsula at the head of Massachusetts Bay and the mouth of the Charles River. The old centre near the harbour declined as a residential area on becoming the central business district of Boston. Commercial invasion of the subcentre led to the flight of better-class residents. The upper class moved to Beacon Hill and there entrenched themselves as Boston's aristocracy. The middle class was more mobile. It moved first to the North End, away from the harbour. But as the harbour then expanded northward, the North End declined and the middle class fled to a hilly area to the south known as the South End. But the port then expanded south, and the railways came into the south from New York, so the

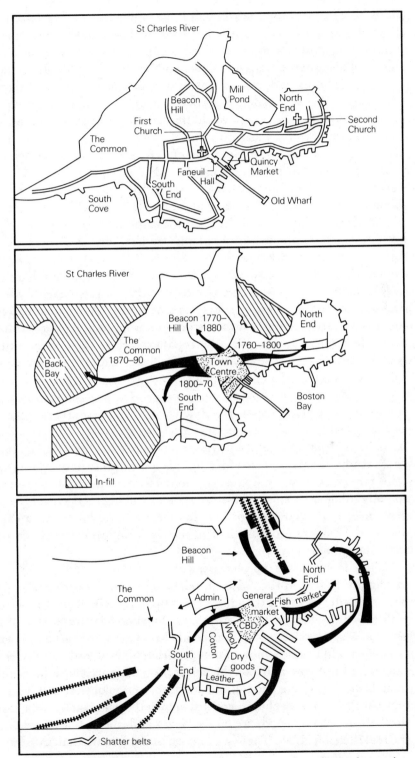

Fig. 7.5 *The changing geography of Boston, seventeenth to nineteenth centuries.*
The 'dignity of the district' led to a 'peregrination of prestige' in Boston,
with marked changes in social geography through flight to, or fight for,
status areas; this is very typical of the American city.

middle class fled to the Back Bay, a large embayment of the Charles River above Beacon Hill. Lapham is involved in these latter movements; as he climbs *up* in Boston's social circles he moves *out* to districts of increasing dignity. This progression is still typical of the American family on the make.

Having made a success of himself, Lapham likes to look back on the days when, 'We were patched all over, though we wa' n't ragged.' He had moved to Boston to contact a world market for his product. Already, by the 1860s, central Boston was in decline. Lapham took up an office in an old mansion not far from the docks. One infers from a conversation he had with a young reporter that he and his wife boarded in the vicinity. But 'the streets were all narrow and most of them crooked in that part of the town', and though he might like the fact that, at the end of the street, 'the spars of a vessel pencilled themselves against the cool blue of the afternoon sky and the air was full of a smell compounded of oakum, leather, and oil', yet he found the district increasingly irksome. This was especially true when he became the owner of a gig with a very mettlesome horse. He complained that there was 'no chance to speed a horse here, of course'. He had to make way for heavy drays drawn to the wharf by slow-plodding shires. Giving a lift to the young reporter who was doing a success story on his life, Lapham asked where he lived. 'Just round the corner', the reporter replied. 'But we don't live: we board. Mrs Nash, 13 Canary Place.' 'Well, we've all got to commence that way', suggested Lapham, consolingly.

But he himself had soon given up that way of life, and as success came he climbed to the open, tree-lined 'ovals' on the southern ridge, known as South End, which became for a while, a district with some dignity. Actually, by the time the Laphams went there, the flight to the South End had already been recognized as 'a mistaken move of society'. But the shrewd countryman for whom it was status enough to move into a neighbourhood till recently still good, exploited the situation by buying 'very cheap of a terrified gentleman who discovered too late that the South End was not the thing, and who in the eagerness of his flight to the Back Bay threw in his carpets and shades for almost nothing'.

However, as the years passed, Lapham was made to feel it beneath his dignity to live in the faded grandeur of a failing district. The problem became acute when his daughters grew up. They chanced to make contact with a wealthy family, the Coreys, who lived on 'the water side of Beacon Hill', a very favoured neighbourhood. Mrs Corey, disturbed at what she thought might develop into an inappropriate liaison for her son, decided to call on the Laphams, and look them over. When she arrived at the South End, though she was polite enough, she let drop, in apology for calling almost at nightfall, 'that the coachman had not known the way exactly'. She explained that 'nearly all our friends are on the New Land [the in-fill of Back Bay] or on the Hill [Beacon Hill]'. There was a barb in this remark that 'rankled' in Mrs

Lapham's breast, and after Mrs Corey had gone, comparing notes with her daughter, Mrs Lapham found that a barb had been left to rankle in her mind, also. She told her mother, 'They said they had never been in this part of the town before.' All of a sudden the Laphams came to realize that they had made a mistake in moving to the South End and had been there long enough. The wife felt compelled to admit, 'I don't believe but what we're in the wrong neighbourhood'. Lapham told her he had speculated in property and bought a lot at Back Bay. They decided to move yet again.

Having planned to break away from the South End and invade the Back Bay, the Laphams were made aware of what the change meant through the need to build a new style of house. Their old home was *infra dig.* beside the dignity of the new district. Howells makes a distinct point of this in his story.

> *The Lapham drawing room* [in their South End house] *was in parti-coloured paint which Lapham hoped to repeat in his new house. The trim of the doors and windows was in light green and the panels in salmon; the walls had . . . a wide strip of red velvet paper running up the corners; the chandelier was of massive imitation bronze; the mirror over the mantel rested on a fringed mantel-cover of green reps, and heavy curtains of that stuff hung from gilt lambrequin frames at the window; the carpet was of a pattern in crude green which, at the time Mrs Lapham bought it, covered half the new floors in Boston. In front of the windows were statues . . . representing allegories of Faith and Prayer.
> . . .*

Lapham wanted to carry all this over to Back Bay but on a grander and more opulent scale. But the architect insisted that the upper-class mode (to which, if he were to move to Back Bay, he would have to aspire) centred in 'light and elegance'. Howells points the contrast in describing the Corey home. This was in

> *a handsome quiet old street,* [where] *the dwellings were stately and tall. The Corey home was one of two designed by the same architect built opposite Boston Common. It has a wooden portico, with slender fluted columns, which have always been painted white, and which, with the delicate mouldings of the cornice, form the sole and sufficient decoration of the street front; nothing could be simpler . . . within, the architect has again indulged his preference for the classic; the roof of the vestibule . . . rests on marble columns, slim and fluted, and a staircase climbs in a graceful, easy curve from the tessellated pavement. A rug lay at the foot of the stairs, but otherwise the simple adequacy of the architectural intention had been respected. The place looked bare to the eyes of the Laphams.*

The Coreys, of course, live on the Hill. They are not too sure about Silas Lapham who has not been rich long enough to have given his family any dignity in society. But they admit that 'the suddenly rich are on a level with any of us, nowadays. Money buys position at once. Money is to the fore now. It is the romance, the poetry, of our age. It's the thing that chiefly strikes the imagination.' Mrs Corey finds it increasingly distasteful that her son should be linked with the Laphams, but her husband reminds her that birth and breeding 'represent a fading tradition'. The Corey's own family after all, 'had followed the trade from Salem to Boston when the larger city drew it away from the former'. They, too, had had to make a breakaway to make good. They were only Laphams at two or three removes, though their successes had carried them to the security of the Hill. Here social pre-eminence had been protected by geographical seclusion. The ascent to social distinction where they were 'in savor just beyond the salt of the earth' (though just a little short of 'the real aristocracy'), had become entrenched on the commanding heights of geographical distinctness.

All status-seekers are not, of course, American, but all Americans are status-seekers. This is what makes the social breakaway so significant, and why it breaks up the city so much and so frequently. Class helps to keep the American city on the move. What between the push of economics and the pull of society the city is constantly changing. Each American family moves five to seven times in its life. Howells's novel fits the facts.

All areas but Beacon Hill saw a trooping of the classes. What triggered it off was the expansion of the central business district (Ward, 1966; see also Fig. 7.5).

The first business area ran from the Long Wharf, on the eastern cove of the Boston Peninsula, up State Street towards the old market and the tower hall. In the early days most merchants conducted their business at their residence and there was little differentiation of function. Then, as Firey (1947) shows, specialization began to occur in the early nineteenth century. Between 1812 and 1837 banks grew from 4 to 37; 22 of these were sited on State Street. Insurance and brokerage companies also moved in. Households had to move out. Those with real wealth went *up* to Beacon Hill, others – still well off – went *out* to the North End. This was a pleasant elevated spur between Boston Bay and the Charles River, and had clean air and beautiful views. But business began to move north: the green market, and markets for meat and fish spread out between 1835 and 1875, and then the wholesale food business in general extended north from 1890 to 1920. Meanwhile in the great railway building era of the 1840s to 1870s, four major railway companies built their Boston terminals on the inner side of the North End, when the old Mill Pond was filled in. Caught between the southward thrust of these railroads and the northward drive of business, the North End was squeezed in a vice; it was shattered as a pleasant middle-class residential area, and swiftly changed into a working-class tenement district. As the old Yankee merchants and professional men fled, the Irish moved in (1850–80), followed later on by the

Italians (1880–1920), then by Jews, (1900–20), and now by Negroes (1920–present). It is one of the least desirable of all Boston's living quarters.

Meantime, those middle-class white Anglo-Saxon Protestants who had fled to the low elevation of the South End found themselves in difficulty. After 1830, warehouse construction south of the State Street business strip began. A huge dry-goods wholesaling area developed, especially after the 1860s, until by the 1890s business pressed right on the heels of residence. The textile and leather industries, and the manufacture of clothing, required large stores of wool, cotton, and hides. The factories themselves moved in, particularly when main-line railways built terminals on the inner flanks of South End. The South Cove was filled in for big railway stations with their sidings and depots. South End was also caught in a squeeze between business and transportation and its calm soon shattered. Upper-income families fled to Back Bay, and South End became a low-middle to low-class rooming-house area. Eight major arterial roads carrying heavy traffic and an elevated commuter railway pass through it. Before it had changed in this way it became a refuge for the more ambitious of the Irish trooping out of the North End. The poorer Irish still remain, but French Canadians, Greeks, and Syrians have moved in, making essentially an ethnic district. It is here that these recent immigrants are opposing the bussing of negro children into their schools.

The retail portion of the central business district had pushed west from State Street, beyond Faneuil Hall and the Quincy Market towards Boston Common. So had the administrative parts. The new State House on the edge of the Common became the nucleus of the main administrative district, and deflected retailing down Washington and Tremont Streets, between the South End and Back Bay. Here was yet another pressure that destroyed the residential quality of the South End. It was a pressure that kept probing west, and by the 1920s had moved into the Back Bay. Between 1865 and 1920, Back Bay had been the refuge of the middle-class flight from South End. The in-trooping families, like Silas Lapham, included the next-but-top business men and many leading professional men. They fought the further incursion of business. But their area was too near central Boston, and too much in the path of main roads and bridges between Boston and Cambridge, to remain residential. However, by allowing urban invasion to take the form of a cultural institutional movement, with art galleries, libraries, the Harvard Medical School and MIT, the upper-class 'tone' of the area was maintained. Although many residents wanting more room and peace moved out, others, accepting apartment life or row-house development, stayed on.

Beacon Hill has been the only inner area in Boston that has resisted changes of class trooping through it. Taken over in 1795 by the Mt Vernon Proprietors it was laid out in large lots exclusively for the upper class, and has resisted extensive subdivision and physical deterioration ever since. In 1922, the Beacon Hill Association was formed specifically to keep out invasion. Very ingeniously the original Proprietors had planned the streets to make discordant junctions with the rest of Boston, and this minimized the flow of through traffic, especially from the rapidly declining area of the Hill's north slope. That slope saw the movement west into it, from the North End, first of the Irish and now of the Negro: hence there is an astonishing *fault-face* between the highly ethnicized north slope and the homogeneous native-white south slope of the Hill – surely one of the great 'interfaces' in the social geography of America.

In most American cities, the central areas have been abandoned by the wealthy, particularly by upper-class Whites, and there has been a great flight out. This has now turned into a positive outward thrust and has led to the 'exploded city' – especially in the West, where freedom of movement has always been greater, and where so much of the growth of the city took place in the automobile age.

Los Angeles – the spatial breakaway

This means that there is a spatial breakaway in America of unparalleled dimension. The urge to get out literally is exploding the city. As Vance Packard (Packard, 1959) shows

> . . . the desirability of an address can be determined by its distance from the downtown business district. As you move outward from the centre houses become progressively less aged, and more desirable for those who can pay. A few old high-prestige neighbourhoods manage, by investing in paint and polish, to maintain their status; but most areas lose their élite status within thirty to fifty years. Their middle-aged mansions become funeral parlors or Moose lodges. The pressure is always outward.

As a result the American city has exploded completely beyond the built-up area to spatter the whole countryside. In Gottmann's (1972) words, in his now famous study of the Atlantic metropolitan belt, from Boston to Washington (the whole of which he treats as one community, called Megalopolis) the American city is 'the cradle of a new order in the organization of space'.

This new order is due to two very American things, first the breakaway mind of America, and second a breakaway technology, that is to say, the readiness of the road for the road-ready mind. As has already been mentioned, for Kerouac (1961) the American people, and especially young Americans, are people *On the Road*. It is not surprising that Kerouac wrote in California, because California, now the fastest-growing State in the Union, attracts the go-ahead and the get-about from all over America. San Francisco and Los Angeles are noted for the tremendous sprawl of city into country, made possible by the greatest rush of freeways in and out of town anywhere in the world. People can work in any one of a score of cities, yet live out in the countryside; and, thanks to 'phones, telex, TV, expressways, the car, the vertical car park, drive-in restaurants, even drive-in banks, theatres and churches, together with planes, helicopters, and heliports, they can keep in touch with each other through a fantastic web of contacts. There is nothing else like it. City life is dispersed by a system of leap-frogging over an immensely wide area: (see Fig. 7.6). Los Angeles suburbs have broken away beyond the rim of the San Gabriel, Santa Susana, and Simi Mountains to far-flung satellites reached not by train or even by car but by plane. This is the world of people for whom to live is to move.

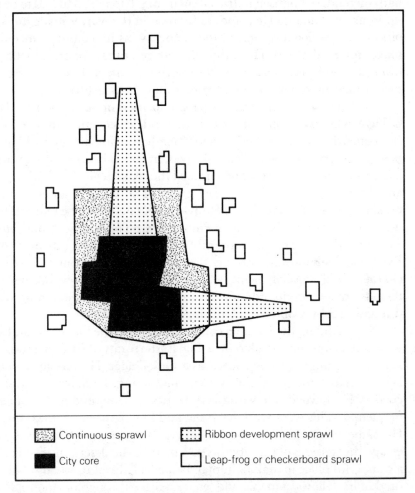

Continuous sprawl

City core

Ribbon development sprawl

Leap-frog or checkerboard sprawl

Fig. 7.6 *The exploded city.* The exploded city in the Los Angeles region, with an ever wider 'fall out' of suburban and satellite communities, has been accelerated by the spread of freeways and the 'land-grab' policies of speculators buying up big blocks of land in the countryside and then inducing a leap out of the city.

So much of California is, as Steinbeck said of Cannery Row, both 'the gathered and the scattered' – the place where people gather from all over the United States but where they live, none the less, in a scatter. This is best seen, perhaps, in Mailer's (1957) *The Deer Park*, the story of a Hollywood colony full of both a geographical breakaway as easterners have come out West to make good, and the social break as people have torn themselves from their past to 'put themselves on the map' – and have thus changed the map of California.

The tale is told by Sergius O'Shaugnesay – an Irish/Slovene mix from eastern America who, because his mother had died early and his father had 'surrendered himself to travelling from job to job', had had to be brought up in an orphanage. He comes to his own in the war, is made an Air Force officer, shoots down several of the enemy, wins his country's medals, and – makes for Hollywood. He is thus the image of that American who, coming from nowhere, and springing from nothing, can still hope to rise. He was surrounded by others who had gone as far from as little.

He joined a clique of people focused on an ex-actress, Dorothea O'Faye, who 'had been born in Chicago and "discovered" in New York', and subsequently moved to Hollywood. 'She had made money and lost money, been a celebrity and a failure' – she was, in fact, a breakaway character. She had moved across country and climbed the social scale. She had seen enough and been enough to live her own way. The whole community had this breakaway mind: a satellite of Hollywood it could only be reached by a long drive or a plane trip, yet its members were constantly in and out of Los Angeles. They were as constantly off to other cities, all over America. Everyone had moved, was on the move, or was about to move. 'What characterized most of them', we are told, 'was that their business allowed them to travel. Sergius admired the convenience of their itinerary, which was triangulated by California, Florida, and the East.'

Among the members of the colony was the film director, Eitel, 'the only son of an auto-dealer in a big Eastern city. His father was born of Austrian immigrants and started as a junk-dealer. His mother was French.' Having had some success in writing and acting, he moved west and made good in Hollywood. He was a very restless person, and had changed home frequently. This went with marrying and having been divorced three times. He came to the growing movie-colony of Desert D'Or because he could escape the tensions of the city there. 'You take the desert,' he liked to say, 'it's a wonderful place to make a human being feel alive.' It was also a site where, tired of his fellows, a man could 'go for a drive through the mountains . . . or take a boulevard to the ocean and cruise along the shore for miles'.

Here, people were using the land as an escape from society: the spatial breakaway was a social flight. People were buying freedom from each other by making free with the countryside. Hence the exploded city, the compulsion to get out. Hence the restless drive to start new suburbs, or promote new towns. When Sergius was asked by Eitel, 'What are you doing here at Desert D'Or', the young man first replied, 'Nothing, I'm trying to forget.' 'Do you have money to do this forever?' 'For a year or two.' 'Then what?' 'I'll think about the next town.' That kind of freedom had made America; though unhappily in this case it was a freedom to break away *from*, rather than to break through *to*. Later, Sergius was more positive and said he was not only trying to forget the old life, 'but I'm looking for another'.

Another life in another place – America has made this the way out. As a result it has gathered into areas of attraction, like Los Angeles, an extraordinary array of talents. At the same time it has scattered its opportunities, by the expulsive power of land-values and of social status, over a tremendous range of sites. Freeways lace suburb to city and town to town by an immense community of movement. This not only allows for but tempts people to shift from place to place in their ever-restless drive for the end of the road.

To do this, people like to keep their options open. Sergius describes how an actress, Lulu, had made such an impression in Hollywood at the age of 13 that Magnum Pictures had wanted to sign her on as the teenage heart-teaser for a 7-year contract. Had she accepted, Lulu told him, 'I'd be making a stinking seven-hundred-and-fifty a week now, like other poor exploited schnooks, but daddy wouldn't let me. "Free-lance", he said – he talks that way – "this country was built on free-lance".'

Free-lance geography has been the result – the ability of millions of Americans to develop the homes they like in the place they like, and thus explode the city all over the countryside. The total area of the so-called Los Angeles Economic Region is bigger than Northern Ireland and not much inferior to Belgium. Thus, one community has spread over space providing enough room for whole countries in Europe. The outer satellites and suburbs are knit to the centre by freeways which in the five counties area of Los Angeles had made up 1,500 miles in the mid 1970s, or more than the then length of motorways in the whole of Britain. And although Los Angeles is the archetype of the new geography, all the states of America have followed suit: the American landscape as a whole is a spatter of atomized central places.

It might be supposed that their central functions would thus be imperilled. Some are. Less shopping is done downtown and far fewer people live there. But Los Angeles has met this problem by building up a different kind of downtown – one which is very lively and has tremendous pulling force – in making its centre the hub of art and music, a great convention meeting-place, and a sort of arch-club for business men in top-level financial offices. Consequently, although there is a tearing away of the urban fabric into far bits and pieces, these are still woven together by a marvellous web of roads tied to a living and dramatic centre. The tearing away, then, has not really disrupted urban life, it has only given it a new dimension and meaning.

This spatial breakout is something very American. Observers from America have often been amazed at how tightly packed European cities still are and at how abruptly they end where the countryside begins. Green-belt reglations have, of course, sharpened this cut-off, yet it has been a longstanding feature of at least the historic European cities. R. C. Weaver, author of *The Urban Complex* and one-time Administrator of the US Housing and Home Finance Agency, certainly comments on this (Weaver, 1966): 'Those who have travelled in Europe,' he declares, 'have noted the relative ease with which Scandinavian countries, Great Britain, and France can control the land use in the periphery of the central city. In the United States this is practically an impossibility.' Although most cities have zoning regulations, these take into account the outward thrust of the city. Moreover, that thrust usually passes beyond city control into neighbouring counties and townships. Orange County, for example, contiguous to Los Angeles, is a huge grouping of settlements in itself. Very often county administrations invite city sprawl in order to catch the upper-class ratepayer. Thus, county zoning may not only allow for but encourage the breakaway city.

Consequently, as Weaver explains, we have to think of the American city in different terms. Certainly, 'When we talk of the city of the future, we can no longer think of an independent [i.e. self-contained] urban community, or even one that is the focal point of just a metropolitan area. Rather, we must think in terms of urban communities that must function as one of many nerve centres in a vast, complex, interconnected organism' – a human ganglion, in fact, with cells of control and networks of impulse creating a whole citified countryside.

Helping in the rise of this new social geography has been that old American character, the land speculator. In America, land is an excuse for speculation as much as a basis for production. Many make their living by selling it rather than working it. Frontier history consisted of finding land, breaking it, selling it at a profit, and moving on – to do the same elsewhere. A great number did not even break it, but held it vacant until they could sell for gain. The speculator looked for the trends of movement, bought ahead, and then tried to draw people along the paths of profit. Hence, speculation has played a great part in the shape, direction, and scale of urban growth.

Once people became affluent and mobile they could be induced to move out of town: to do so was to move into status. Farmers literally sucked the town into the country by selling their land to city suckers – who then found how rocky or sandy or swampy it was, but who nevertheless felt attuned to nature with trees and birds around them. A great deal of marginal farmland has thus earned itself a higher return that it could otherwise possibly have got. But even farmers on good land sell out, some because this is a way to get a retirement fund, others because their children are not interested in carrying on the farm, or some to use the high profit accrued to buy a better farm further away from the city.

City speculators themselves, either rich business or professional men, or those in the real-estate trade, induce farmers to sell out, and city dwellers to take to the country. To do this effectively they must obtain a reasonably large block of land. It is difficult to trade with many small patches on the urban–rural fringe. Hence, as Sargent (1976, p. 30) has said, large-scale developers buy up big areas so as to 'locate their planned communities on the outer-edge of the urban fringe'. This has especially been the case where, like Los Angeles, metropolitan areas have allowed for large block grants. As a result, the grace of the countryside has been traded for more and more urban space, carrying the city far out into the rural scene.

There is little coordination in such work. Hence the city simply sprawls out; its expansion is usually quite haphazard. This *sprawl-scape* is one of the unhappiest aspects of American geography, but since 'each speculative agent can be viewed as an independent profit center', private judgement is the chief space-maker. Most cities are private affairs. As Warner (1971, p. 4) insists: 'The tradition of privatism in America has meant that the physical forms of American cities, their lots, houses, factories and streets have been the outcome of profit-seeking builders, land-speculators and investors, and not of community action.' He certainly found this to be the case in 150 years of the development of Philadelphia, though it started out as part of Penn's 'Holy Experiment'.

The community breakthrough

Nevertheless, community concern has not been wanting, and has grown with time until it now vies with private profit as a principal city-shaper. One of the earliest government bills passed in America was the Virginian Town Planning Act of 1691, by which the beautiful towns of Williamsburg and Annapolis were plotted. Colonial America rose in the age of Wren and Inigo Jones. The whole of Western Europe was interested in architecture; there was a Vitruvian revival throughout Italy, France, Britain and Holland. Bath and Edinburgh had some of the finest examples of new-town development, with spacious squares and gracious crescents. Edinburgh town council called for a new town that was to become at once 'the centre of trade and commerce' and also of 'pleasure and beauty'. Social as well as economic criteria were to rule the plan. Something of this sort of thinking had crossed the Atlantic. Pillsbury (1970) shows that New Haven, built in a large square divided equally into nine lesser squares, 'was laid out following the ideas of Vitruvius to the letter, including the orientation of the streets to catch the Italian breezes from the Adriatic!'

The rectilinear 'classical' model which did so much to shape the towns of the late seventeenth and early eighteenth centuries, was modified by the more 'romantic' views seen in later models, such as Washington, where, in addition to the great east–west and north–south streets, there were the angled boulevards, planned by Pierre L'Enfant, joining in hub-like circles or squares to draw neighbourhoods together as in a spider's web. Buffalo and Detroit had a central rectilinear plan that then broke away in a dramatic radial system. Edinburgh's 'New' New Town, growing up in the 1830s, favoured crescents and circles rather than squares, and it is interesting that many plans for American cities being built at that time – as for example, Missouri – adopted the same ideal.

America, like England, had its 'garden-city' enthusiasts. One of these was the Englishman, Robert Owen, who went to America for a time, and tried to set up his working-class Utopia at New Harmony, Indiana. The very name is redolent of early nineteenth-century idealism, when industry could still be held in balance with housing, in an integrated community. According to Brown (1827:1972) who visited New Harmony, 'Mr Owen seemed to have for his single object to introduce a new system of society to supersede the old by which . . . at the present point of degeneracy in human morals . . . reasoning men could throw themselves into . . . the perfection of our nature'. Owen envisaged a geometrical form of perfection, in which, as he advertised it:

> *The general arrangement of the buildings is a square, each side of which is 1,000 feet. The centre and the extremities are occupied by the public buildings. The parts between them are the dwellings of the members. In the interior of the square are the Botanical and other gardens, the exercise grounds, etc. The whole is raised above the level of the natural surface to give fine views and surrounded by an esplanade.* [The factories were to be set in along the four main roads leading into the square, but clear of both the peripheral housing and the interior gardens.] *The disposition of every part is so regulated by a careful attention to the most important discoveries and facts in science as to form a new combination of circumstances capable of producing permanently greater physical moral and intellectual advantages to every individual than have ever been realized in any age or country.*

Owen's idea never caught on, perhaps because it was too disciplined for its would-be followers, but similar attempts were made elsewhere: all over America Utopian communities sprang up. One of the more successful of these was the Oneida group, where in a beautifully planned, spacious, green and airy settlement people used their individual talents to serve the common good. This differed from most in that the main industry chosen, that of making silverware, found a wide market and thus lifted the community from mere self-subsistence. Although in the end it was the industry that lasted rather than the ideals, and communalism gave way to individual enterprise, nevertheless the plans expressed in the initial settlement continued to grace the landscape.

It was the strength of planning, and of such ambitious planning at that, which struck Trollope (1862) on visiting America. He compared European with American cities mainly on this basis. He wrote:

> *Our towns in England have been built as they have been wanted* [i.e. by rule of thumb]. *No aspiring ambition . . . warmed the bosoms of their first founders. But in America, the founders of cities have had the experience of the world before them.. . . A city at its commencement is laid out with an* intention.. . . *The sites of towns have been prepared with noble avenues and imposing streets.. . .*

If that were so, what led to the very grave unevennesses that then sprang up, and stamped themselves on the well-planned layout? The reply is simple: relatively unrestricted competition for land, and the dominance of the commercial mind. These stimulated the intense struggle for status areas as between classes; these led to the rise of American ghettos, with the segregation of conflicting ethnic groups; and above all these created the economic zones that contoured the use or abuse of the land. Economic usage took precedence. Individualism and competition, 'the twin pillars of the capitalistic system' as Mann (1954) calls them, came to the fore and dominated the nineteenth-century scene. Whatever the town had been before, it had to realign itself – down to brick and concrete – to the prevailing state of mind. Money more and more controlled morphology.

However, as Mann (1966) shows in his *Yankee Reformers in the Urban Age*, the fount of idealism continued to flow through the land, even during the height of opportunism and power. Reform was there as an undercurrent, gradually gathering volume and strength. Business was made to have a conscience. Many of the positions resulting from the naked show of power were criticized and modified in favour of the rising tide of reform. Men were tired of 'the fact that the governments of most of our important cities have for a long time been more or less rotten, and in some cases little more than gigantic systems of fraud'. Wealth was challenged where it was contemptuous of welfare. Boston, 'which had once been the cradle of . . . the public school movement and feminism, temperance, prison reform and abolitionism' remained true to its 'concern for the welfare of the many'. There, Hale denounced extreme *laissez-faire* as un-American and urged on Americans that 'public enterprise expressing the public will' should be a part of the nation's tradition; Sanborn cried against the extreme individualistic views of 'non-interference by government' . . . which he said were 'conjured up to thwart . . . the ethical relations of government'; Phillips called for 'the overthrow of the whole profit system' in favour of a system based on public good.

In the midst of this clamour for a community breakthrough came the Chicago World Fair, 1893, with its magnificent exhibition of 'the city beautiful'. Space, light, greenery, ordered lines of houses of regular height, wide streets, frequent parks, lakes – an environment of elegance and distinction cried out for change. Here was 'an appropriate atmosphere for work and living . . . so antagonistic to the selfishness, pride, arrogance, contention, belligerency and barbarism that characterize existing society', to use Ballou's words. Even business was impressed and sponsored designs (here and there) for 'garden factories', associated with working-men's suburbs.

The great architects of the day, Frederick Law Olmsted, Frederic Adams, Frederic Delano, and John Nolan pressed for beauty and amenity, and urged attention to *plan* as well as *façade*. In 1909 the first national conference on city planning took place, in which the debate was started to clean up the slums and control the suburbs of America. New York, especially, went ahead, supporting a Regional Plan Association to look at roads, open spaces, housing, and land-use on a broad basis; it published its first plan in the late 1920s.

The public responded with growing support. Although many argued that planning was the grave of liberty, yet, to use the ringing words of the Oneida experiment, it was only 'the grave of the liberty of selfishness, which has done mischief enough to deserve death – but it is the birth of the liberty of sociality. The whole gains more than individuals lose. Individuals have the liberty of harmony instead of the liberty of war'.

A new state of mind emerged that called for a social use of space. By 1927 at the nineteenth annual conference on city planning no less than 176 American cities, having a total population of 25 millions, had planning commissions and city plans. True, many of these plans, like the ones for Philadelphia, 'were to improve the commercial environment of the city'. As Warner (1971, p. xi), points out, 'they were downtown oriented – to bring traffic to the downtown, to beautify it, and to raise or maintain downtown business property values'. Even so, they marked space with grace. Eventually they turned a disaster like Pittsburgh's 'golden triangle', a jungle of dirt, noise, crowdedness, and confusion, into a triumph of elegance and comprehensibility.

In 1929 came Radburn, NJ, a remarkable example of the social use of space, with streets curved to the contour, houses staggered to get the view, motor routes separated from pedestrian ways, open gardens with a flowing sense of connectedness, and countryside brought into the town. But this was really planning *for* a community, not *by* a community; it imposed ideas of what was good for people, without getting people to work out their own good.

In the Great Depression the will of the people was itself stirred. Government leadership for example on the Tennessee Valley Authority

(1933) met with increasing popular support. This was the world's greatest regional planning effort, including water, power, soil, forestry and recreation, with industrial and urban spin-offs. The whole New Deal Program went with a new state of mind; it certainly produced a new social geography. The Conservation Corps drew in 2½ million people to regenerate soil and forests; the Agricultural Adjustment Administration put marginal cropland back into range and woodland; the Works Program Administration built thousands of much-needed schools and hospitals; the Public Works Administration improved and expanded roads and initiated the first important urban renewal projects in America; while the Home Ownership Loan Corporation assisted scores of thousands of low-income city dwellers to buy or repair low-cost homes. Finally, the Social Security Act of 1935 took fear out of the lives of a great many Americans by providing unemployment insurance, assistance to the disabled, and pensions to the old.

A social breakthrough in thought led to a breakout in social landuse. In 1937 Roosevelt set up the US Housing Authority which was the first nation-wide organization to clear the slums and extend low-cost housing. Private landlords were not finding enough profit in building or refurbishing downtown tenements, and those private speculators buying up downtown housing were selling out to office developers. Public intervention was necessary.

As Ulmer (1969) has argued in *The Welfare State - USA*, America in a sense became the father of the welfare state - that great new development in the progress of the Western world.

> *Under the crushing impact of the Great Depression, problems were thrust to the forefront of national consciousness everywhere.. . . Tentatively and pragmatically, government moved onto the scene as innovator, decision-maker, and regulator - under the pioneering leadership of President Franklin D. Roosevelt. The object was at no time to displace private enterprise in its prime job of producing and selling goods and services for profit. More conservatively, but still quite radically, the intent was to assert the public will, through government, to administer the economy by making the central decisions on matters of collective interest. At the beginning . . . business everywhere bristled in opposition. For the ears of some, amazingly, the polished, aristocratic diction of F.D.R. acquired a fearsome, proletarian accent! But gradually the new approach attained familiarity and respectability.. . . Within two decades, the basic . . . transition was accomplished, at least by the vast majority; the fundamental premise of the welfare state was accepted.. . .*

And with this change in state of mind there came about a widespread change in the American landscape: it became increasingly cast in the image of the planned community. The 1949 Housing Act had as its objective, 'The realization as soon as possible of a decent home and a suitable living environment for every American family.' No state had ever expressed a higher welfare ideal. To carry it out, the federal government required that any development to be supported should be part of an approved community plan. Thus, local planning was called for in the strongest terms. The 1954 Housing Act insisted on a 'Workable Program for Community Improvement' as the basis for a grant, underscoring a breakthrough to community participation. An overall look at municipal housing had to be taken including community facilities, routeways, and traffic, and the zoning of land-use. In Section 701 of this Act provision was made for an Urban Assistance Planning Program to give municipalities the money to make their own comprehensive development plans.

In 1964 the Civil Rights Act encouraged multiracial housing schemes by proclaiming that no person should be excluded from any federally aided urban renewal project on the basis of colour or creed. The following year, 1965, saw housing and urban development put into the federal cabinet itself, which meant that planning received the highest national recognition. Further improvements came with a National Land Use Policy in 1973, and the Better Communities Bill of 1974, making block grants to states, and through them to local authorities, to provide support for local initiatives. Thus, communities were urged to survey their own problems and come up with their own answers.

Seattle, and public housing

Mercer's (1977) study of federal housing in Seattle is a case in point. Here 'governments, whether national, state or municipal are now among the more important locational decision-makers in urban growth'. Important to realize is the fact that above direct federal outlays are indirect subsidies, such as the support of the mortgage market for housing loans, and tax relief on mortgage interest payments. In these ways government is underwriting, and not merely paralleling, private market initiatives: here the public and private sector are both at work to meet people's needs. However, government does not play anything like the large-scale directive role that it does, say, in the mixed economy of socialized Britain. In Seattle, publicly owned or assisted housing only makes up about 5 per cent of the total housing stock. The US government has taken the view that its role is 'largely residual – to assist those in the general population who cannot compete effectively to secure adequate housing in the private market'. Nevertheless, its functions are widening. They have gone well beyond the Low Rent Public Housing and Urban Renewal Act of 1968 (interested in resuscitating downtown decline) to the rehabilitation of individual homes (Section 115 of the Housing Act); leased public housing (Section 23) by which landlords lease private tenements for public rent; rent supplement (Section 236); and home ownership (Section 236). Perhaps the main thrust today is in assisting people to rent or buy their individual homes. Of special significance is the Rental, Elderly Only Program (Section 202) which has enabled thousands of old people to rent a house or apartment of their own, rather than become dependent on their children or go into an old-folks' home. In Seattle there has been an actual preference, in the 1970s, to use its limited funds for senior citizens. Geographically, the result of all this is a gradual shift from centre-city to the metropolitan fringe. Sargent (1976, p. 33) claims that, 'More than any single program, FHA insurance for single family homes has transformed the shape and social characteristics of American cities.. . . Suburbia is its monument.'

Thus, government is helping in the two major crisis areas of the American city, through downtown renewal and suburban control. In giant cities like Chicago, where downtown and the shatter belt around it have deteriorated so much, the central city/suburban ratio of commitment is 80:20; in Seattle, a city of 1.4 million, it is 58:42. Here, as in most western cities, the home-ownership programme of the US government has proved increasingly attractive and has helped to give plan and significance to the suburban fringe: 24.4 per cent of federally supported housing is for subsidized home ownership in planned suburban communities. Interestingly, many of the single-family homes are in areas 'undergoing racial change and are accelerating racial turnover' as middle-class non-whites are given a chance to move out to the suburbs – something that would scarcely happen under privatism afflicted by status resistance.

The American city, then, is a spectrum of private and public interests which make it a cross-section of American life. As Zelinsky (1976) says in his essay, 'The Pennsylvania town,' '. . . of all the works of man that dense, complex, totally artificial creation we call the town or city is . . . the most profusely charged with cultural signals'. It is in fact the culture of a nation in concentrated form. How the nation thinks becomes crystallized here in how the landscape looks.

References

Berry, Brian, J. L. (1972) 'On geography and urban policy', in Adams, J.S. (ed.) *Urban Policymaking and Metropolitan Dynamics*, Cambridge, Mass., p. 6.

Brown, P. (1827:1972) *Twelve Months in New Harmony*, 1827, Porcupine Press reprint, 1972, Philadelphia, p. 13.

Burnaby, A. (1760:1960) *Travels through the Middle Settlements in North America, 1759-60*, Cornell Press edn (1960) Ithaca, pp. 94-5.

Carey, G. W. (1976) 'A vignette of the New York-New Jersey metropolitan region', in Adams, J.S. (ed.), *Cities of the Nation's Historic Metropolitan Core*, Cambridge, Mass.

Chettle, H. (1592:1916) Quoted from Onions, C.T. (ed.) *Shakespeare's England*, Collins London, 1916, p. 40.

Crèvecoeur, J. H. St J. de (1782:1963) *Letters from an American Farmer*, 1782, Signet edn., N.Y., (1963) Letter 111, 'What is an American?' p. 61.

Dollard, J. (1949) *Caste and Class in a Southern Town*, Anchor N.Y., p. 65.

Firey, W. (1947) *Land Use in Central Boston*, Harvard U.P. Cambridge, Mass.

Gottmann, J. (1972) 'The city as crossroads', in *Ekistics*, No. 204, Nov. 1972, p. 309.

Howells, W. D. (1885, 1963) *The Rise of Silas Lapham*, 1885, Signet edn., N.Y., 1963, pp. 8, 15, 20, 24-30, 63-65, 92-5, 173.

Jackson, J. B. (1972) *American Space*, Norton N.Y., p. 144.

James, H. (1908, 1946) *The American Scene* (1908), Scribner's edn, N.Y. (1946) p. 78 ff.

Kerouac, J. (1961) *On The Road*, Pan edn, London, p. 23.

Mailer, N. (1957) *The Deer Park*, Signet edn, N.Y., pp. 7, 11, 35, 67, 147, 187.

Mann, A. (1954:1966) *Yankee Reformers in the Urban Age*, Belknap Press, 1954, Harper Torchbooks, 1966, N.Y., pp. 65 ff.

Mercer, J. (1977) 'National policy and the geography of housing: Canada and the United States'. Paper read at the Bellingham Conference, Pacific Coast Geographers, Mar.

Packard, V. (1959) *The Status Seekers*, McKay N.Y. pp. 83-4.

Park, R. E., Burgess, E. W., and **McKenzie, R. D.** (1925:1947) *The City*, Chicago (1925) reprinted 1947, p. 103 ff.

Pearl, V. (1961) *London and the Outbreak of the Puritan Revolution*, Oxford U.P., London, p. 40.

Pillsbury, R. (1970) 'The urban street pattern as a cultural indicator: Pennsylvania, 1682-1815', *Ann. Ass. Am. Geogr.*, Vol. 60, No. 3, Sept., p. 437, footnote 21.

Powell, S. C. (1970) 'The origin and stability of a New England town', in Reinitz, R. (ed.) *Tensions in American Puritanism*, N.Y., p. 182.

Robson, B. (1973) 'A view of the urban scene', in Chisholm, M. and Rodgers, B. (eds) *Studies in Human Geography*, Heinemann London, p. 54.

Sargent, C. S., Jr (1976) 'Land speculation and urban morphology', in Adams, J.S. (ed.) *Urban Policymaking and Metropolitan Dynamics*, Ballinger's Cambridge, Mass.

Saul, S. B (1970) *Technological Change: the United States and Britain in the Nineteenth Century*, Methuen London, p. 54.

Smith, A. (1776:1843) *The Wealth of Nations* (1776) Wakefield edn, London (1843) Vol. 1, cxxxv.

Trollope, A. (1862) *North America*, 2 vols, Chapman & Hall, London, Vol. 1, p. 182.

Ulmer, J. J. (1969 *The Welfare State: U.S.A.*, Houghton Mifflin Boston, p. 4.

Underwood, A. C. (1947) *A History of the English Baptists*, Carey Press London, p. 47.

Von Hübner, Baron (1871:1949) *Promenade autour du Monde*, quoted in Handlin, O., *This Was America*, N.Y. (1949) p. 298.

Ward, D. (1966) 'The Industrial Revolution and the emergence of Boston's Central Business District', *Economic Geography*, Vol. 42, pp. 152-71.

Warner, S. B. (1971) *The Private City, Philadelphia in Three Periods of its Growth*, Philadelphia U.P., p. xi.

Weaver, R. C. (1966) *The Urban Complex*, Anchor N.Y., p. 7.

Zelinsky, W. (1976) *The Pennsylvania Town* (preliminary draft) Penn. State University, p. 1.

The Whole America

The fount of idealism in America

Although the role of freedom in the making of America cannot be overstressed, it was the freedom to achieve the common good, as well as to secure individual interests. Social idealism is essential to the American dream, and much of American geography has been the attempt to give ideals shape and form in the landscape. In early New England, idealism was as much a communal, as it was an individual, expression: the hope was to set up a community of individual believers. The Mayflower Compact, between the Plymouth Fathers, was a great step forward in human cooperation. And from that day the interest in the community as a whole, as well as in the individual, has been a central part of American life. Although the New Englanders competed with and at times went to war against the Indians, they also tried to convert and care for them. In Bradford's *History* he tells how epidemics swept the Indians 'wherein thousands of them dyed', but Christian charity led many of the Pilgrims to 'tend to the sick, and bury the dead'.

Americans are proud of the fact that so soon after their fathers landed they founded Harvard College, in 1636. A few years later, in 1653, an Indian college was built there, for the education of the Massachusetts Indians: shortly after that, in 1693 William and Mary College was set up in Williamsburg, also with an Indian college. Though Wright claims that 'efforts to educate Indians in colonial colleges were futile', none the less the efforts were made.

So too were the still more idealistic attempts to live with the Indians and form joint White–Indian communities. In 1737, John Sergeant, a graduate of Yale, set up a 'wilderness community' in an undeveloped part of up-state Massachusetts and the so-called 'Stockbridge experiment' began, at what is now the lovely New England town of that name. In this experiment, so well described by Elizabeth Speare, a minister, a schoolteacher, and four white farmers went with their families to live among a tribe of Mohican Indians 'to teach them by force of example the virtues of the Christian religion and the English way of life'. Once more, that this experiment proved futile, need not detract from the faith and hope that lay behind it.

Idealism had its adherents in the South as well, where not a few outstanding voices were raised against slavery. This took a lot of courage, especially as the system became entrenched. That they may have vented no more than a despairing *cri de coeur* is true, but at least they showed a touched heart; they helped in the ultimate breakup of the system. Cable (1880) in his book of the South, *The Grandissimes*, has the leading Creole character become aware that his civilization lay in 'the shadow of the Ethiopian. It is the Nemesis' he cried 'w'ich glides along by the side of this morhal, political, commercial and social mistake. It drhags us a centurhy behind the rhes' of the world. It rehtahds and poisons every industry we've got.. . .' And much criticized though Styron may have become for his version of the Nat Turner story, yet he was correct in conceiving that Turner's masters might have been tired of a system which bound them to the slave as much as the slave to them. It was not beyond belief that the very judge who sentenced Turner was sick of the order he had to uphold, and cried out, in all honesty, 'Is not the handwriting on the wall for this beloved and foolish and tragic Old Dominion?' Had he in fact protested like this he would only have been echoing Jefferson who was deeply distressed at men having the mastery of, or being subject to, men, and proposed the voluntary liquidation of slavery. Justice would not sleep for ever.

Nor did it, but, at length rousing the sense of justice in the vast majority of Americans, led to that emancipation of the slaves which brought a new sense of humanity to the fore. This great act of idealism alone, changed the face of the whole country, as nothing else – not even the Revolution – had, and created a new American geography. Thus, from the beginning there has been the healing American – the American with a mission – who has done a great deal to keep the fount of idealism flowing throughout the land.

Strangely, the idealism that flowed out to Indian and Black, seemed often to stop short at women and youth. Yet to achieve wholeness in society, to develop the whole America, required that each person should be whole, whatever his race, age, or sex. This ideal came to the fore in the latter part of the nineteenth century, running side by side with the goal of self-interest. Both were driving forces in the American character. For the interest of the individual is in developing himself as a whole and this can only come from wholeness in society.

Emerson (1837) has been taken by many as the great protagonist of the individual, with his cry for non-conformity and self-reliance; but he wanted individual freedom for the sake of the Whole Man. Certainly he asked men to free themselves from the conventional, the artificial, and the traditional – but only to bind themselves to the total and the ultimate. He was, after all, a leader of the new Eudaemonism, a philosophy which under its distinguished Scottish proponent, Seth, urged men to revive the balanced view, and relive the balanced life. Only in this way could the breach between nature and spirit, science and religion be healed: in the truly well person. But this meant a person working for the well community. No person can be well in a sick state. What America is sick of, is that welfare sought by each individual at the expense of the well-being of the whole person. Emerson wanted everyone to stand up for himself, a free individual: but free for what?

To be the Whole Man

This is also part of the American dream – indeed, it is the only part that will keep it from becoming an American nightmare! This is the only thing that can hold Sartoris and Snopes, Maggie and Gatsby, and all those other so unequal people, and powers, and positions – and keep them in the one mind, and come out with a land that is one. And this is, of course, what a lot of people have worked for; a wholeness of mind that will make the land whole.

But the land has been very lop-sided, it has been a male land, and a male adult land, at that, dominated by male occupations, male interests, and male institutions. There may have been some excuse for this in colonial and in pioneer American days when male strength and aggressiveness pushed back the Indian and cut out the forest. Of course women tried to feminize the landscape as soon as possible with home and garden, school and church, and with their protests against brothels, gambling halls, and saloons. However, these continued to flourish, albeit off the main street, and settlements were still dominated by male-run businesses, law-courts, churches, and colleges. Even the public toilets were all male till the reforming 1890s. The women's business or social club, women's recreational associations, a women's hall at university, a woman doctor's clinic or lawyer's office, banks designed for the woman, these and similiar things, which are part of the concrete landscape today, only came into American geography as the American mind changed. How much fuller town and countryside now are – particularly when the geography of youth is also taken into account, or, for that matter, of old age. A fullness, a roundness has come into the American scene because at length a wholeness has taken over the American mind. Few things could more underscore the value of values in the geography of the land.

The female scene

As wives and mothers, women have always played a great part in society through the family. Yet in many cases the family frustrated as much as it fulfilled women's talents, particularly in the days of many children and large households. A time came when women began to think that their main role was no more to bring up a family than the men's to seed it. If men could regard their profession as at least as important as their family, why should not women? The family was something that ought to be shared so that women had time and energy to share the life outside it. Even in connection with their homes women often had little say – as, for example, in its site, its decoration and furnishing, the mortgage or maintenance. These were traditionally – and sometimes, indeed, legally – in the hands of their men. Women rarely decided the religion of the family, what church they would go to, or by how much they should support it. Even holidays and recreation were decided by the men. No doubt there was considerable satisfaction in playing a supporting role, and in getting behind the career of the husband and the interests of the children. But what of women themselves and their interests and propensities? Should not the family get behind *them*? There was an immense world outside the family that was closed to women – politics, business, the professions, higher education, sport; yet in all these fields women believed that, simply as human beings, they had as much to offer as their fathers, husbands, or sons. The trouble was that, in many instances, they were not legally entitled to enter these worlds, even if they wanted to. In 1884 Helen Gregory McGill was the only person to receive first-class honours in the Cambridge external music examinations, which could be taken in North America at a recognized institution, but she was denied a degree because she was female. Her grandfather had to fight a court battle to have her enrolled in university. In 1917 she was one of the first women to be appointed a judge. It took the better part of her lifetime, and the First World War, when there was so much need for help, to get anywhere. Henry James (James, 1885) wrote about the women's emancipation movement in *The Bostonian* of the 1890s; it took another 50 years before they were in positions of public significance. In the meantime society had been denied the free and full operation of their talents.

The female emancipation movement

This ran into a lot of trouble, but persisted. When Olive Chancellor invited her cousin, Basil Ransom, to an Emancipationist meeting, she could hardly believe he would accept. And he probably wouldn't have, except that he loved 'to reform reformers'. The most distinguished of these, Miss Birdseye, 'belonged to any and every league that had been founded for almost any cause. She languished only for emancipation' and now that the slaves were liberated she was determined to liberate that next most exploited race – women. She seemed to Ransom 'the revelation of a class who . . . had spent their life on platforms. In her faded face there was a kind of reflection of ugly lecture-lamps.. . .' Nevertheless, poke fun at them as Henry James might do, it was the zeal of such people that turned exploitation into recognition for women. The movement was already in full swing when James wrote about it. In June 1848, the first women's convention was held at Seneca Falls, NY, demanding equal rights to learn, preach, and vote. The movement rapidly snowballed and in 1850 a truly national convention took place at Worcester, Mass., led by Susan Anthony and Elizabeth Stanton. They formed the National Women's Suffrage Association in 1869 and pressed for a suffrage amendment to the US constitution. Sometimes called the Anthony Amendment, this was put to the Senate, but defeated in January 1887. The very regions that were keen on reform – New England and the mid-Atlantic States – were also seats of the Establishment, where men had immense power. The West was much more hopeful. Women had played a big part in opening it up, and it became an area where new things were tried. When Wyoming was made a State of the Union, in 1890, it provided for the woman's vote in its constitution. Between 1893, when Colorado followed, to 1914 when Montana and Nevada gave support, every Mountain and Far West State had enacted women's suffrage.

With the advent of the First World War, and the mass efflux of men, women were needed in factory and office in a big way. They pressed their advantage home, and formed a National Women's Party in 1914, under Alice Paul and Lucy Burns, to influence elections in their favour. The Suffrage Amendment was revived and put to Senate and Congress but was defeated. However, as the war progressed many more women were involed in national affairs, and on 18 August 1920 the Suffrage Amendment finally became the 19th Amendment to the US Constitution.

Yet women still found themselves discriminated against in many occupations and associations. Consequently, they went much further and demanded an equal rights bill that would open every profession, association, club, or trade union to them. Again it took a war to shake things up. In the Second World War women's participation in war work and indeed in the war itself, as members of the Armed Forces, made it evident that they had to have greater recognition. The Business and Professional Women's Association was formed to press for a greater share in their important fields. Nevertheless, progress was slow. Consequently in the decade of violence, during the 1960s, when Negroes were on riot in every major city, and students on sit-ins at almost every major campus, women, too, decided to move forward, and the Women's Liberation Movement was formed, as a revolutionary and not just a reformist force. Caroline Bird, author of *Born Female* and editor of the new journal, *New Woman*, came to the fore. An Equal Rights Amendment was advocated, to put women on absolute par with men, indeed, to gain real equality for everyone and end not only sex discrimination but racial and religious intolerance. The government answered cautiously by setting up the President's Committee on the Status of Women in 1963, and establishing a

Women's Bureau in the US Department of Labor. But quick and widespread action was demanded. In 1966, a more radical leader, Betty Friedan, set up the National Organization for Women, or NOW. The very title sounded insistent. Two years later a still more active group, led by Ti-Grace Atkinson, formed the New York Radical Women, from which the really radical group emerged calling itself the Women's International Terrorists' Conspiracy (WITCH). The pace was not only quickening but the action was threatening to be more violent.

An interesting development was the sudden rise of black concern. Blacks on the whole had been pushing for negro rights without too much attention to the rights of their women. But in 1970 Mrs Hermandez, a black woman, was elected President of NOW. Shortly after, the National Black Feminist Association was founded. This came at about the time when many black nationalists had turned against birth control and abortion as measures of black genocide. They soon had the black feminists turn against them! Women's Lib meant, if anything, the right of women to their own bodies, and how they would be used. Dara Abubakari, a Vice-President of the separatist Republic of New Africa to be set up in the USA, claims that, 'Women should be free to decide if and when they want children. Maybe in this phase of the game we feel that we don't need *any* children because we have to fight the liberation struggle.' The Black Women's Liberation Group has gone much further. It 'indicts black men for making black women the real niggers in this society oppressed by whites, male and female, and the black man, too. Having too many babies stops us from supporting our children, teaching them the truth . . . and from fighting black men who still want to use and exploit us.' (Population Bulletin, 1975.)

These bitter remarks show how strongly women feel. Although their efforts eventually got the Equal Rights Amendment through both Senate and Congress, in 1972 (still to be ratified by two-thirds of US states, at time of writing) they are in fact after a deeper and greater change, that in the mind itself. They know that conditions on the ground will not be revolutionized until there is a revolution in the mind. They are in fact very good social geographers, realizing that values must be changed, to change the scene. They want a complete revaluation of sex, marriage, the family, and the community. They wish to get away from talk about women's nature or men's nature to the nature of humanity. 'Children should be given human models to emulate at home not just male and female models.' They want society to accept that women have their own views of sex, and sex needs, and that they should be as free in sex relations as men. Love should result in sharing and sharing alike in the care of children and home. Having or not having children should be as much the option of women as of men. Women must have the right to birth control and the right to terminate pregnancy. The rearing of children should not be left mainly to the mother and should not interfere with a woman's career more than with a man's. Above all, the family must be rethought. The family ought not to take precedence over the individual, but serve each member in trying to work out his/her life style. The wholeness of the person will alone keep the family whole; any family that frustrates the best interests of its members should come under close scrutiny and perhaps be changed. Society should pay as much respect to one-person-headed as to husband-and-wife-headed families and there should also be equal recognition for childless families, homosexual unions, and communal living arrangements. Only then can there be real equality between men and women, and older and younger people. Only then can we get communities of equality. Such at any rate are the ideas being mooted – and pressed for.

The American family and household

Emancipated ideas affect the family and household. Here is perhaps the most basic and widespread geography of the new woman – a geography of smaller families, of more space per member of the family, of more apartments and condominiums, of greater movement from home to home to find the right town and the right neighbourhood, of more breakups of

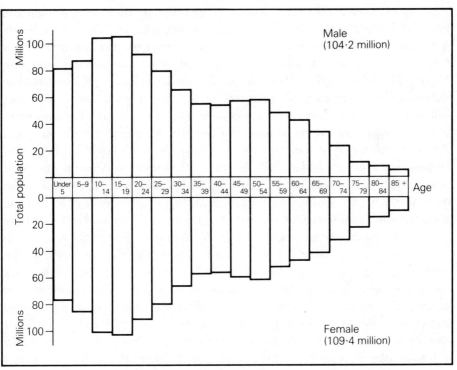

Fig. 8.1 *Population pyramid, 1975.* The population pyramid for America shows how female the country is, how important is the group 29 years and under, and how significant the over 60s have become.

one family arrangement to try another, of a greatly extended use of cafés, clubs, and halls in which to entertain or find the life that used to be centred in home. All these things have had a tremendous impact, to be measured in brick and stone, on town and country landscapes. They have made places quite different from what they were when women were expected to stay at home and run the household for husband and children. Women are now one of America's chief geography-makers.

To begin with there are more women than men (see Fig. 8.1). There are more female public toilets than male. The geographical consequences are as simple and evident as that! Cities have to make their adjustment to women. And because these women work and have more money to spend, there are more cafés and boutiques. And since these women are much better educated than before, there are more libraries and galleries. And because all these facilities cater for women and help them entertain and interest themselves more, there is less need to depend on the home for emotional, intellectual, or social satisfaction. Consequently fewer women feel the need to marry. There is a much larger population of single women. And more institutions spring up to meet their needs. It is an endless circle, with spin-offs constantly adding to the scene.

Consider it in more detail. Whereas in 1910 there were 106.2 males for every 100 females, now there are 100 females to 96 men. The United States is a female world. Women are the largest consumer group: of course the shops realize that. A great number of speciality shops have appeared for the purpose. Walk down Main Street: there are more women's clothing shops and shoe shops and hair stylists and magazine stores than men's. There are more billboards advertising women's goods, more cinemas with programmes out to attract women: the whole commercial world is geared to the 100/96 ratio. And the training of women becomes more evident, with typists' colleges and beauticians' colleges, and so forth. Women are being invited not only to spend a lot of their time, but most of their time, out of home. They can study, entertain themselves, eat, have a massage and sauna bath, get a hair-do, meet their friends, go to bingo, be trained to work, or work, all in places that have sprung up in the last 30 years to meet their numerical superiority.

This fuller life is one reason why so many stay single or, if they marry, delay the marriage date longer than they used to (US Bureau of the Census, 1976a). In 1975, of the women of 18 years or over, 31.7 per cent were single: this compared with 25.17 per cent of the men. One would expect those between 18 and 24 to get married, nevertheless the proportion of single girls of this age remains high enough to suggest that many prefer to stay single. This is reinforced by another figure: the adult population under 35 years who had not married, was proportionately much greater in 1975 than in 1960. The increase in singleness characterized both sexes, but was significantly greater among women.

The fashion to stay single represents a new state of mind. Thirty years ago girls disliked the prospect of being spinsters and hated that name: now, those who do not marry call themselves singletons and set out to enjoy it. And they can, because of the great number of facilities that have sprung up to cater for them. Singles clubs are an example, either all women, or mixed. There are singles'·bridge clubs, dining clubs, sports clubs, travel clubs, night clubs – you name it. Some of these simply book a room in a hotel for a given night a week and so do not make much visual impact. Others have separate club rooms of their own and add to the urban fabric. As this element grows it will make a more conspicuous geography. Already whole blocks of flats have been built as 'girl Friday bed-sitters', with launderettes, massage parlours and hairdressing salons for the singleton too busy to 'do' for herself. In the meantime many old houses near the city centre are being turned into singles' apartments to exploit the new trend. Downtown cafés have adapted themselves as well, with more single-seat coffee bars, or double-seat tables. Some cafés specialize for singles, and have no four or six-seater booths. Indeed, everywhere one goes one can see concrete signs of the transforming power of the single woman.

Many are single of course for only a relatively short time. Yet this time is being stretched out by later and later marriage. According to the Census (US Bureau of the Census, 1976b):

> *More and more young women are delaying their marriage. During the last fifteen years, 1960–75, more women under thirty have been postponing an early entry into marriage. Only 87 per cent of the women who were in their upper 20's (26–29 years) in 1975 had entered marriage compared with 92 per cent in those years in 1960. Indeed, the ones now in their late 20's will make the smallest proportion of those who eventually marry of any group in over a third of a century.*

This delay in marriage means that a girl has more choice of mate, can presumably make a more mature choice, or, in the end, decide on not marrying at all. Yet in any event she will set up a separate household. She no longer stays with her parents as she used to.

One of the most remarkable developments of these times is the proliferation of households with single heads, and of such households headed by a woman. In most cases this means that the girl simply leaves home to get her own apartment. But in a growing number of instances it signifies living with 'another unrelated person', either another girl, or a boy with whom she has a shorter or a longer association. Between 1970 and 1975, in but 5 years, single-person families increased from 11 to 19 per cent of all families. Of great interest as far as women are concerned is that households with a female head increased by 33 per cent: these represented 13 per cent of all families by 1975. How swift this advance in female responsibility!

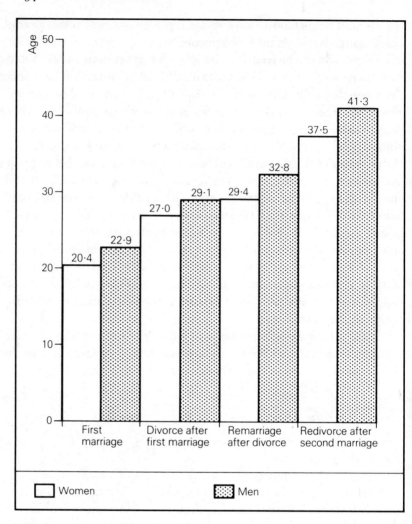

Fig. 8.2 *Marriage, divorce and remarriage, 1975.* Duration of marriages and frequency of divorces have changed dramatically in the US during the last 30 years, indicating a new life style among women, with fewer marriages, more divorces, more second marriages, and greater redivorce.

Of course, in many instances the woman did not choose to be responsible, she was abandoned by a man, or she and her man separated or were divorced. The divorce rate in the United States is now one of the highest in the world (see Fig. 8.2): but though this brings a lot of difficulties, it gives the freedom to make a new start. Women feel that they have come of age – they are not going to subject themselves to tensions and indignities just for the sake of the home. Moreover, they are not the young things they used to be, dominated by a husband 4 or 5 years their senior. 'The age gap between bride and groom is narrowing', we are told. 'Twenty years ago it used to average four years. Now it is two years or less'. Women are in a better position to make up their own minds on family issues.

Marriage is no longer looked on mainly as a source of income or as a means to status; nor is it thought of as the chief means of personal satisfaction. Women can get jobs: they can fulfil themselves outside as well as inside marriage. They enter it mainly for personal motives – love and companionship. If these do not flow from it, they are willing to give it up. Marriage is a more fluid arrangement than it has been. People move into it or out of it largely for their own purposes. Hence one-third of recent marriages will end in divorce. Present projections imply that at least that proportion of marriages made in 1975, between persons of 25 to 35 years, will end in divorce. This level is three time as high as for persons in their early 70s. Furthermore, the increase has been far greater for the 5 years, 1970–75, than for the preceding 10 years, 1960–70. Perhaps as many as 40 per cent of those married at 20 years in 1970 will become divorced. This dramatic change, which is taking place mainly among the young, is already making itself evident in the American city. Broken homes leave streets strewn with at least temporarily abandoned houses, they swell the transport of household effects, they fill the pawnbrokers' shelves or the second-hand dealers' stores and, of course, they support the springing up of divorce lawyers, their offices and office signs.

Again, the pace of events is quickening. The most typical interval between marriage and divorce is now only 2 or 3 years. Thereafter, most divorcees get remarried within another 3 years! Thus women can be in, out, and in marriage again within 5 to 6 years. However, if they remain together, when they marry, for longer than 10 years they are not likely to get divorced!

All this hardly sounds like the development of the 'whole person'. And this may well be so. The frequency of broken marriages may go back to a much-fractured person. Here again this could be one of the curses of freedom – that too many people make free with marriage: such are the risks of American freedom. On the other hand, one might argue that this is one of the new things that America is doing, to bring about new kinds of family relationships for the 'new race of man'. These new relationships do often help people to fulfil themselves, do give them a chance to search round for that kind of association that really does satisfy and will embody their idea of the whole life. For some, it appears to be quite a long process, since divorces after the second marriage have been increasing, especially at a younger age. Four times as many men who had reached their 40s in 1975 were likely to break up their second marriage than was the case with the same age group in 1960. For women the contrast was even greater: whereas in 1960 only 1.8 per cent of those in a second marriage were divorced again by the time they were 40, in 1975, the percentage had risen to 11.3. This is more than a sixfold increase.

The new idea of making marriage serve people rather than of

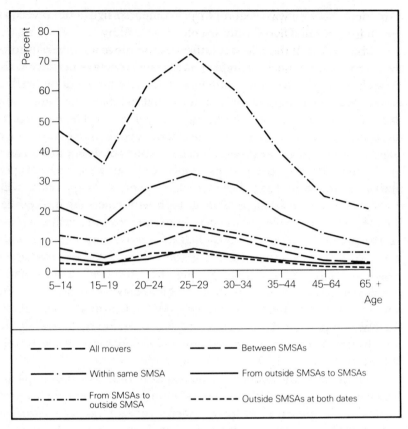

Fig. 8.3 *Percentage of population moving by age-group and destination, 1970-1975.* Population mobility is one of the most distinctive and distinguishing features of American social geography.

having people adjust to marriage is creating a fluidity in American relationships not known before. As a result many families are now headed by women who have no husband present. This forms a growing pattern. Indeed, 87 per cent of all divorced families are headed by women. On the basis of the evidence before it the US Bureau of the Census suggests that a lot of women are passing through a life cycle in which they start up female primary households while they are looking for marriage, repeat the situation after their first divorce, and return to it after their second divorce. 'Many more women are passing through this increasingly common life cycle than in the past.' (US Bureau of the Census, 1977a).

Several geographic effects spring from this. The home being unstable, the house itself is not given the position it had in the community: it is evacuated, it is left abandoned for a time, it goes out of repair – if occupied again, it may pass through the same round. This is especially true in lower-class areas, and is at least a contributory reason why 7.2 per cent of all

American housing was vacant in 1975 – a higher figure than ever (cf. 6.4 per cent in 1960). Divorcees are often unwilling to stay in their own neighbourhood. If they do move, they tend to move well away from what they have come to regard as having unhappy associations. Some move to a neighbourhood across town, others move much further – to a different town altogether. They thus contribute to that astonishing mobility that possesses America, where one-sixth of the whole population move to a new address every year – there's newness for you! Six times the population of Scotland moving house every year, what a game of musical chairs! Indeed, in the age group 25–29 years, 72 per cent of the population moved house between 1970 and 1975 (see Fig. 8.3).

Finally, when divorce breaks up a home, whether the woman leaves with the children or not, the need for her to be supported by employment, welfare and child-care arrangements can, as the Census remarks, 'constitute a major challenge to governmental and private agencies'. Hence the growing presence of these agencies in modern geography.

As a consequence of the new life style, women remain in, or return to, singleness for a longer time, or decide to be childless, or have fewer children. The purpose of marriage is no longer regarded as procreation. Many enter it simply for the companionship it can give while husband and wife continue with their individual careers. If that companionship does not work out, then to break it, while still childless, does not affect a family. Even when they are with child, many women decide not to give birth. An AP release, 28 July 1977, announced that in New York, 1976, there were 106,000 abortions to 105,000 live births. This did not include 'back-alley' abortions. In addition, of course, a lot of women avoided conception by birth control. The childless woman is forming a distinct subculture, creating childless areas distinctive enough to become noticeable in the landscape. Today, 5 out of every 100 women who marry expect to be childless, which is nearly twice the number of 30 years ago. But *that* many women cannot have changed physiologically: this is a mental change. If it continues it will make itself noted in not only childless apartment houses but *areas* of apartment housing without a child: a geography that is already coming.

One of the freedoms the new woman wants is not to be cumbered with a large family, or rather to plan the family she would like to have. To most, this has meant planning for a small family which can easily be handled, where the child need not interrupt the woman's career, or make it difficult or costly to obtain house and car, entertain and travel. Indeed there is a marked increase in women having only one child. In 1975, 11 per cent of women under 25 expected to have only one child, compared with 6 per cent in the 1960s. Another interesting change is that in the 1960s only women of higher educational level wanted a small family; in the 1970s there was 'a reduction in the lifetime birth expectancies for all women at all levels of education'. This marks a major social shift which is, of course, already having its geographical impact: there are many more couples with a small family, living in apartments or semidetached 'town houses' than was the case with their parents. America used to be almost the pre-eminent place for the family home. Now many of these are either being made into flats, or being sold off to be replaced by 'walk-up' apartments. Here is a big difference in at least the city scene. Why have a family home when 'more mothers of young children work outside the home today than ever before?' (US Bureau of the Census, 1976c). On returning from work, does one want a lot of house-cleaning or of gardening to do? Many home functions have been taken over by city businesses and institutions – the geography of the spattered home. In 1977 one in every three food dollars was spent in restaurants. According to AP, 28 July 1977, supermarkets were getting so worried over declining sales that they were not only selling prepared foods, but hot take-out meals. Parenthood no longer went with the preparation of food.

Why clean house and provide meals for 0.8 children per family? Yet this was the number the average woman of 18–24 years had had in 1975. Her lifetime expectancy of births was then only 2.2. These figures had dropped in 15 years from 1.4 and 2.9 in 1960.

Women are not only not having but are not going to have even medium-sized, let alone large, families. They are barely going to reproduce themselves. And the change is happening very quickly. In 1970, of the women between 35 and 39 years of age, 1,000 had 3,167 children; in 1975, but 5 years later, 1,000 women of the same age had borne 2,994, and over 900 of those women would then have no more children. In the next 5 years, the 1,000 women reaching the same age, will have had 2,200 children – or less. Indeed (US Bureau of the Census, 1975a) the total fertility rate fell in 1974 to 1,862

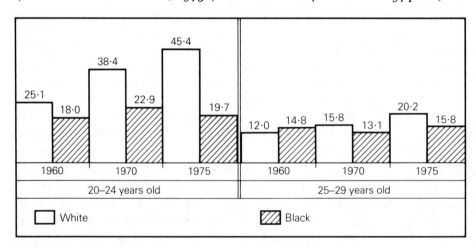

Fig. 8.4 *The changing fertility of American women, 1960–1975.*

children per 1,000 women, or less than 2 children per woman (see Fig. 8.4).

And that will mean that in the 1980s there will be zero growth in schools, in the late 1980s zero growth in colleges, and in the early 1990s zero growth in houses. Events today are already making tomorrow's geography. If 90 per cent of women have now finished with child-bearing by 35–39 years, in a short time, those of 30–34 years will have quit. Does that mean that in the decade after that, very few women between 25 and 29 years will have any more children?

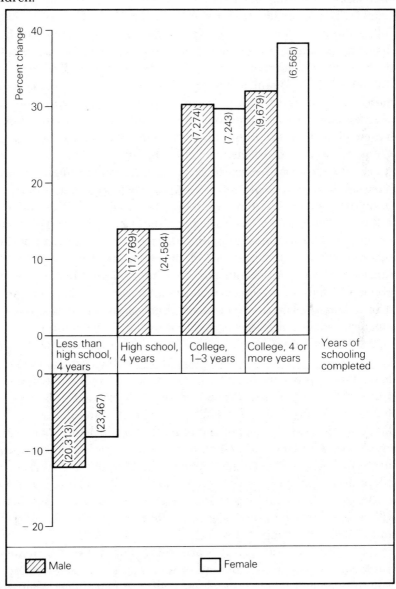

Fig. 8.5 *Change in years of schooling completed, 1970–1975.*

But while the family might decline, its members would be better off, for, if there are to be fewer persons, and yet the personal disposable income is substantially to rise, each member of the family could have a better education, be in better health, have more interests, and travel more. Perhaps this is the new American race? This may be the new way in which Americans of today fulfil Crèvecoeur's dream of the 'new man'?

Women in education are certainly trying to help bring about emancipation and change. One of the most dramatic things in the last 15 years is the extraordinary increase of women in high school, university, and colleges of education (see Fig. 8.5). In fact part of the reason why they are delaying marriage, postponing childbearing, and having so few children in the end, is their eagerness to spend time and energy on education. The loss in the one case, is a gain in the other. That girls have put back the age of marriage for at least 2 years between the 1960s and the 1970s, from an average of 20.8 to 22.8, has been used to add just that much time to their education: it has enabled them to finish high school and have at least a year at college. Think of the impact on institutional geography!

What was the privilege of the rich woman in Henry James's *The Bostonians* is now the right of the ordinary girl. Although it is true that the children of better-off families are more likely to go to college and, once there, to finish college, than those of the poor, the fascinating thing about the recent survey of 'College plans of high-school seniors' (US Bureau of the Census, 1976d) is the high proportion of those coming from incomes below the American median who wanted to go on into college. In 1975 no less than 38.6 per cent of high school seniors whose families were earning less than $10,000 a year had made plans to enter college. (The median family income in that year was $13,700.)

This is, of course, part of the new man pictured in the great American dream. In fact, it is more a part of the new woman. For we read that 'fewer males who were High School seniors in 1974 had any plans to attend college than did their counterparts in 1972'. At the earlier date, 76 per cent of the seniors wished to become college men; at the later date, only 69 per cent did. 'This decrease in the percent of male High School seniors with plans to enter college is an indication that the current college enrolment rates of young men could persist in declining.' The momentum of past habit and tradition still pushed them forward, and there will be an overall increase of 12 per cent in the 1970s, but if mid–1970 trends represent a new way of thinking, there will be zero growth in the 1980s and a decline in the 1990s, regardless of the shut-down of the supply of babies.

By contrast the 1970s are seeing a 60 per cent increase in female enrolment in college (US Bureau of the Census, 1976e). In many cases it is only the women that are keeping the colleges going. Their eagerness to learn and to improve themselves – and thereby improve their status – is one of the most dynamic aspects in American life today. Once again, one is astonished at how rapid the change has been. In the first 4 years of the 1970s the number of women in college made for 63 per cent of the total college increase. By 1975 they accounted for 44 per cent of all the students in college and, what was more important, over 50 per cent of the freshman year. And they are staying on longer, forming a third of the post-graduate enrolment.

The geography they make! More lavatories again! And halls of residence: new lounges, enlarged cafeterias, beauty salons on the campus, and the campus bookstore expanding – to sell nylon stockings! But in all seriousness they add such verve, grace, interest, distinctiveness, and force to college they have enormously increased the range and power of American institutions.

And of course they add to the whole educational chain. When they marry and have a child, they try to ensure that it will be well educated. In all probability, one of their reasons for restricting their family to 2.2 is to give each child a fuller life – including a fuller education. They know too well that 'High School seniors from families whose head attended college are more likely than those from families whose head had not gone, to have college plans

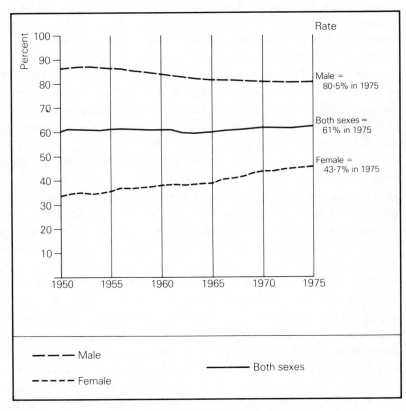

Fig. 8.6 *Change in participation in labour force by sex, 1950–1975.*

themselves'. (US Bureau of the Census, 1976f). They work for this end. They use their own schooling to get a job, and thus help their husbands to bring in the fuller tomorrow.

This does require an enormous outlay of work and will. As the Espinshade report makes out, the average husband and wife must spend the equivalent of 4.6 times their annual earnings – that is to say, $4\frac{1}{2}$ full years of their life – to raise a child, including education at a state-supported university. On the median income of $13,700 in 1975, something between $53,000 and $66,000 would be required in raising a child to college age. Thirty-two per cent of this would go for housing, 24 per cent for food, 16 per cent for transportation, 9.5 per cent for clothing, 5 per cent for medical care, and the rest for education and recreation.

Women's part in the labour force

A very notable contribution has been made by women in the labour force (see Fig. 8.6). They have not only rounded out and satisfied their own life but have assisted their families to reach a wholeness they might otherwise not have known. The Espinshade survey (AP, 1977) shows that, high though its estimates are, these 'do not include the cost to the family if the mother has to give up work to stay with her child. That child, in a middle-income family, costs an extra $107,000 in "lost" earnings if the mother gives up [even] a half-time job to stay at home. The comparable loss for a low-income family is $77,000'. This shows the value of the woman's work to the modern family: many a household would collapse without it, or at least, not have, or would have to give up, the 'whole' life.

Women are making a very great contribution to the income not only of the family but the whole community. That this is not yet as great as they would wish it to be, when equal work ought to get equal pay, should not diminish from the importance it has in fact commanded. Women now constitute 38 per cent of the total work force, which is a significant increase on 31 per cent at the 1960 census (US Dept Labor, 1970a). In fact, the number of women at work in 1975 (35.5 million) was a 37 per cent gain on the numbers for 1960. To have added over a third of their force in 15 years is no mean feat. Since most of this growth was in the clerical group, and the greater part of that group works downtown, the impact of women on downtown has been tremendous. Except in the financial core itself where there are few stores, a whole new range of small shops selling women's fashion clothes, fashion shoes, fashion jewellery, wigs, luggage, umbrellas, women's magazines, and so forth, have come in among the big stores and offices and invaded the large hotels. At the same time there has been a marked increase in 'intimate' cafés, hairdressing salons, massage parlours, women's clubs, gymnasiums, and other service facilities: many banks now have a women's section with lounge and powder rooms.

The feminization of the downtown is a major feature of American urban geography. It will grow greater because more women are getting into top managerial and municipal positions where their decisions count. Thirty per cent of women are now in the financial, professional, and kindred occupations, where today there are more women than men. Without question many of these are in secretarial posts, but, thanks to the high proportion with degrees, and with post-graduate degrees at that, more and more are themselves running branches of banks, insurance, mortgage and real-estate offices, and municipal administrative offices. These are all insisting on back-up facilities for women where they work, and not just at home. The author once went to a high office building in Chicago from which, as a geographer, he had hoped to be able to photograph the whole central area, only to be told he could not go up because the top had been turned into a swimming pool and gymnasium for the women employees. 'They go up there at any hour of the day', he was warned, 'and if it's sunny they sun-bathe. Topless! It would never do for a man to be let loose up there!' The idea was intriguing, but suffice it to say here was a bit of downtown geography, albeit at the fortieth storey, that had grown out of the female touch.

In the period from 1970 to 1975, the American work force grew by 8.3 million people, 4 million of whom were men, but 4.3 million of whom were women (US Bureau of the Census, 1975b). The greatest growth was female. What it will be when the greater part of women go to work can only be guessed at. Presently, 45.6 per cent of women are in the work force. Married women account for just over a quarter of this, i.e. for 11 per cent of America's work strength. But if, as we have seen, married women delay having children still longer, or more of them choose not to have children, or they only have 1.2 instead of 2.2 children – a position that could well be reached in 25 years – then a far greater number of women will flood into the professions and high-level service occupations. At present, growth in the female labour force is mainly in the age group 18–35 years. But in fact there was growth in the 35–45 age cohort as well. Actually (US Bureau of the Census, 1975c) 'the absolute size of the female labour force increased for each age group' whereas, after 1970 'the labour force rate for all men decreased'.

Here's a cat among the geographical pigeons: a lot of old ideas about urban geography will not be able to roost around much longer. The 18–35-year-old women will soon be the 36–70-year-olds who, having had a taste for work, and for the much fuller life which it can support, will want to have an environment where it can go on. For instance, the married woman with the second family car is not going to use that simply to go round for coffee at a neighbour's or pick up some items at the neighbourhood shopping centre, she will want to drive it every day to her downtown office – as much as her husband now drives the main car: it is in the downtown restaurant that she will have her coffee, and in the downtown store she will pick up the things for home before driving back in the evening. On the way to and fro she will drop off or fetch her child at day-care centre or school. The car will be central not accessory to her life. And the urban planner will have to put that in his pipe and smoke it – because the greatest number of voters today are women, and will have their say.

Once the Equal Rights Amendment is passed, and at the time of writing only four more states had to ratify it to make it law, women's say will have to be acknowledged. The South and the Plains West, which have held out against ratification, cannot be King Canutes against this tide. The social change is too great and too general. Already a new social geography, based on that, is emerging. If America as a whole is to fashion the whole life it must accept the whole woman as well as the whole man: when this occurs the whole person will come into being in what will truly bring about a 'new race' in America.

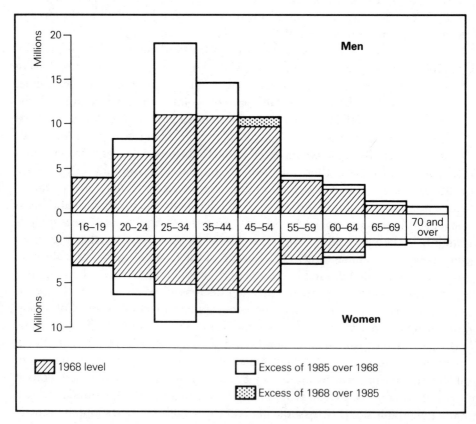

Fig. 8.7 *Age–sex profile of the total labour force, 1968 and projected 1985.*

Youth in the American scene

This will happen largely because youth is behind it, and youth are bulking larger in American affairs. By 1985, the 20–30 years group will be the largest in the nation (see Fig. 8.7). Their ideas may well dominate. Young people's concepts of 'unisex' have already scrapped the differences between men and women: men have long hair, beads round their neck, and rings on their fingers, women go round in shirt and trousers. Much more than that, they work together, play together, and live together. They have together created the 'youth culture' which is one of the most dynamic parts of American society. A great social force like this is bound to have its effect on the landscape. Youth geography in America is one of single-head households; of household mobility, indeed of personal mobility on a scale never seen before, as the youth launch themselves 'on the road', of youth rallies and conventions, of 'pop' festivals, 'pop' art often exhibited on roadside hoardings; of craft camps; of youth communes of all kinds – Christian as well as secular; of youth hostels, youth clubs and other organizations; recreation and sports grounds and facilities; of highly specialized shops for youth (clothing, shoes, music, book, art shops, to mention but a few) and youth cafés, bars, dance halls and other support facilities. The whole face of America has been changed. Everything, from evangelism to crime, featuring youth in a new way, and does so as if youth were not only the main problem, but the principal destiny, of America.

The rise of the youth-scene

The youth scene has had its ups and downs, but really started with the First World War when American youth, on an unprecedented scale, got together, learned about each other, saw the world, had their ideals tested, and began to come up with new ideals. Before that, as Debra Parks has said, 'youth followed close in their parents footsteps, family life and everything that went with it was important' and the young met each other, studied, played, and travelled in that context. Camps to which youth were sent by their parents were becoming popular, but were hardly run by the youth, they were highly supervised by adult staff. Schools and school playing grounds, Sunday schools, community baseball parks, and ice-hockey rinks were perhaps the only obvious signs of youth in the landscape: they were subordinate features, and really an extension of the home complex.

After the First World War things changed a lot. The returning soldier, though he was a young adult, wanted to change or at any rate shake up the adult world proper. Youth followed quickly behind. The automobile made a big difference. It set youth loose. They had a chance to get out of the neighbourhood of home, indeed, out of the home town, and meet with other youth in *places anonymous*, where they could act in anonymity. This gave them much more freedom, and that freedom began to be exploited. Roads were straightened and macademized, bridges were widened, traffic was speeded up and drawn out: 'road houses' sprang up for drinks and dances in the outskirts of town. In town itself night clubs mushroomed in dark alleys off main streets. The 'Roaring Twenties' came in with jazz, cocaine, and speeding tickets. The young did not seem to be able to settle down. This was the time when young Bayard Sartoris, having distinguished himself in the air force at the front, came home – not to help his ageing father run the estate, but to go tearing around the countryside like a madman in a high-powered car. A kind of savage dissatisfaction took hold of him, he delighted in driving full tilt at mule and cart and only at the last moment when he saw the white of terror in the aghast eyes of the driver would he swerve to the side. He died in a few years as a test pilot, trying out a new type of plane. Aeroplanes, too, quickened the whole pace of life, and the air circus gave dare-devil youths the chance to perform aerobatics that made the hair stand on end.

The whole element of space was being shot through with youth. The staid old days were over.

In the late 1920s youth broke away not only from parental values but from parents themselves, and set up house on their own. The day of the bachelor flat was ushered in. Youth found work in new-style jobs to which the old were not adapted, and spent their money on themselves. Stores with prepared foods, eating places, the cocktail bar, burlesque shows, popped up in urban geography like a lot of leeches to such the new blood. The young bloods in the meantime poured out their substance on a whole world of travel and entertainment – who was exploiting whom?

The bubble was pricked with the Great Depression, and the so-called 'Dirty Thirties' came in. This was actually a term that grew up in the worked-out and eroded countryside where clouds of dirt, whipped from the wasteland that many a farm had become, darkened the sky, blew along the street, sifted under door and window, and smirched the entire scene. In their poverty people could not paint their houses or wagons, they wore their clothes until they were threadbare, and everything went dull and dispirited. Dirt invaded the towns, litter filled the alleys and yards, tenements grew stained with smoke and acid, and the Depression deepened. Youth lost so much of their youthfulness. Many could not finish school, a lot were out of work, they could not afford to go anywhere – they just hung around. The pool hall, that great killer of time, came into its own. Other things that spun time out also appeared, cafés, card rooms, and, above all, the cinema. This was Hollywood's gift to forget the Depression. The shows were long, exciting – and cheap. The author can remember as a boy getting into a show for two jam jars: boys brought these along, or beer bottles, or anything on which the proprietor could get a penny return, and then went through the doors of oblivion. Cinemas sprang up at every major centre-town crossroads.

The disillusionment with life was challenged by at least two movements – communism and fascism, and these swiftly began to gain youthful adherents. They never became the popular movements in America that they grew into in Europe, in a sense they were too opposed to the American way of life; but they, too, started a new geography – of political halls, political 'schools', political printing presses, political camps, and above all political marches. Both radical and reactionary students worked for their cause, and political cells grew up in the 'shatter belts' of most inner cities in the great metropolises. Political handbills became part of the city flotsam and littered the streets, especially after open-air meetings. One shuffled through them like the dry leaves of autumn.

The Second World War changed things dramatically. Once more youth were called on to save their country, and this time saw even more of the world from Burma and Japan to Italy and Germany, and had more responsibility laid on them and more power given into their hands. Those who stayed at home had plenty of jobs in the war industries that sprang up, and a lot of money. Large amounts of money also became available upon demobilization.

A lot of this was wasted on drink and gambling, night clubs and strip-tease joints, and the geography of sleaziness invaded the city as never before, seen in a rash of porn shops. Pornography began to be big business. It did not stay in the back alleys, but invaded the city broadways, it affronted the passing citizen and boldly courted the tourist. Prostitution also walked out on the streets, or waited at cafés and hotel bars, for whom it might devour! Organized crime found new wyas of mulcting the youth. Marijuana was introduced as a come-on to hard drugs. There was a great leap in young crime.

But both the young veteran and the youth that trod at his heels also spent their new-found affluence in getting a better training for a better job. Colleges of all kinds began to boom. New specialized colleges sprang up in the central areas of the city to teach better business, better cooking, better potting, better English, almost anything that could help widen interests and improve skills. The geography of regeneration flourished side by side with degeneration. It won out, on balance.

The youth of the Busy Generation made the 1950s an industrious and relatively stable period. The business man was the model. 'The man in the grey-flannel suit' – well dressed, well mannered, well spoken and, perhaps as important as anything – well connected, came to the fore. Some youths were almost smarmy in copying the type: one remembers 'Yours sincerely, Willys Wade' in which Marquand scores the insincerity of being too sincere, and gives the sycophant the edge of his tongue. Nevertheless it was true that 'getting on' became at least the middle-class ideal and to do this many 'polished the apple' in trying to gain favour in the status chase. As Debra

Parks remarks, 'Political interest and activity were out, youth culture became privatized and conformist; boys were expected to be clean cut, athletic and anti-intellectual – girls, well-groomed and marriage-orientated.'

It was the day when the golf and country club came into its own. The whole geography of the suburban fringe was changed. Golf clubs that were in fact social clubs for the élite, where upper-class families entertained each other and gave wedding receptions for their daughters, vied with one another not only in better pros but classier chefs. Tennis clubs, too, ran up their wire-net surrounds in the suburban scene, and riding-schools bought out farms in the city surrounds.

All this was very well at upper-income levels; for the lower class the youth culture expressed itself in disgruntlement and disillusion. Radicalism, which had been down-graded during the war and in its aftermath, started to raise its head. Drug-taking and violence formed an ugly underswell.

These things broke through and almost engulfed youth in the Violent Sixties. The black revolution touched off the spark. Black youth had waited too long for the promises, made when Negro and White fought side by side in the foxholes, to be fulfilled. Many white youth were wholly sympathetic. An explosion of protest and riot shook America like nothing else had since the Civil War. At times it looked as though a new civil war were about to break out – youth against age. Both white and coloured youth joined in the spectacular 'freedom rides' into the South when hundreds and thousands of demonstrators expressed their fury at Southern opposition to the Civil Rights Acts of Eisenhower and Kennedy that had insisted on desegregation. Although these cannot have been said to have left a permanent geography, they were very much part of the scene for their decade. However, geography-making forces did leave their mark, especially in the black riots, referred to earlier, that burnt out whole sections of cities, and made Detroit and Watts, LA, look like battle-torn wastes.

Meanwhile white youths organized take-overs and sit-ins at schools and colleges where, again, the scars of their anger were imprinted on the landscape. Their protests so democratized many campuses that the old divisions between – yes, here is this geography marker again – staff lavatories and student lavatories disappeared, along with the division between staff refectories and common rooms and student ones. The author hardly recognized some of the institutions he knew in the 1950s on visiting them in the 1970s, the brick and stone of staff privileges had gone, students drank coffee and smoked in staff lounges once private to the professor, and each relieved himself side by side in the most democratic of porcelain ware. If this isn't a new geography – what is?

Curiously, while throwing rocks at police and burning down slums, the youth were strangely pacifist, and did not volunteer to fight in Vietnam. Their philosophy went with peace and meditation: they were very much against materialism, they did not want to get on at all. As the to them dreadful war in Vietnam dragged on they put their draft-cards to the flame, or tried to dodge the draft by fleeing to Canada or Mexico. What they wanted to do was to dabble with Buddhism and Hinduism, become the flower people wearing leis and cultivating gardens, rediscover folk ways, sing folk-songs, wear folk-dress, get back to the grass-roots, forget team sports and turn to group art, blissfully fudge the distinctions between class, race, and sex, and live together in joint relationships that could be made or broken with the mood. They hated the idolized American words *property* and *possession*, *I* and *mine*, and lived in a fraternal we-ness that was free of all bounds. Drugs and rock music, which gave a heightened sensation to life, were their new symbols – along with long hair that, like Samson's, was the secret of their strength.

The Permissive Seventies followed in which all that youth wanted was the permission to do what they liked, even if this meant upsetting their parents and the rest of society. In fact an unprecedented number (although one should remember that they really formed only a modest minority) eschewed society and set up communes of their own. In cities these are often referred to as youth ghettos. They ghetto-ized themselves, and thus formed a new geography within the old. And it is still there, visible in the streets. He who runs may read, the signs are so clear: old houses taken over and packed full of the young, mother-earth foods (never sprayed with insecticides or pumped full of hormones) sold in food cooperatives run by the youth themselves, underground book stores with underground novels, poetry, and tape cassettes excoriating the bourgeoisie, child-care centres for the young adults who have had a child but must go out to work, therapeutic centres where they practice on each other with herbs, acupuncture, and group meditation, group art work in art shops that also advertise how to make and smoke your own pot, dress boutiques full of caftans from Nigeria or saris from Bangladesh: in the most vivid and palpitant form – the townscape of American youth.

For those who cannot find a spot in the run-down areas (which youth can alone afford) for their organic gardens and ecology centres, the answer is the rural commune. Here young people can get away from the terrors of technological affluence by milking goats, spreading down chicken manure, and raising greens in their vegetarian Edens where, at last, they can be the new American Adam. This movement out to the wilderness in search of a new purity and grace will be discussed later, but should be noted here as not unlike the 'wilderness working wonder' of the early Puritans that started America on its way.

Lifestyle of the young

The youth life style is confirmed by statistics. The young of today are observable as being statistically different. At present, one out of every three people in America is aged 17 years or under. The numerical strength of the young gives great weight to their ways. One should also include the young adult, since much of the youth culture has been created and sustained by people aged from 18 to 24. These included, the 'young' amount to 46.4 per cent of the Americans. It is no wonder that so much American business is aimed at them in the selling of clothes, shoes, books, music, sport, and travel. Downtown America is full of youth boutiques, youth discotheques, youth bookshops, youth sex shops and pin-ball alleys, and cafés patronized almost entirely by youths. The teenage market is one of the most rewarding in America. Youths still living at home but working out have a lot of disposable income, a powerful factor in the retail trade. Black youth, though poorer, are proportionately more numerous: 41 per cent of Blacks are under 18 years. Here, too, is a large group to cater for – and it is a big spender.

Youth break away from home sooner and stay on their own longer than they used to, and this stresses and reinforces their separateness. The tendency to break away has become almost a tradition. Boys, especially, will move out even before they leave high school, while a major aspect of college life today is for both young men and women to have their own apartment. In this way they can get out from under their parents and dress as they like and amuse themselves in their own fashion. The Census (US Bureau of the Census, 1975d) notes 'an increase in the proportion of younger persons remaining single for longer periods'. It is at that time that they build up their youth culture, among themselves. Even in the last few years singleness has grown. In 1970, just over three-quarters of the males under 20 were single: this became four-fifths in 1975.

Most of these singletons have established their own households in non-family situations. This means either living by themselves or with another unrelated person. About a quarter of all American households are of this type, a proportion that is growing each year. While the total numbers of households expanded by 15 per cent between 1970 and 1976, primary individual families grew by 41 per cent. (Two-parent families increased by only 9 per cent.) These changes result from different views of household arrangements held by the young: many are content simply with their own 'pad', or room. A lot link up with another young person, either of their own or of the opposite sex, in a two-person household. Such two-person households now amount to 18.5 per cent of all American households. A 'gay' association recently criticized city planning officers for not recognizing this trend and planning for gay quarters in the expanding city 'instead of fobbing us off with back-alley rooming-house areas'. Gay condominiums may be the order of the day.

There is thus a tremendous demand for rooms within shared apartments or for small two-person apartments, which has altered the housing pattern quite appreciably in the American city. These are either downtown, in lower-class tenements or in old town houses of families in flight (in which case the homes are swiftly altered, with separate entries marking out different suites), or else they are near to the universities. They now form well-marked no-family, no-children household districts. In most cases they are a part of the gay geography that is rapidly transforming these quarters: in other cases they mark trial-marriage areas, from which, however, people tend to move out when establishing a husband-and-wife family.

A good number of the singles, gays, those in a trial liaison, or newly married couples are in college. This author was interested to see in a recent visit to an American university the number of posters in the corridors advertising singles' clubs, gay societies, and lesbian associations, obviously

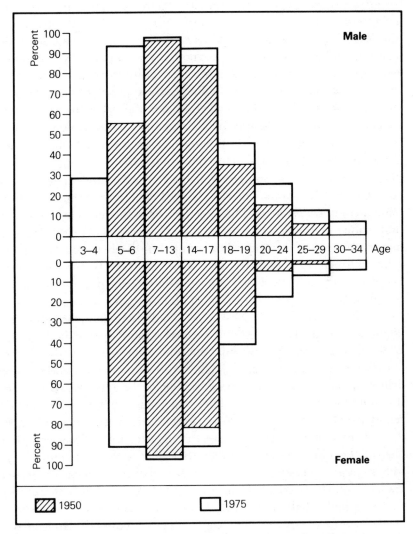

Fig. 8.8 *School enrollment rates by age and sex, 1950 and 1975.*

indicating that these were as much a part of the social life as film clubs, operatic societies, or the Student Christian Movement.

In any event, colleges have become the target for more and more young people between 18 and 29 years. Today, 24 per cent of men who have reached 25 have graduated from some form of college or another, as compared with only 9 per cent of those who aged 65 years. This represents a much greater thrust in high-school enrolment, much higher in 1974 than in 1950 (see Fig. 8.8). Thus, the level of educational attainment is higher for successively younger age groups. This is particularly true for black students. Constituting 7 per cent of all students in 1970, in 1975, only 5 years later, they made up 9.2 per cent. This is a notable increase. In the most recent survey of the future plans of seniors at high school only 19.2 per cent do *not* plan to go to a centre of further or higher education – 19.6 per cent Whites, and 17.8 per cent Negroes (US Bureau of the Census, 1976g). The vast majority chose college. This is now the norm, and will, as another survey points out, 'influence many aspects of American life. It will affect spending patterns, as the educational level of consumers rises. It will influence the types of jobs the educated youth or young adult seeks and for which he qualifies' (US Bureau of the Census, 1976h). It should also shape the course of the political vote.

With college behind them these young people have a wide choice not only of what work to go in for, but where to work. They move from one job to another, or from a job in one place to a similar one somewhere else. They launch themselves upon America. Indeed the United States has never seen so many people *On the Road*. This was the title of the novel by Jacques Kerouac that made him the in-writer with young America. There is still no plot except movement, except this vague but compelling desire to go out and see life that gripped Moriarty and his friends. There is no hero but youth, but the young people telling each other their story and discovering how they thought. If there is a philosophy it is that of tasting all philosophies and sucking any good that any of them has. Finding New York too divisive and frustrating a group of young people head out West, but sweep the South up, too, in their experience. Everyone ended up in California, but it became too crowded and competitive so they rushed back East again. The Southwest appealed and in Mexico they drifted off once more – this time searching for the old earth symbols in Mexico that might give them new life. They married and broke up, had children, and remarried. They drank, took drugs, and talked the sun down to the sea. They did not really know what they were doing except that they were shaking the dust of the old ways from under their feet and were determined to find something new. They slept with others of their kind in vacant houses, under viaducts, on the beach; they hived about the exits of cities thumbing rides to wherever luck would take them; they were like a new Tartar horde sweeping resistance before them – but there was this gain, the concourse of their thought became the whole of America.

Such extraordinary gadding about was not fictional. Nor is it today. Nearly 40 per cent of all Americans change their address every 5 years; actually, about 17 per cent may be expected to move in any one year. In fact the Census report on mobility for 1975–76, issued in 1977 (US Bureau of the Census, 1977b) showed that during that year 35,645,000 or 17.1 per cent of the total population had moved house. Among these movers 'the highest rates of residential mobility reached their peak at ages 20 to 24'. Thirty-eight per cent of all that age group had moved, in contrast to 5–7 per cent for those 55 years and over (see also, Fig. 8.3).

This tremendous urge of young people to drive about seeking new jobs, new places, new households, which is far greater in America than anywhere else in the world, this cult of movement, again has affected geography – with an unequalled demand for super highways, for roadside restaurants and service stations (not to forget lavatories, of course!), for motels, gift shops, flea markets and, increasingly, country clubs or city-fringe night clubs, which flap their flags by day and flash their neon signs all through the dark. But more than that, there are whole areas for transients in every large city, and not only for car-thumbing hippies but car-driving hopefuls heading for new things.

The America of the aged

By 1980 there will be nearly 11 per cent of the American population over 65 years of age. This group is as large as that of the Negroes: indeed it includes 2.2 million Negroes. Yet they have not bulked as large in public attention: in fact, for a long time, they were not a concern of the public so much of the individual. American individualism has often been hard on the aged; as individual power, so position, declines. The competitive system calls for enterprise and effort, but in age these often fade to uncertainty and dependence. For the aged poor, competition often means the loss of home and car, with consequent suffering and isolation. Since 25 per cent of all the old live in centre-city conditions in the great metropolitan areas, they are confined, in any case, to regions of crowded and inferior housing with few local amenities. Of applicants seeking 'assisted shelter', 58 per cent live in rented flats and 19 per cent in rooming houses. While the competitive system has built in it the competition to bring up one's children and to protect one's aged, enforced migration or ill-health or death may make this impossible. Of all old people, 25.6 per cent live on their own and another 4.6 per cent are confined to institutions. Hence a third of them are outside the bosom of their families. This does not mean that they cannot live well, and, thanks to the high level of savings in the United States, most of them do manage for themselves. Only 9 per cent of all the old live in unsatisfactory, unsafe, or unsanitary conditions. None the less many find themselves in difficulties. A house that was costing them 25 per cent of their full wage, may cost 40 per cent of their pension income. Indeed, 30 per cent of the elderly would be paying 43.1 per cent of their pension on their house were they not in receipt of income supplements. And yet even then merely living on, safe and sound, in their own homes, or in the home of a son or daughter, may not meet their need: they may be far from a doctor or nurse, have no access to bus or subway, and live in a neighbourhood without a senior citizens' centre.

The sense of community among American people has shown more and more concern for the elderly. This is indeed one of the major changes brought about by the welfare state. Old-age pensions, old-age housing, old-age medical facilities, and old age recreation are a built-in part of the communitarianism which is now general to America as a whole. Shelter allowance programs 'assist the old in age to maintain their dwellings'. Citizens see, in Golant's (1976) words, 'that the physical attributes and social environment of the residential setting for old age should . . . help the older person cope with declining physical energy, poorer health, smaller funds, lower social status and a sudden lack of spouse or of good friends'. Above all, the residential arrangements should enable him to 'engage in a lifestyle of his choice'. This involves a new old-age geography, as for example of ground-floor housing, access to public transportation, pedestrian crossings, small urban parks, local libraries, and old-age recreational centres.

All levels of government are now active in creating this sort of environment; however, the federal government has the chief share of the costs and has shown the main initiative. The costs for old-age housing and recreational facilities are usually on a 75 per cent federal, 25 per cent municipal, basis, provided proper local plans are drawn up and approved. As early as 1937, the New Deal had passed a US Housing Act to build or make available low-rent accommodation for the elderly. This was confirmed and enlarged in the Housing Act of 1959, Section 231, when buildings designed particularly for the elderly could gain federal support. Incidentally, this recognized the wish and need of many to retire earlier than at 65 years of age, by allowing them to benefit when becoming 62. The Housing Acts of 1961 and 1968 enabled associations building homes for the elderly to get low-interest, long-term mortgage rates. The Housing and Development Act of 1965, Section 101, created a rent supplement programme to subsidize old-age tenants. Furthermore, under this Act, help was given to municipalities to set up health and social service centres for the aged; later, recreational facilities were included. Indeed, an Old Americans Act was also passed in 1965, amended in 1973, offering 'Grants for State Community Programs for Aging'. These grants covered the broadening of old age centres to include further education, cheap transportation services to such old-age centres, assistance to pensioners to use centres, and 'services designed to assist older persons in avoiding institutionalization, including home-help, etc'. Nixon slowed down but Carter has (1977) accelerated the whole old-age programme.

Life expectancy is in many ways the best measure of the fullness of life. Americans have a better chance of living to old age than any other people (US Bureau of the Census, 1973a). In the mid-1970s men could expect to live to 70–72 and women to 75; the total population could hope to reach 71 or 72. Even within the 1970s the numbers reaching 65 years and over rose by 9.2 per cent to about 22 million people. This was the equal of the whole population of Canada! Think of it, the whole of Canada with white hair – looking for a place in the sun.

In 1900, life expectancy could promise hardly more than 50 years. A man kept working up to that age. Unless he was rich he could not look to a significant period of retirement. The geography of the day took little impression from him; there were not many forms of recreation for him, or travel arrangements, or learning programmes, or specialized retirement resorts. Today, at 50 he can still contemplate a future of 20–25 more years. This might mean as much as 50 per cent more life than his grandfather had. This gives time for retirement, and time for retirement-geography.

Especially if he should have good health. And here again he has the best chance to live on and enjoy himself that any person could have. Most of the so-called killing diseases, with the exception of cancer (and admittedly that is a big exception) are less lethal today than before: the incidence of strokes has fallen from nearly 90 per 100,000 of the population (1940) to 62 (1975); pneumonia from 70 to 18; heart disease from 290 to 250; accidents (even including car accidents) from 75 to 50. Consequently, he has much more opportunity to break through to calm.

If he does he will have more money and property and other things behind him to keep him going. He can cease from the strain and worry of work and do what interests and pleases. Taking the median earnings at 65 years they will, it is true, be less than half the median for the total population, yet, at the same time they will be 60 per cent above the median poverty level. The average man at 65 does not face penury, starvation, and despair as is the case in many lands (US Bureau of the Census, 1973b). With his children off his hands, his house paid up, a serviceable car, and a TV set – which are the American norm – he can not only get by but hope to have a reasonable time. This means having enough for home, food and clothing, for reading and recreation, and for a moderate amount of travel.

Because of this most men can in fact retire at 65. There has been a consistent reduction of the number of men who feel they must go on working after that. In the labour force projection made from 1947 (at the end of the Second World War) until 1985 (regarded as 'the foreseeable future'), the decline in the labour force participation rate for the over 65s (that is, the percentage of their total group actually at work) has been most revealing, as shown in Table 8.1.

Table 8.1 Percentage of population over 65 years of age at work.

	1947	1950	1960	1970	1975	1970	1985
65 years+	47.8	45.8	33.1	27.2	23.9	22.7	21.8

Thus, four out of five men may feel that they do not have to work to keep them going (US Dept. Labor, 1970b).

So much is this the case that government and business are now encouraging early retirement. Both government and business offer good retirement schemes. Both realize that in order to give younger men a chance at promotion, and to maintain a high and continuous level of work, earlier redundancy should be aimed at. The Social Security Act now allows retirement at the age of 62, although with reduced benefits. If a man has saved up enough to augment these reduced benefits then he might very well retire and enjoy his years while he still has them. And many do retire, and do enjoy that.

In doing so, a lot now leave the big city for a small town or for a place in the country. And they are doing so in such numbers as to have set in trend, or at least helped to set in trend, a major shift in American geography, which is the decline of the SMAs (the standard metropolitan areas) for the rest of the country. As the Bureau of the Census (1975e) points out, since 1970 there is evidence that, on balance, metropolitan areas are no longer gaining population through migration from the rest of the land. Among factors involved in this development are (1) increase in jobs outside the metropolitan areas (with decentralization into ex-urbia); (2) the growth of retirement communities in non-metropolitan areas that attract older migrants from metropolitan territory; and (3) the explosion of suburban areas beyond metropolitan bounds. Here is a complete, even if not a very large-scale, reversal of all previous trends.

The attraction of 'retirement communities' is now one of the principal makers of American geography. These have grown up very rapidly, to a most sophisticated degree, in Florida, California, parts of Texas, and the Southwest Mountain States, where conditions are warm and sunny and free from commerce and industry. Whole towns have been built for the old, with houses designed to save them from exertion, with roads, shops, banks, and churches built for the use of the car, with recreational and learning facilities that will exhilarate but not tire, and with that careful balance between beauty and efficiency that will both inspire and satisfy.

In the mid-1970s the population of the US was growing by barely 1 per cent per annum; the South and Southwest, however, grew by 1.75 per cent, and together accounted for 83.3 per cent of the total US growth (US Bureau of the Census, 1975f). The most rapid expansion occurred in

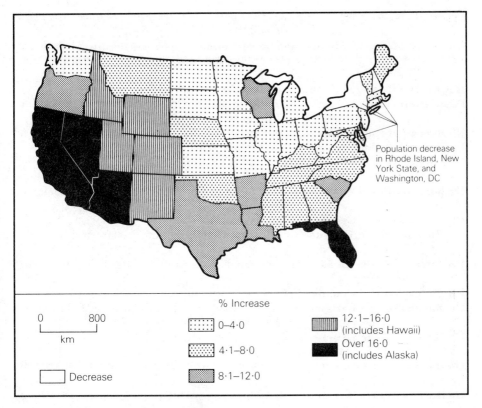

Population decrease in Rhode Island, New York State, and Washington, DC

% Increase

0   800
km

Decrease

0–4·0

4·1–8·0

8·1–12·0

12·1–16·0 (includes Hawaii)

Over 16·0 (includes Alaska)

Fig. 8.9 *Population change, 1970–1975.*

Calfornia and Southern Mountain States, with a 3.4 per cent per annum growth, and by the Gulf-side Southern States, 2.07 per cent. The leading growth States were Arizona, 5.35; Florida, 4.8; and Nevada, 4.32.

Thus the one social factor of not only a riper but a more rounded and fuller old age has made the swampy flats of Florida, now well drained, and the desert desolations of Arizona, now well irrigated, into the desire-line geography of America. Admittedly these are middle- and upper-class havens, and there is a class, to which most poor-Whites, Negroes and Indians belong, that will never retire beyond the end of their street, yet well-being is so advanced that more and more people are advancing into it: America is achieving a wholeness not known before.

To many, this·is its destiny now; this is the new thing it is doing in and for the world.

References

AP (1977) Associated Press news release, Washington, 1 May 1977.
Cable, G. W. (1880) *The Grandissimes: A Story of Creole Life*, Amer. Cent. edn, N.Y. (1957) pp. 41, 158.

Emerson, R. W. (1837) 'The American scholar', in Wicker (ed.) *Selections from Ralph Waldo Emerson*, Riverside edn, Boston (1960) p. 64.

Golant, S. M. (1976) 'Housing and transportation problems of the urban elderly', in Adams, J. S. (ed.) *Urban Policymaking and Metropolitan Dynamics*, Cambridge, Mass., p. 387.

James, H. (1885) *The Bostonians*, Bodley Head edn, London (1967) pp. 28, 35, 37.

Population Bulletin (1975) 'Family size and the Black American', Population Reference Bureau Inc., Washington, D.C., p. 12.

US Bureau of the Census (1973a) 'Population', *Social Indicators*, spec. pubn, Ch. 6.

US Bureau of the Census (1973b) Op. cit., Ch. 5, Charts 5/3, 5/11.

US Bureau of the Census (1975a) 'Population profile of the U.S.', Ser P-20, No. 29, p. 1.

US Bureau of the Census (1975b) 'U.S. population profile', section on Labor force, Ser. P-20, No. 279, p. 25.

US Bureau of the Census (1975c) Op. cit., p. 25.

US Bureau of the Census (1975d) 'Household and family characteristics', Ser. P-20, No. 276, p. 3.

US Bureau of the Census (1975e) 'Population profile of the U.S.', Ser. P-20, No. 279, p. 19.

US Bureau of the Census (1975f) Op. cit., p. 26.

US Bureau of the Census (1976a) 'Number, timing and duration of marriages', Ser. P-20, No. 297, also 'Fertility of American women', Ser. P-20, No. 301.

US Bureau of the Census (1976b) 'Number, timing and duration of marriages', Ser. P-20, No. 297, p. 8.

US Bureau of the Census (1976c) 'Daytime care of children', Ser. P-20, No. 298, p. 1.

US Bureau of the Census (1977d) 'College plans of high school students', Ser. P-20, No. 299, p. 2.

US Bureau of the Census (1976e) 'School enrolment in the U.S.', Ser. P-20, No. 303, p. 4.

US Bureau of the Census (1976f) 'College plans of high school students', Ser. P-20, No. 299, p. 2.

US Bureau of the Census (1976g) Op. cit., p. 2.

US Bureau of the Census (1976h) 'Educational attainment in the US, 1975', Ser. P-20, No. 295, p. 1.

US Bureau of the Census (1977a) 'Population characteristics, marital status and living arrangements', Ser. P-20, No. 306, p. 5.

US Bureau of the Census (1977b) 'Geographical mobility in the U.S.', Ser. P-20, No. 305, p. 1.

US Dept Labour (1970a) Bureau of Labor Statistics, 'The U:S. labor force: projections to 1985', *Special Labor Force Report*, No. 119, p. 7.

US Dept Labor (1970b) Op. cit., p. 11.

The communitarian landscape
—the geography of the anti-self

The Communitarian Mind

Although individual competition has played a powerful role in American society, the concern for community has also been critical. Hence the rapid rise and spread of the communitarian ideal where, as Noyes (1853) wrote: 'Egotism is abolished . . . by the extinguishment of the pronoun *I*. The grand distinction between this ideal and the world, is that in one reigns the *We* spirit, in the other the *I* spirit. From *I* comes *mine*, and from this the exclusive appropriation of money, women, etc. From *we* comes *ours*, and from the we spirit . . . a universal community of interests.' Consequently, a geography of the anti-self grew up in the landscape seen (1) in the abandonment of uses of land and forms of settlement based on self-interest, and self-esteem, individual competition and individual specialization; and (2) in the rise of the group-self, featuring group-planning, group-activity, group-structure and form. This pricked itself out in the scene, in the brick and stone of housing, industry, religion, and recreation, through patterns patently different from those which prevailed in self-ridden America. Hence, their great significance for social geography.

The famous Plantation Covenant of New Haven, 1640–62, tried to set out the perfect rule for the government of men, and bound its members 'to establish such civil order as would be likely to secure *the greatest good*'. They built a common meeting house, regulated the price of labour and of goods, and based further entry into their numbers on the consent of the community. In 1690 Conrad Beissel was born who came to America in 1720, and set up at Ephrata (in Pennsylvania) what the title of his colony itself proclaimed as an other-worldly communal settlement in his *Solitary Brethren*.

After the Revolution, America carried on these early colonial traits. It accepted Mother Ann Lee, from England, who started up the Society of Shakers. Her doctrine was one of rigid self-denial and involved celibacy (giving up selfishness in personal relationships), together with common property (denying selfishness in material possessions). The Shakers chose relatively isolated places where they could 'seclude themselves entirely from contact with the outer world'. Nordhoff's reaction to them in his famous study of *The Communistic Societies of the United States* was that, 'To a man not in love with the ascetic life nor deeply disgusted with the world, Shakerism would be unendurable' (Nordhoff, 1875, p. 167). This disgust was directed most of all against the world-in-the-self, as in the Shaker hymn, 'I mean . . . to cross my ugly nature'.

Likewise, America made a place for Rapp, the German separatist, who organized his followers at Harmony, Indiana, into the Harmony Society, agreeing to pool all possessions, and to 'labor for the common good of the whole body'. The Rappist experiments of 1805-15, were followed by those of the Zoar Separatists, 1819-45, in Tuscarowas County, Ohio. Separation from the prevailing faith in Germany led to separation from the prevailing ethos in America.

Independence from the established system was also sought by Robert Owen, the English socialist, who set up New Harmony, in Indiana, opening it in 1827 with 'a declaration of mental independence against the trinity of man's oppressors – private property, irrational religion, and marriage'. He was not able to translate his mental geography of a world rid of individual competition and of entrenched selfishness into the geographic harmony of the planned and socially centred community: he had to return to England, admitting failure. But at least he realized how important the state of the mind was in the development of the land.

Another attempt to 'dissolve selfishness and demonstrate the doctrine of perfectionism on earth' was made a few years later in 1848 at Oneida, NY, by John Humphrey Noyes. Among other things, Oneidans 'rebuked the propensity toward the exclusive and idolatrous attachment of two persons to each other [in what they called *selfish love*] as sinful, and tried to break it down rigorously' in a system of propagation controlled by the community. In 1855, the True Inspiration congregation, newly settled at Amana, Iowa, took pride 'in the conscious surrender of the individual will to the general good'. Among their Rules for Daily Life, rule 5 read, 'To abandon self with all its desires, knowledge, and power.' They were urged to keep themselves separate from the world. In the same year, Dr Keil founded the Aurora commune in Oregon, preaching against selfishness and praising self-sacrifice. Nordhoff found the members 'practiced in self-sacrifice knowing that selfishness is evil and the source of unhappiness' (Nordhoff, 1875, p. 314). The Progressivists of Cedar Vale commune, set up in Kansas, 1871, put things a little more positively. The preamble to their constitution states: '. . . man is not only an individual having rights of his own but also a person owing duties to others: we believe that our highest development can only be obtained by a union of interests and efforts'. Freedom was necessary, otherwise how could one 'come out' from society, but the freed man was at the same time, in the Pauline sense, the bound – bound to the common good. This was a strong American view until the social Darwinism of the late nineteenth century replaced it with rugged individualism.

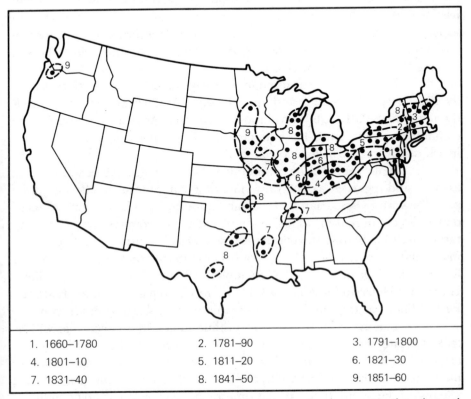

1. 1660–1780	2. 1781–90	3. 1791–1800
4. 1801–10	5. 1811–20	6. 1821–30
7. 1831–40	8. 1841–50	9. 1851–60

Fig. 9.1 *The spread of the communal idea in America, seventeenth to nineteenth centuries.* Starting in the mid-Atlantic and New England States, where religious freedom was the climate of development, the communitarian movement spread into the Old Northwest, and then to the Pacific Northwest. Subsequently, it extended into the Old Southwest. It tended to be an essentially rural feature.

These examples, spread over 250 years, from the Atlantic to the Pacific, reveal the full strength of that mind in America pitted against the self and the self-centred world (see Fig. 9.1). However, it was at all times a minority mind. As already indicated, landing from the *Mayflower*, saints were mismatched by strangers. These last founded Merriemount, the *aperçu* of individualism, which put up its maypole and danced with self-gratifying joy as New Plymouth wrestled in its common corn. Self-interest and self-gratification, individual enterprise and individual competition, came to dominate America and become its central image. To be an American was to be free, to be free was to compete with every other American. The power of this position made it more and more difficult for the communitarian way. Furthermore, individualism increasingly viewed communism as its opposite, and did not see how a common mode of living could free individuals for a fuller development of the self. As European communism ceased to content itself with the experimental commune and wanted to communize the whole of society, it evoked a still greater belief among Americans in the merit of individualism. All men are born equal – equal to compete with others in making the most for themselves.

The climate of the mind in the early half of the twentieth century is dynamic, restless, unstable, and full of change. At the heart of that change is the individual. Although a revolutionary country, America has rejected the communist revolution. It has clung to the individual revolt, and put its faith in self-discovery and self-reliance.

Hence, most of its communistic experiments have been looked at askance and regarded as aberrant. The title 'communist', itself, once quite proudly worn by sectarian and secular communities alike, became watered down to communalism, or its modern inoffensive counterpart, communitarianism. One by one the communist colonies died out, very often rent by individual discord: many of them only came to stay on in the landscape as historic buildings or sites, as for example Plymouth Rock in New England, Harmonist House in Indiana, the Old Colony Church in the Bishop Hill State Park, Illinois, or the Sunday-school picnic park at Aurora, in Oregon.

The cycle of growth and decline in communitarian life will be looked at later. Meantime it should be noted that even in their heyday, which occurred between 1845 and 1875, the pioneer American communes were numbered only in their hundreds, and probably accounted for no more than 150,000 of the population – at that time already between 50 and 60 millions. The vast majority of Americans rejected the communist mode, preferring the reform, to the remodelling, of individualism.

The geography of the counter-culture

However, communalism is by no means dead or dormant in America. It has raised its head not as the anti-self, but as the counter-culture; as a positive assertion of the commune as an alternative way of life, often referred to as *The Alternative*. This is not to be taken as state communism – in fact, many communes are very much against the state. A considerable number are anarchical cells, hoping to change American society from within not from above, by a kind of cellular multiplication that will take over and replace settlement, in explosive growth.

Protest forms the link between the old- and the new-style communes. Present protest is not against the ugliness of the self, or the inadequacy of the individual, in a retreat to a more social life (although that does come into it), but against the American society itself, in favour of a new set of values. Here again, a mental geography is shaping up, that has already brought new shapes to the landscape. A new social landscape is being sculptured, that springs to the observant eye.

Since it springs from a different mind, it takes a different form. Many of the new communes, while out to protest selfishness, are all for self-expression, while against individual competition, support individual callings: they are in fact centres of a super-individualism that would give people enormous licence in a highly permissive association. Hence, although association is important, it is no longer the goal to which individualism is subordinate, but the means for greater individual scope.

The new mental geography may have been foreshadowed in the Cedar Vale experiment in Howard County, Kansas, where in 1871 people came together 'to achieve both communism and individual freedom'. Thus, while that commune considered themselves 'as a family, their property in common for the use of all', they agreed that 'each member shall be free to hold whatever his conscience may dictate'. This idea of greater freedom of the individual through 'mutualism' is now seen, by many, as the best way of freeing people: as long as they associate with those of like mind they are more free, through mutual help and understanding, to do their own thing.

The mutualistic mind must come first: only in this way can individualism, and especially a self-centred individualism, be broken up; thereafter the individual is set free for fuller self-expression. These points are well brought out in Albertson (1936) and Melville (1972).

The first heralds the new attack on individualism in favour of mutualism. For him 'the chapters of American history . . . marked by the most outstanding individualism in the world . . . have just closed'. Up to the mid-twentieth century 'men have struggled alone, climbed alone, failed or succeeded alone in America more than anywhere else in the world'. But now, following Roosevelt's New Deal for the nation, 'there is a new page in history. Everybody is either helped or helping as never before. No one stands alone any more as in the old days of uncurbed individualism. There is a feeling . . . that the days of every man for himself are gone . . . that some more co-operative form of community life for the future is imperative'. (Albertson, 1936:1973.) Melville (1972) regards this cooperation as a means to greater selfhood. It supports 'uninhibited self-expression, an alternative to authoritarian leadership, and a sensitivity to alienation', i.e. to the alienation that would 'impede personal contact'.

It is out of these mental constructs that the new counter-culture has arisen, counter 'to the dominant assumptions that are the ideological underpinnings of Western society'. The prevailing culture of rugged individualism 'tends to give preference to property rights over personal rights, technological requirements over human needs, competition over co-operation, the producer over the consumer, social forms over personal expression, striving over gratification . . .' (Melville, 1972, p. 26). It is to reverse these priorities that the communitarian counter-culture has been created. For it tries to 'set the assumptions of the dominant culture on their heads'.

As a result there has been a widespread revival of communalism in America, and an explosion of mutualistic communities across the landscape.

Their difference from earlier counterparts may be seen, among other things, in attitudes to sex. Most eighteenth-century and early nineteenth-century communes regarded sex as an arch-bastion of individualism – *my* wife and *my* child ill went with *our* land and *our* labour – and consequently they circumvented it through celibacy, or controlled it by planned propagation. Mental concepts have changed. Although actually few in numbers, a significant development of communes based on 'the joy of loving' has sprung up in recent years, such as Greenfeel's (Vt) 'community of lovers'; Kerista's (Cal.), 'free love organization'; or the Alternatives Foundation, (Cal.) dedicated to 'total sexuality'.

That these are not merely questions of the mind, but form answers in the landscape may be seen from both nineteenth- and twentieth-century examples. There was a distinct architecture of anti-sex at, say, Mt Lebanon, where 'brothers' and sisters' workshops shall not be under the same roof', or at Pleasant Hill (Ky), where 'in most of the dwellings there were two doorways, for the different sexes, as well as two-stairways within' (Nordhoff, 1875, pp. 176, 213). By contrast, the modern free love commune, especially in the Buckmaster Fuller 'dome house', is designed to bring the sexes together with as little obstruction as possible. Here is a sex geography that answers to a new sex-mentality.

The communitarian landscape

The material impact on the land of these various social and personal ideals has been quite impressive. However, one should point out that – many minds, many manifestations – patterns have varied quite considerably. Different ideas have occurred about the nature and function of the commune. Different relations have been made with the world outside. These things themselves have created different geographies. And then there have been variations within each theme, especially as men moved west and, later, as the cities grew. Some groups have singled out a community of property and work; others have featured common living conditions. Most experiments have been agrarian, though urban communes are becoming more significant. Some have been strongly religious in their idealism, others purely secular. Most have chosen a plain life, others have tried to live 'in-the-round'. The fact that all of them existed in mainstream America forced them to deal with a world dominated by individualism: some tried to get away from this, others to strike a compromise with it, and a few – to exploit it! A settlement here will have a communal core but an individual periphery, a place elsewhere may have accepted individual homes but stuck to communal worship or work.

Most classifications have been made by historians or sociologists and thus miss the geographic connection. Maddeningly, no mention is made of the type of settlement, the land system, the road network, the use of the soil, the siting of institutions, and so forth. Were it not that the author had seen many of the places listed he would have found it difficult to have filled out the terse descriptions – or even lack of description – given. However, there are distinct *patterns* which enable a geographic classification to be made. Basically, this divides the communes into two, the unitary forms, with a highly nucleated settlement where common living and working quarters are centred; and binary structures, where some buildings exist for common purposes along with those for individual need or gratification. These are again split into two, according to the balance between communal and individualistic features found in each settlement (see chart below).

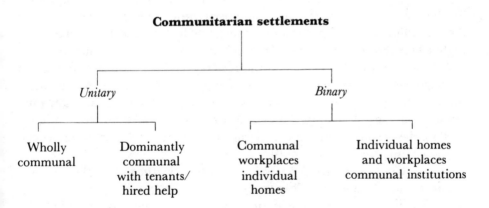

Communitarian settlements

Unitary		Binary	
Wholly communal	Dominantly communal with tenants/ hired help	Communal workplaces individual homes	Individual homes and workplaces communal institutions

Unitary settlement forms

Unitary settlements bear perhaps the most characteristic stamp of the commune. Most people wanting to do something against individualism rely on groupism, and concentrate themselves into a compact, homogeneous settlement. This is so different from the heterogeneous, loosely knit, and uneven forms of mainstream America. Indeed that was Nordhoff's instant reaction when he saw the Aurora commune in Oregon. He wrote (Nordhoff, 1875, pp. 305, 308):

> As you approach the settlement, you will notice a large wooden church, a saw-mill in a deep ravine, and a number of 'houses', different from the usual dwellings in the United States, because of their uncommon size and the entire absence of ornament. They are three stories or more in height, a hundred feet deep, and look like factories. Community of property and work is basic. The commune is dominated by a large communal dwelling-house, in which however each family has its own apartment. . . .

This was in 1871. At the other end of the country, in Mt Lebanon, the Shakers had a similar colony, founded in 1793, but still going strong in Nordhoff's day, and described by him as a collection of large communal buildings 'forming a distinct community, with industries of its own, and a complete organization for itself. As you drive up the road the first building to meet your eye is the enormous barn. This huge structure is 296 feet long by 50 feet wide and five stories high.' It was, in fact, a compendium of the barns that would otherwise have been scattered over several sections of land on individual farms, drawing together into one the byres, stables, corn mill, hay lofts, and tool rooms usually disseminated through the landscape. This was an eye-filling measure of mutualistic geography.

Next to the barn lay the 'sisters' workshop, three stories high, used for the women's industries' in a commune structured for celibate women and men. Beyond this rose 'the "family" house, 100 feet by 40 feet, and five stories high' where the Shaker 'family' of the gathered, lived in their all-male and all-female dormitories. 'Then an enormous wood-shed, three stories high, and a carriage shed can be seen, with, beyond that, the brothers' house where different industries are carried on. Farther still are the grist mill, saw mill, laundry and herb house, the last 100 feet by 40 feet and three stories high' – used for drying out, sorting and packing medicinal and culinary herbs needed in the community and sold outside.

Could this have described, or would it be true today, of the typical country town of America? That town of lines of irregularly spaced, custom-built, highly idiosyncratic homes and shops and vacant lots and billboards and service stations with an episcopal church here, a baptist one there, and a Kingdom Hall somewhere else, two saloons, and a baseball diamond?

The unitary pattern covers both religious and secular, pioneer and contemporary, isolationist and activist groups: it springs from the group mind working groupism out in its most logical and at the same time necessary form. It was more prevalent at the time of the opening frontier, when technology was less advanced and made group work more incumbent than today, but it is still a potent style. It still, of course, sets itself off from the highly individualized – almost atomized – American settlement of comparable size in the mainstream tradition. It embraces living, working, worship, and play conditions. In its quintessential structure it is separate, exclusive, largely self-sufficient, and homogeneous – what might be called type U_1, unitary simpliciter. Where.it has yielded to the outside world, to a certain extent, and its members go to outside jobs using routes developed to connect with the general network, or outside labour is brought in for which single-house accommodation is found, it dilutes itself to type U_2, unitary complexitas.

Some examples of the unitary landscapes, in either or both of its forms, are as follows: of religious persuasion, the Shakers, the Separatists, the Inspirationists, the Bruderhofs, the Hutterites, and various kinds of modern fellowship groups; of secular origin the Fourierists, the Icarians, the earlier Perfectionists, and in our own day the New Learning groups and most of what might be called the drop-out communities.

The Solitary Brethren

This Community of Seventh Day Baptists was one of the first truly unitary, mutualistic, settlements in America. It was set up in 1735, in late colonial times, at Ephrata, in Pennsylvania. Its founder, Johan Beissel (1690–1768) had been a Dunker. This was a separatist group that admitted members only on believer's baptism performed in the triune manner – a threefold immersion in the name of the Father, Son, and Holy Ghost. Persecuted by the Established Church in Germany, Beissel fled to America. A separatist, Beissel separated out of the Dunkers to form his own Seventh Day Baptist community which he then persuaded to adopt celibacy. He thus established a very exclusive and self-isolated monastic community, the brethren and the sisters living separately in large communal houses run essentially as dormitories. They ate together in a common dining house which also served as a meeting place. They tried to be self-subsistent, and ran a communal farm and a common wood lot, the proceeds of which supported community mills – grist, saw, fulling, tanning, and paper-making. They also had a printery and published religious literature including hymns. They existed in supreme simplicitiy; they wore Capuchin habits, kept their buildings undecorated and strictly utilitarian, and had no institutions for the arts or recreation. In all this they stood out against the normal Pennsylvania village, with its well-painted houses, flower-filled gardens, inns with decorative inn signs, and its churches and schools of German baroque, Queen Anne, or Georgian architecture.

Here a fault-like interface in the mind produced a distinct fission in the landscape. Geographers are used to the impact of geological faults; they should become sensitive to the influence of mental fission, in the scene.

The only entertainment the Solitary Brethren allowed themselves was the singing of hymns. Beissel's choir was quite famous. But since it sang in the community meeting place (which was also the dining hall) it made no mark on the land. Compare this with the music halls, assembly halls, conservatories, music shops, piano-teaching houses of rural towns in the mainstream America of that day, and once again the mental differences come out as marked physical contrasts. Mappa mundi in mentis humani est.

Ephrata continued for a long time in its cocoon-like state, indeed a Seventh Day congregation still exists, although the old monasticism was abandoned by 1800.

The Shakers

These too, have persisted, though with a waning presence in the land. With anti-self at the front door, they allowed self-interest at the back: they shifted from U_1 to a U_2 status, as their geography clearly showed. They began by supplying their own needs through their own work but, agrarian-minded as they were, they invested their savings in land, and soon acquired more than they could handle: the balance was rented out for profit to tenant farmers. Hence a mixed communist–capitalist economy developed which increasingly strengthened the individualistic as against mutualist trends in their life.

Mental concepts soon became concrete modes. The Shakers organized themselves into two orders, the so-called Church Order of fully accredited members, and the Novitiate Order, of those on trial. The geography of living and working arrangements at once showed this up. To the Church Order, we are told, 'belong those who have determined to seclude themselves more entirely from contact with the outside world' – they chose isolated sites, indeed, as Dolores Hayden (Hayden, 1976, p. 43) points out, they liked mountain sites off the chief roads, when most Americans were competing for nodal meeting places in the mainstreet network, along the great valleys.

The geography of segregation then segregated the full members from the novitiates, who often still lived in their own homes, or on separate farms rented from the commune; furthermore, it segregated the sexes and the age groups from each other. In most Church Order communes, adults lived together in a unitary home, 'divided as regards its upper storeys into rooms accommodating from four to eight persons. A wide hall separates the dormitories of the men from the women.' The ground floor was reserved for the kitchen, communal dining room, and stores. They eat in a general hall; men at one table, women at another, and children at a third. [Since adults are celibate, children are adopted to keep up numbers and perpetuate traditions.] The sexes, both old and young, are kept apart. Even the walks between the buildings are so narrow that a man and a woman, or boy and girl, cannot walk abreast.

Now there's the geography of apartness for you, if ever there was!

As Nordhoff (1875, pp. 166, 176) found, 'The sexes eat apart, they labor apart, they worship – standing or marching – apart.' And this comes out in the micro-geography of the settlement, with separate men's and women's entrances to the common dwelling house and the common dining room, and the insistence that, 'Brethren's and sisters' workshops shall not be under the same roof.' How different again from mainstream America where men and women lived, worked, worshipped, and played next to each other!

Work was an important agent for communizing people, and, in especial for breaking down the family, seen by Mother Ann Lee as Satan in the woodpile. As Hayden (1976, p. 69) shows, 'different spheres of activity – agricultural, horticultural and mechanical operations for the men; domestic work, tailoring, garden and craft activities for the women – discouraged personal contact, since members could not visit the workplaces of the opposite sex without a specific reason'. Moreover, the paths were so made that there was a circulation of separateness: men and women simply did not meet going to or coming from work. 'Short-cuts were forbidden.' As Hayden (1976, p. 69) remarks, 'Distancing regulations created envelopes of space' that kept work groups apart, and yet made movement contribute to the communal order. What ingenuity! How different from the secular city where all routes were avilable to all individuals, with short-cuts galore, and diagonal lines cutting off right-angled corners in a way expressly forbidden in Shaker geography.

Work separated out the Shakers in many ways: it was agrarian, therefore they had no impact on the city; it was self-subsistent, and consequently as non-commercial as possible; it was all-embracive, making a multiple-use pattern of the soil that contrasted with the increasing specialization in farming, forestry, and processing that went on outside; and it was highly regulated, compared with the experimental freedom enjoyed in the mainstream economy. 'Not a single action of life, whether spiritual or temporal, but has a rule for its perfect and strict performance.' Work was planned by the community-in-council, and carried out under appointed foremen, responsible to the group.

Certain special features singled the Shakers out. Most were vegetarian, hence the concentration on orchards, market-gardens, and food grains in their pattern of land-use. Meat eaters were in the minority; furthermore they were not allowed to eat pork. By contrast, outside America had gone hog wild, and today more than half the hogs in the world are in America! Both Cincinnati and Chicago have been given the title, Hogopolis.

As the Shaker proverb says, 'Every force evolves a form'! Certainly hamburger stands do not form part of the Shaker landscape.

Nor do pin-ball stands, stand-up bars, grand-stand doors at

theatres, stands at ball parks or football stadiums, cab-stands, stands of flags or any other kind of stands, except music-stands! The geography of social life must be an important part of social geography, but here it is almost absent – except for the choirs that meet in the common hall. Even their music is limited. At Groveland commune, NY, 'They sing finely, but are opposed to instrumental instruments.' (Nordhoff, 1875, pp. 199.) All pursuits, even those apparently secular, were centred on religion. At Union Village, Ohio, 'They have what they call a Lyceum, a kind of debating club, for the discussion of set questions. The question last discussed was "Whether it is best for Shaker societies to work on cash or credit?"' (Nordhoff, 1875, p. 203.)

The lack of recreation is, of course, a part of the geography of the anti-self. Joy should not be in self-expression or self-gratification. This means, too, a lack of joy in the beautification of the self or of one's surrounds.

The geography of the unembellished scene has characterized the Shaker down to this day. Their personal appearance, their architecture, their landscape is one of dedicated plainness. A religious poem by a Shaker girl affirms that 'Beauty's self was never worth a pin'. Nordhoff (1875, p. 118) though a great admirer of their communes, nevertheless could not get over the plainness of their architecture 'whose peculiarity is that it seeks only to be useful, cares nothing for grace and beauty, and carefully avoids ornament'. This was written in 1873, almost at the height of the Victorian era, when mainstream houses were decorated with French-baronial towers, Gothic windows – often with coloured glass, and rococo decoration of the most florid kind. 'Considering the homeliness of the buildings', Nordhoff wrote, 'which mostly have the appearance of mere factories or human hives, I asked . . . "Why not aim at some architectural effect, some beauty of design?" The Elder replied, with great positiveness, "No, the beautiful as you call it, is absurd and abnormal. It has no business with us."'

Could there be a better example of mental geography?

As a result of such views, which represented 'an almost total repudiation of worldliness', and also of their 'penchant for stifling the individuality of their members' (*Encyclopedia Americana* 1976) the Shakers began to lose their appeal, and from over 6,000 members by 1850, they have decreased to barely 1,000, at Mt Lebanon, NY, and Hancock, Mass. Part of this decline was because more and more of their groups traded with the outside world, and began to rent land out to individual tenants, or hire in labourers for whom they had to build individual homes on the outskirts.

The geography of returning individualism began to invade them, until less than 10 per cent of the children they adopted (to sustain them in their traditions) stayed with them. They themselves gave up trying to be self-sufficient and entered the commercial economy, specializing in certain products from which to get a sufficient surplus to trade for goods on the open market. Communism became mixed up with capitalism in a country where the overwhelming force of thought favoured the capitalistic form of life. In slipping from U_1 to U_2 there was little to stop a slither out of the unitary system altogether into individualism.

The Rappists

This community also started with a bang but ended with a whimper. George Rapp, 1757-1847, founded Harmony in Indiana and Economy in Pennsylvania. His followers agreed to put all their possessions into a common fund, to labour for the common good, to adopt simplicity of dress, and live in a uniform style of house. They tried to make everything they needed and to depend as little on the world as possible. Rapp exhorted his followers 'not to care overmuch for riches, but use their wealth as having it not', i.e. not for personal comfort or status but for community expansion. In spite of this they made trading posts of their communes, rapidly increased in wealth, and entered into the prevailing economy, investing in coal mines and oil fields.

Thus, although they held that 'in the renewed world [of their community] man would be restored to the . . . Adamic tradition', reflecting Lewis's claim that the American dream saw in America 'the New Adam in the New Eden', it was the Old Adam in them that increasingly took over, and led them to their fall. In doing their 'new thing', Americans so often simply let the 'Old Adam' have a new chance.

Zoar

Another communitarian experiment, Zoar was also separatist. It bought 5,600 acres of military grant on the Tuscarowas, Ohio, thus all but ensuring a separated condition at the outset. Unlike the highly individualized landscape with its disseminated farms going back to Cleveland and Pittsburgh, not far away, it built a tightly nucleated village with large community dwelling houses, each holding several families, a single church, a school, and some community mills. Segregated from the outside, it was split by segregation within. Children were segregated away from their parents, not long after they could walk, and put into dormitories, 'the girls in one and the boys in another, and did not come again under the exclusive control of their parents'. Sexes were likewise segregated, even at worship. 'The church has two doors, one for the women and the other for the men, and the sexes sit on different sides of the house' (Nordhoff, 1875, p. 113).

Oneida

This community too, built up a unitary geography, at least in its early phases. Its aims were somewhat different, because Noyes, the leader, believed in making the individual perfect. In a sense, a higher individualism was the goal. But this could only be done through a more controlled community. Founded in 1848, on the site of an old Oneida Indian reserve in up-state New York, it tried to get away from monogamy and the one-family home – those bastions of the corrupted individual who equated self with self-interest and self-gratification. Hence, it put people together in large communal dwellings where 'every woman was the wife of every man and every man the husband of every woman' so as to 'dissolve selfishness and demonstrate the doctrine of perfectionism on earth'. For 'a community home in which each is married to all', as Noyes (1853, p. 57) proclaimed, 'will be much more attractive than an ordinary home where love, in the exclusive form, has jealousy for its complement, a jealousy that brings on strife and division'. Children remained with their mothers until they could walk, but were then taken away and put in a communal nursery.

Once more it is important to realize the strength of mental geography in the actual geography of a settlement. As Noyes asserted, 'The community must be Perfectionists before they are Communists', principles come before patterns. These principles (Noyes, 1853, p. 59) included not only 'the surrender of private property, but of *personal identity*, to the use of the whole'.

The pattern was of a very large central community dwelling, with a long dining room and kitchen behind, all set in a big square carpeted with lawn. In the unitary building was an extensive hall for meetings and lectures. Above this was a floor divided into sleeping rooms, partly for single women and partly for couples. Half of it was made into a large 'tent room', that is to say, it had twelve tents erected against the walls. These left a hollow square in front of them, which as Hayden (1976, pp. 212 ff.) describes it 'became a comfortable sitting room for the occupants of the tent. One large stove in the center was found sufficient to warm the twelve "rooms" around. Although their neighbours were scandalized by these flimsy and unconventional bedroom arrangements, the residents were pleased. "Much might be said of the increased sociality of the tent Room, as compared with the cold isolation of ordinary apartments."' The topmost storey was for men, with two tiers of dormitories, one above the other, the uppermost opening off a gallery.

Many of these ideas were worked out by the members themselves who were thus able, in Hayden's words, 'to satisfy the spiritual requirements of Perfectionism through collective design. . . . The presence of communal activities outside bedrooms obviated the possibility of loneliness for residents and at the same time decreased the chance of exclusive relationships. Encounters essential to increased sociability were fostered by circulation spaces passing through areas of communal activity.'

Thus, form fortifies faith; faith is justified of form.

However, faith was at risk when the Oneida community hired

outside help, building private houses for them. They employed over 100 women in their silk factory, and 70 men in their metal-working enterprises: yet they themselves only counted 238 members. 'With increasing prosperity they even began to hire household servants' (Nordhoff, 1875, p. 263). These practices changed Oneida from a truly unitary to a binary system with the individualized and communized societies side by side. Shortly after this there was a move against communism, and in 1880 the commune was replaced by a joint-stock organization centred in the manufacture of Oneida silver-plate. Thus, Oneida has become successful, but as a conventional commercial town.

Brook Farm

Established near Boston, Brook Farm, said to be the most celebrated of American Utopias, was contemporaneous with Oneida, operating from 1841 to 1847. Though started by a minister, the Rev. George Ripley, it was in fact a secular organization that had its inspiration from the French socialist, Charles Fourier (1772–1837). One of his ardent admirers, Marianne Orvis (Orvis, 1847:1972) claimed in her *Letters from Brook Farm*, 'Our individualities must be forgotten' for 'Oh the blessedness of association.' Fourier believed that 'the free play of individual desire in co-operative association would bring about the most harmonious living'. Fourierism promoted community living and work, but had a place for individual talents. It was based on voluntary association, and worked through local cooperatives or 'phalanxes', the optimum size of which was set at 1,800 people, i.e. the size of a small town. Each phalanx would live in a large unitary building and would cultivate a farm, specializing in one or two products. Godwin (1844:1972) describes what this would involve:

> Let us suppose . . .a township of 400 families of from 1,600 to 1,800 souls. It will no longer be worked in isolated farms – many of them hardly worth cultivation; the enclosures, fences and many of the roads will disappear, and the whole territory be thrown into a single domain for general cultivation.
>
> In an isolated farm every family must cultivate its own fields, vines, gardens and orchards, and it is clear no one can be occupied with so many different tastes with success. In an 'associated' township, among 1,800 inhabitants, there will be a certainty of finding persons, capable of every particular kind of labor. The type of soil, too, best adapted to each kind of cultivation, will be chosen, which can not always be done by isolated families.
>
> A township thus organized will soon feel that it has gained immensely by replacing 400 poor granaries and its 400 bad cellars, by a large central building, perfectly adapted to the reception and preservation of its

harvests. It will soon understand that it must substitute 400 kitchens occupying exclusively the time of 400 women, by a common kitchen managed by a few persons. Thus seven-eighths of the women, now absorbed in the details of housewifery, would be emancipated from their petty cares, and turn their energies to productive labor.

These changes being executed, each one would require only a small number of chambers for the accommodation of his family and friends. . . . These apartments for the sake of simplification would be found in the same edifice which contained the kitchen and dining hall, the cellars, the school rooms, the work-shops, and the children's dormitories. . . . Then the 400 dwellings which composed the township would disappear . . . and all the people be established in a grand unitary edifice. . . .

This is nothing if not social geography!

At Brook Farm everything ran to talent and not production, and so in the end it failed. But with men like Nathaniel Hawthorne as members and Emerson as well-wishers and lecturers, it attracted a lot of attention. A large 'phalanstery' was built and an attempt was made at the cooperative development of the farm. But the communal activities were unbalanced; writing, art, music, and debate got the better of farming. Actually, the communal house was so busy, Nathaniel Hawthorne had to get away from it to write! He remarked of the experiment, 'Persons of marked individuality – crooked sticks as some of us might be called – are not exactly the easiest to bind up into a fagot.' The binding enthusiasm faded, and the fagot broke up.

Hutterites

The Hutterites have been more persistent in carrying on the unitary tradition, with still active communes in Pennsylvania, Florida, and North Dakota. In the latter case, the author visited a colony of about eighty people living as families in two large unitary dwellings, that dominated the scene. The village is unlike its neighbouring loosely knit and individualized one in being off the highway. It is built around a small green. This is enclosed on the north by one of the big living units; on the west by the schoolhouse (also used as the 'meeting house') and the leader's house and office; here, too, is a large dining room with separate entrances for men and women; on the south, by the children's house, with their own dining room and a nursery; and on the east, but at some distance, by a large byre and barn, for stock raising. Chicken houses and a duckpond are behind these with, opposite them, a big garage, repair shops, tool house, and electric generator. All property is held in common. Work is divided up in groups, the women in the houses, kitchens, laundries, and school; the men in the stock pens and yards, chicken houses, the equipment depot, and the corn and barley fields. Each group works under its own foreman. A council of the leader and foremen runs the commune.

The buildings are well painted and kept, but of simple design; borders of flowers run beside the living quarters and children's house; the youth have a volleyball and a baseball pitch, at the side of the green: there is a magnificent choir. Thus, life is well rounded and full. It is strictly communitarian with no tenants or hired labourers or their homes on the 2,000-acre property. Here the essence of the unitary system prevails.

The Society of Brothers

This Society has carried the Bruderhof movement of South Germany across America and has several unitary communes from New York State, Pennsylvania, and Connecticut, to the West. These are small enough to be based on a single unitary home, with a school-cum-meeting house, and common work units. They are very simple, clean but without decoration, and are dedicated to Christian communism. Their amusements are few and their social life limited and without variety. Some of them gain money to buy the goods they do not raise by making crafts and toys and selling them outside, but otherwise their contacts with the individualistic–capitalist system are minimal.

Modern secular communities

Modern secular communities based on the unitary commune are small at present, but they are widespread. A new agrarianism, anarchism, and, simply, escapism seem to dominate as motives for settlement, but the settlement type is fairly constant – large dome houses, prefabricated army-style huts, and big old farmsteads. The majority have tended to opt out of mainstream America because of their abhorrence of violence, pollution, militarism, a centralized bureaucracy, government intervention, and big business. Some are completely isolationist and exclusive and as such do not play much of a part in the landscape. Only the geography of the unique would pick them out – the Ahimsa community, Kans., Buddhist, 8 people; the Democratic Republic, Vt, 13 people; Tolstoy Farm, Wash., 26 people; USCO, NY, art community; Yasodhara Ashram, Kootenay, 9 adults; the Lama Foundation, NM, 10 people; Free Folk, Minn., 6 adults, 2 children; or Resurrection City, Ala., 4 adults.

By contrast, there are some nation-wide associations with linked-up communes that try to present the same point of view in numerous states. Among these the society calling itself either Resistance or Any-Day-Now is quite prominent. With its headquarters in Philadelphia it gives encouragement to protest not only against war, but against the whole military–big business–centralized government syndrome. It has also taken a stand against that type of urban renewal which puts out people for offices, on behalf of higher urban taxes. A great number of small rationalist societies have sprung up, usually on a scale where they can occupy one old house, frequently selling crafts, herbs, and literature. There is today's *New Harmony* group, echoing the social ideals of Robert Owen; the *New Learning* group or Chelsea commune, NY, concentrating on anti-alienation and interpersonal sensitivity; the *New Light* movement, echoing that first of American protests against 'the Establishment' when Mrs Hutchinson had a tilt at the Puritan theocracy, and still concentrating on the role of conscience in society (in this case expressed as group conscience): the Children of Light, Arizona, and City of Light, NM, carry on the same motif; various *Humanist* societies, like Humanites, Vt and the Cooperative Humanist movement, Wis., which are all pacifist, and some of which are anarchist (so strongly opposed to the state that, although themselves communitarian and living and working in common, they would oppose a communist state). The *Walden Two* movement has spread from Boston, where it is called 'The Association for Social Design', to Virginia, at the Twin Oaks commune, La.; to Kalamazoo, Mich., called EC2: in these a revived Thoreau again influences men to get back to nature and live the balanced life.

The back-to-the-land movement

Mainly in the form of farm communes, this is one of the major examples of the new mutualism. So many people are tired of – and indeed disgusted at – the atomized, individualistic, competitive, polluted, and often corrupt life of the American city, still gripped in the capitalist system in spite of the modifying effects of urban planning, that they have fled into the country, bought an old and generally run-down isolated farm and given themselves up to the country virtues. These are regarded as sharing, joint decision-making, fellowship with simple life styles, and a clean environment. They stress unitary dwellings, common property, and working in common. They eschew chemical aids and are devoted to organic farming. The *New Alchemists* at Woods Hole, Mass., dedicate themselves 'To restore the Lands, protect the Seas, and inform the Earth's Stewards'. In 'arks' of glass they use solar energy to produce garden foods, even in winter.

The author visited a similar commune in South Dakota. A farm had become run down to the point of desertion. Several families sold out their town homes and, buying the farm together, moved into the big old farmhouse. A large communal garden had been worked up by hand hoeing and was neat, weedless, and productive. It was manured by chicken droppings from quite a large chicken house in part of the barn. The rest of the barn, especially where the old horse stables had been, was festooned with lines of herbs hung out to dry. These were natural herbs culled from the rest of the farm which had been left in the semi-wild state into which it had fallen. Marijuana had been grown and dried – until the police intervened! The wood lot was being carefully cut out, mostly for firewood, since the women cooked on old-fashioned wood stoves, but also for cord-wood, sold for pulping. In front of the wood, half hidden in juniper bushes, tall goldenrod, and a sea of Michaelmas-daisies, were eighty beehives. 'Natural' honey was collected; a separating shed next to the house was used to cull the liquid honey from the combs, and the distilled honey was sold off the farm as the main source of income. The women also made rag dolls' clothing for sale at country fairs. They breast-fed their babies, and encouraged the young children to run around bare on nice hot sunny days.

How different this was from the neighbouring farm where the flash of the combines, and the clack of the bailers was heard all day, where tractors were out, and waffle machines turned over the cut barley so that it could be dried in the sun. In its yard was a high pile of bags of chemical manures, and of chemical insecticides. Chemical manure spreaders and spraying machines stood by. Its owner and his family had spent the winter in Florida.

The very names of many of the farm communes are redolent of their new state of mind. Community Farm of the Brethren One, Earth House, RI; Fellowship Farm, Pa.; Green Valley Centre, Fla.; Heathcote Community School of Living, Md. (a return to pioneer-style homesteading); Hutterian Brothers farm commune, Wash.; the Land Fellowship, Ohio; Naturalism, Ill.; New Meadow commune, Pa.; Noah's Ark (refuge for the organically minded), Maine; Peace Action Farm, NY; Peace House, Cal.; St Francis Acres, NJ; Society for the Preservation of Early American Standards, NY (dedicated to the 'back-to-the-land movement'); Tolstoy Farm, Wash.; Unity Village, Mass.; Whole Earth, Cal.

Binary settlement forms

Communities which include individual houses and workplaces but feature communal institutions and either communist or cooperative offices, have also played their part in the mutualistic movement. They are often omitted from study as not being true communes, yet to their members they are sincere and real experiments in communal settlement. The communal element in them is usually quite clear, indeed self-evident, in the landscape – made up of a single communal church or meeting house, a single communal dining hall, a community recreation centre, a large common store, or distinctive community projects like a commune-wide drainage scheme or flood dyke.

These are clear manifestations in the landscape of the mode of mind of the people; they form a significant part of the social geography of communitarianism; they stand out in contradistinction to the atomized, individualistic settlement peppered with churches, vying with each other for members, or with shops cutting each other's throats for trade, or commercial entertainment centres competing for custom. The difference is of the order of two worlds – the worlds of two different minds.

New Plymouth

Here was a complex binary community. The members of the *Mayflower* had lived separately in England and again in Holland. They were in a sense independents, who put personal belief before established creeds. Yet they were strong through their congregation, and this bound them together. Hence the individual and the mutualistic traditions were both in their minds, and they made a place for both in the landscape. On the way over to the New World they drew up a compact to act together and to put group before individual interests. To begin with they shared both the land and its produce. One of the first buildings in New Plymouth was the common store. They also built a common meeting house at the head of the village. They made a common palisade to protect themselves from possible Indian attack. Common features were so strong that some of the wives grumbled at having to wash and repair the clothes of the bachelors, as well as of their own husbands and children! Yet individual habit or interest made themselves evident in the two parallel lines of small private houses, with their private gardens that formed the bulk of the community. Eventually privatism won out over mutualism, and people owned and ran their own farms and businesses: the communal way dissolved.

New Haven

This too, had both its private houses and lots and its communal buildings, in a dualistic system. It is true that 'dividing allotments for inheritance' was, under the plantation Covenant, a matter for the group, but individual heritors then developed the property as best they could. Private choice was limited in that 'no person should settle among them without the consent of the community', and a single meeting house signified the communal nature of their faith. At the same time they traded their goods in the private market, and were in the end subsumed within the individualistic society on which they came more and more to depend.

As unitary communes were founded, the whole debate about the binary mode intensified. 'Understanding the individual's reaction to space', Hayden (1976, p. 42) points out, 'led self-conscious groups to negotiate a balance between communal and private territory – an essential part of subordinating private property to new communal concepts. Boundaries, approaches and vantage points helped to define the communal territory', and these were maintained with force even where private space was catered for in individual homes, gardens, and paths.

Amana

This formed a case in point (see Fig. 9.2). It was set up on a piecemeal basis between 1843 and 1855 as individual families sold out their farms in the East, and moved to Iowa. Here they set up seven villages, which, though based on farming, had mills and stores. Some of the villages specialized on a particular product, Middle Amana on the carding and spinning of wool, Amana-under-the-hill, on tanning leather, West Amana on milling grain, South Amana on sawing wood: only Amana itself, the central village, had a comprehensive economy, with grist- and saw-mills and a woollen factory.

Specialization was an outcome of separate choice. 'Seeing that some of the brethren did not take kindly to agricultural labor', Nordhoff (1875, p. 30) remarks, 'they determined that each should, as far as possible, have employment at the work to which he was accustomed'.

The individual was also catered to in the fact that 'each family has its own house'.

How then did the Amana commune differ from other Iowan villages? First, it took up a distinct block of sections, and thus had a well-marked and all-inclusive *boundary*. Other settlers had taken up individual quarter-sections and thus were lost in the multitude of individual holdings. Second, it fostered the village life. It did not break up its big block of holdings into separate farms, each with its own farmstead. In Hayden's words, it 'resisted the national acceptance of isolated family dwellings located on

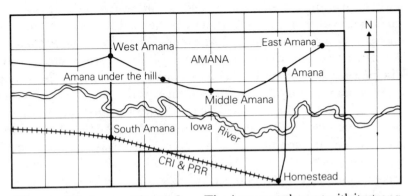

Fig. 9.2 *The Amana settlement, Iowa.* The Amana settlement with its strong village life contrasted markedly with the highly disseminated individualistic settlement prevailing throughout the American Midwest.

individual farms'. Though favouring 'model family homes, it wanted them clustered in model villages' (Hayden, 1976, p. 24).

The village form was so exceptional that that fact in itself became a *landmark* to the communitarian experiment. In each village the single large church was a further mark of group solidarity.

Thirdly, Amana had its own approach and its own network of inner circulation. It had but one major contact with the outside world, a road leading from Amana out to a secular town, Homestead, on the CRI & P Railroad. From Amana main-village, connections then went to the associated villages. All these roads were topographical, i.e. they followed irregular contours, and were quite different from the geometric pattern of roads, following survey lines, in mainstream America. They often climbed up to good *view-points* from which most of the commune might be seen.

Cedar Vale

In Kansas Cedar Vale was also a binary settlement set up, as has been mentioned, 'to achieve both communism and individual freedom . . . and to lead persons of all kinds of opinions to labour together for their common welfare'. The village was made up of individual houses, with their gardens, but with a common assembly, and a cooperative store. Hired labourers had small private homes at the periphery, but there was a common school at the core. In this way it was thought that an American style of communalism had been achieved, making room for both the individual and the common good.

Mormonism

Mormonism went through the search to find this balance. Today, with its world-wide missionary endeavour which puts the onus on each individual Mormon to convert some other individual, the emphasis is on cooperative individualism. The Mormons have fully endorsed that element in American freedom which, in giving man scope for self-interest, requires self-discipline and a responsible being. Hence Mormonism has passed out of the communitarian story, but still has influence in Christian co-operation.

Yet it was involved in mutualism from time to time. At the organization of the Church in Fayetteville, NY, the founder, Joseph Smith, had insisted on a community of believers, but it was not until the Mormons moved to Independence, Missouri, that Smith asserted, 'let every man . . . be alike among his people, and receive alike, that ye be one. You are to have equal claims on the properties . . . and let not any man among you say that it is his own.' The Mormons then formed the United Order to try to develop on a communal basis, but they adopted the binary system of individual homes round a common church, and did not dwell or eat all together. Besides, since the days spent in Missouri were ones of 'bloodshed, of hate, and of injustice' towards them, they did not want to add to their persecutions by thrusting communism as well as Mormonism on their highly individualistic neighbours. Even the United Order, according to McNiff, was forced to '. . . retain individualistic enterprise as the foundation of the economic order, though it built upon the surplus accumulated by individuals a store of goods held for the common benefit' (McNiff, 1940, p. 38).

Brigham Young allowed communalism in Utah, when again, Mormons were faced with severe tensions, but it was accepted only in smaller centres, at Price, Carbon Co., where 'all material possessions, except the clothes they wore, were to be owned in common', and at Orderville, whose members 'entered into a communal association, believing it to be a sacred duty to do so'. But Mormons as a whole did not favour communism. Instead, they relied on cooperation. This became their mark on the American landscape. Brigham Young concentrated on this, and helped to develop a strong sense of community through the Zion's Cooperative Mercantile Institute. At the October conference of 1868, cooperative branches were called for, the shares to be bought by individual Mormons. The Desert Agricultural and Manufacturing Society was a producers' cooperative that 'encouraged the production of articles from the native elements in the Territory'. Through cooperative buying and selling, cooperation in the development of the rather scanty water resources, and cooperative building, Mormonism certainly was 'associated with a strong group consciousness' as McNiff (1940, p. 76) claims, yet it gave individuals opportunity and incentive.

Salt Lake City is a good example of the binary system in the growth of settlement. New Zion was to be both communal and individual. Brigham Young established the original Plat of Zion so that the centre would be reserved for the great Mormon temple and other public buildings and parks. The near-centre went to church and other community leaders. 'After these were determined, the remainder of the Saints drew lots' for their individual portions. The city was surveyed in squares of 10 acres, house plots were $1\frac{1}{2}$ acres and streets 8 rods wide. Wards were set up with a square in each, dominated by 'ward chapels'.

A very rich social, scientific, and artistic life developed, which again reflected both mutualistic and individual endeavour. In the first winter the following groups were organized: the Deseret Literary and Musical Society, the Polyphilosophical Society, the Deseret Mechanical Institute, the Deseret Horticultural Society, and the Universal Scientific Society. This was far from the practice in most communitarian settlements, and gave great scope for individual interests.

Such interests, including room for Gentile institutions and, above all, for free commercial development, has left Salt Lake City today with the landmarks both of strong common bonds and forceful private initiatives. The city centre is like a system of binary stars with the magnificent Mormon temple and other fine community buildings on the one side, and the skyscrapers of mammon – the height of American free enterprise – on the other.

The remarkable achievements made by the Mormons and above all their genius for eliciting the best in the American way of life, have created what Meinig (1965) has called the Mormon cultural region in the American West (see Fig. 9.3) which has been and will continue to be 'of long-standing

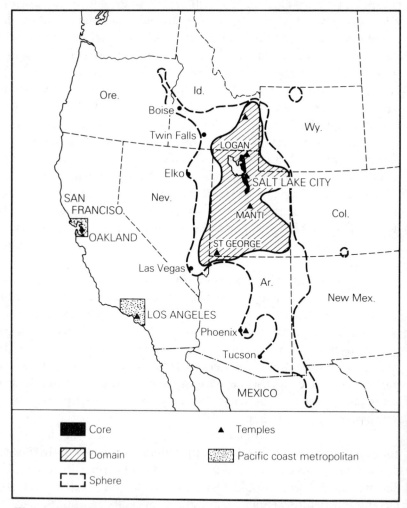

Fig. 9.3 *The Mormon cultural region.* The Mormon cultural region has developed from a remarkable blend of collective and individual effort in which a notable balance has been struck between private initiative and public responsibility.

social significance'. It has made a major contribution to the social geography of the country.

Among other things it has shown an appreciation of the common good that does not limit itself to communalism, and has left room for an individualism that does not go with individual exploitation.

Increasingly, the communitarian movement in America is seeing this, and trying to bring the polarities of communism and individualism – not together, because they are indeed opposites, but into coexistence. Many contemporary 'communards' feel that they do not have to give up private homes and gardens or even private occupations and interests (such as dominate the American landscape as a whole) in order to have mutually beneficial relations with each other in communitarian settlements. In fact, a lot of young Americans have founded communes precisely to do their own thing, to carry out their own crafts, to work out their own personal relations, to till their own plots, to write their own stories, in their own way, joined with, and fortified by, like-minded individuals. The author visited an artists' commune in Washington State where the people bought themselves into deserted or dilapidated parts of a pre-existing community and, in their own homes, carried on their art in their own style, selling the works for their own profit, almost as if they were in private business. Yet they were not. They sold their works not through private agents but their own cooperative; they also bought their supplies, and indeed most of their own food, through a consumer cooperative they had set up themselves. They taught their younger children among themselves. Above all, they met frequently to discuss their ideas and work, offer encouragement, tender criticism, and so create the sense of a community effort.

Modern binary communes of this kind, or perhaps of a more conspicuously organized type, are very frequent. They do not have to isolate themselves in the countryside. Many of them are part and parcel of the mainstream settlements against whose ethos and practice they are protesting. Artists 'and writers' communes are generally of this kind, with their members living and working separately, but linked by real and often visible bonds of mutual relationship. The Artists' Workshop Community in Ann Arbor, Mich., is like this, and so are the Theater People and Friends commune at St Paul, Minn.; Soleri, the architectural commune, north of Scottsdale, Ariz.; USCO, NY, a community dedicated 'to the service of art', and others.

Drop-out communes

Drop-out or 'hippie' communities may sometimes form an individual–communal complex (although many of them prefer to go out into the desert, as it were, and set up a unitary settlement, all living and loving together, under their multicoloured dome). But more often, they occupy, and squat in, old shacks in ghost towns, or abandoned army camps, or on the seamy side of cities, or in city slums. Here, in their own apartments where they can still carry on their individual life-arrangements, they meet in a common place, to discuss, play music, paint, mend their clothes, eat, and smoke drugs together. Often unseen because they are among Harrington's 'invisible poor' (away from the network of middle-class movement and contact), they escape from the pressures of individualistic competition, the degradation of individual conflict, and the alienation of the individual status struggle, to daub murals on shack walls, hang up their incense bowls, display their arts and crafts, and squat on tumbledown verandahs to play pop-music on their guitars. Such are Drop City, Colo., a commune for anarchists and self-elected drop-outs from mainstream society; Fort Hill commune, Mass., for people having 'hip religious ideals'; Head, the hippie commune of the Stone Age folk, Minn.; the hip-style communes of Placentas, NM, where 'anyone can do anything'; or the hippie fellowship of Taos, NM. Here, 'located at the top of a tortuously winding road, and forming one of the regular stops on the hip circuit of communes in the Southwest . . . members live in separate huts of adobe bricks, share a communal kitchen, and work together. The life style is primitive – no electricity, and outdoor "shitters". There is much drug use and mystical orientation.' (Melville, 1972, p. 26.)

Activist centres

These are usually the opposite of 'drop-outs'. Far from an open-ended, aimless, anarchic style, they create associations with definite views and ends, and devise programmes for specific change. They form the true counter-culture, trying not merely to denounce or even bring down the established way of life in America, but to create an alternative one. One of their guiding magazines is called *Alternatives*; it presents the alienated, exploited, corrupted side of American individualism, often in a dramatic way, with scenes of violence and decay, and posits a new situation in which mutual aid and respect will restore men to themselves and enable them to live fuller and more meaningful lives.

Activists deplore the basic escapism that has underlain so much of American Utopianism. 'In this country', as Melville (1972, p. 35) indicates, 'more than in any European country, the utopian urge has frequently taken the form of small intentional communities. If America itself became something less than a utopia, then the solution was to detach oneself from the mainstream of the society and band together with a small group of like-minded idealists to test some notion of the perfect society.' This was not enough. America had to be changed, not circumvented. Nor was change by reform enough: revolutionary change was required, if the American dream was to rescue itself from the nightmare it had become. Schlesinger's 'The American as reformer' was a pathetic thing compared with Thomas Paine's American as revolutionary.

The revolution is rarely political. More often it is educational or social. It is against the ideas and customs centred in competition and status that seem to be transmitted by the family, college, church, the chamber of commerce, trade unions, the city council, radio and TV, sport, and the arts! At Berkley's Free University (the counter-organization to the University of California at Berkeley) some of the course offerings are:

1. *Turning-on social systems:* innovative opportunities for action in reforming, humanizing, and revitalizing social systems.
2. *American romantic mythology:* enlightened alternatives to the bullshit of romantic love handed down to American youth.
3. *Gestalt growth groups:* for those willing to risk the change, *gestalt* awareness through hot-seat work and experiments.

Revolutionary communes include the following examples: Alternatives, Berkeley, Cal. – 'dedicated to total sexuality, peak-experience training, and the cybernated-tribal society'; Bhodan Center of Inquiry, Oakhurst, Cal., 'seminars on human community'; Communes for a New Age, Miami Beach, Fla; New Learning community, NY; Radical Action coop, NY; Resistance, Berkeley, Cal.; and the Yellow Submarine commune, Ore. (reminiscent of the Beatles in their more iconoclastic days).

Most of these communes run on their own, with their own leaders, developing their own programmes. *Centers for Change* is a group of revolutionary communes trying to assert themselves in every major region of the country on the country's major issues. It differs from almost all the communes so far discussed in being essentially a big-city organization challenging the capitalist–individualistic system at its heart and mind. As we have already seen, it is here that the economic values are venerated most. It is here that the social contour is taken from the economic gradient. Here it would be axiomatic that, 'Nothing can be socially healthy that is not economically sound.' Centers for Change would flip this over: America can never be economically healthy unless it is socially sound.

The centers are not very evident in the landscape. Usually they have a number on a door, squeezed between shops or offices, on a street running out of downtown: as for example in Greater New York – Centers for Change, ooo XYZ Ave, Brooklyn; or Chelsea commune ooo West XYZ St, New York; City Island commune, ooo XYZ Ave, Bronx; Clinton Street commune ooo Clinton St, Brooklyn; Coffee House Commune, New York; Park Place commune, Brooklyn; Sedgewick commune ooo Sedgewick St, Bronx; or Woodstock revolutionary commune, Box XYZ, New York. The principal revolutionary communities are found in New York, Boston,

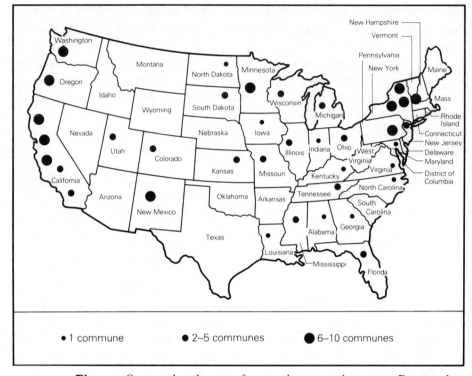

Fig. 9.4 *Communal settlements of 50 people or more, late 1970s.* Present-day mutualistic settlements are found throughout America, but principally in the industrialized north-central and north-east states, as a corrective to urban problems inherited from the heyday of American *laissez-faire*, and also in the traditionally liberal and open-ended society of the Pacific West.

Philadelphia, Chicago, San Francisco, and Los Angeles – at key points in the country (see Fig. 9.4). In spite of this, revolution has not come. This is because of the Nevitt principle that Reaction begets its own reaction – of which, more to come.

None the less, the modern communal movement, in all its forms, has made and is making a not inconsiderable impact, albeit one that does tend to come and go.

The rise and fall of Utopia

Nearly all the Utopian communities in America have fallen apart. As Herzler (1965) points out, 'Utopia is always a fleeting state'. There is a cycle of growth and decay that is all but monotonous in its regularity.

The geography of the *original secession* introduces events. People secede from existing societies and institutions, often fleeing their country or district of origin, banding together with like-minded separatists, to start a new, different, isolated, and exclusive settlement, on strong communitarian lines. Since they are of a mind to break away, this mind may eventually lead to their breakup. George Rapp for instance, founder of the Harmonists, grew up in a climate of secession. 'There were as many sects in Württemberg – his home town – as there were houses' (Duss, 1943, pp. 2–14). No wonder he broke away, but no wonder the harmonists eventually broke up. This was of their mind.

Then comes the geography of *creeping individualism*. The strong individualistic traits of mainstream America make themselves felt. The commune has to sell to private buyers; it has to buy in products from private sellers. If it makes good, it is tempted to hire private labour, to do even better. It starts to get profits, invests these in more land, rents out the land to tenants, becomes in effect a landlord – in spite of Crèvecoeur's triumphant cry that, 'Here [in America] we have no landlords . . .'. In fact it copies the force it had risen to protest. As Richter (1971) shows, American individualism has come to give more than can be taken away from it. Whatever its presumed defects may be the American dream always catches up with and surpasses the Utopian dreamer. In the American Icaria, though land as a whole was held in common, each family was permitted a 'strip of ground surrounding the house for cultivation. This allowed the idea of *meum et teum* insidiously to enter, with its delicious sense of personal ownership.' Thus, as Shaw (1884: 1973) claims, 'the gardens came to introduce a dangerous element of individualism and inequality'.

There follows the geography of *open fission*. Individual interests begin to challenge communal values. People want to give up celibacy or group marriage for the old-fashioned monogamy of the 'outside' world. Furthermore, they break up group working of the land, or even group ownership, for their own job prospects or property. Some choose to work outside, in the competitive system. Enormous stresses arise in the commune which pull it apart. In the Hopedale community, for example, Ballou (1897:1974) notes that, 'Persons favored with the privilege of conducting business on their own account, were led to . . . seek profitable jobs without regard to their moral quality.'

This was the beginning of the end.

Finally comes the geography of *dissolution*, as the commune breaks up. Land is sold off. The mills and factories pass to the outside owners. Members take out their share of the commune and form joint-stock companies to run its most profitable enterprises. The communal buildings become empty and fall into disuse, or are taken over as private colleges or hospitals. A few are maintained for future generations as museums. The settlement is atomized into private homes, private shops, and private institutions – or else, if it is not well placed for commercial development, it fades away and 'is as if it had not been'.

W. E. Nevitt has pointed out that this may well be because of the kind of people the commune has attracted. They were 'come-outers' by nature, and having come out of the mainstream society they then came out of the secessionist commune. The person who finds society difficult to get on with may be idfficult in himself and therefore fails to get on in the new community he sets up. In other words, the reactionary starts a reaction against which he then reacts – till he is back where he started from.

No one is an island in himself, Donne told us, and that is true – yet many people have the mental geography of themselves as little islands. That is why they have wanted to escape to their separate communes. But little-islanders retreating to little islands in the main stream of American advancement are not the answer: they cannot cut themselves off. Furthermore, on setting up their little islands in the stream their little-island mentality soon breaks up the selfsame islands and they are left to sink or swim in the main current.

What has happened is that, having shut themselves up, they have been shut out. In a sense they imprison themselves in their differences and so become treated as the people of a prison by those outside. Then they are irked until they break the prison and rejoin mainstream America. People anxious to be divided off are often divisive, and therefore divide up the community which has made itself apart.

In that event, what is the gain? Many a leader must have asked himself this when his dream collapsed around him and the commune he called out melted away. But – he had made the experiment! He had proved that America gave scope for ideals that challenged America itself. The perpetual rise of these new forces and new forms showed that the fountain of idealism in America could never fail. Part of the American dream has been to dream of better things: that some men and women have dreamed of an America devoted to mutual aid and, more than that, to a mutualistic society, must constantly challenge an America committed to individual freedom and the satisfaction of the self. As John Humphrey Noyes said when Oneida, the commune he had founded, began to disintegrate, 'We made a raid into unknown country, charted it, and returned without loss.' Men have been speaking of it ever since. The counter-country of mutualistic America is being more and more explored. To maintain itself, mainstream America must turn from self-interest and self-gratification to self-fulfilment, which means developing the whole self in terms both of the individual and the common good. In geographical terms this would mean developing the whole environment, or rather, creating the environment of wholeness.

James Russell Lowell once said that Utopias failed since they had everything in common but common sense. If this were true it was because Utopians had not considered the whole man. Yet on balance America has gained through the Utopian experience, since the nobility of Utopian intent has reinforced the thrust of the American spirit. As Duss (1943, p. 2), among the last of the Harmonists, has said, 'I learned as one who learned to think in terms of the welfare of all.' This kind of thinking has never been lacking in America; it has always had its devoted adherents; once again, it is coming to the front and is, as a matter of fact, influencing America as never before. It creates a mental climate favouring all co-operative groups. The Amish for instance who saw two out of every three of their colonies in America fail in the 18th and 19th centuries, when the tide of individualism ran high in America, are now so rooting themselves that their 'landscape impact is obvious' (Crowley, 1978). Although scarcely communes, 'since the Amish family rather than the community has been the social unit', their strong concern for the group has revived as mutualism has become a yearning for many Americans. Indeed everywhere concern for the community is challenging individual interest – to force on America a more balanced mind.

References

Albertson, R (1936) 'A survey of mutualistic communities in America', *Iowa J. Hist. Pol.*, *Vol. 34, p. 000*

Ballou, A. (1897:1974) *History of Hopedale Community*, 1897, AMS Press edn, N.Y. (1974), p. 183.

Crowley, W. K., 'Amish settlement, diffusion and growth', Ann. Ass. Am. Geogr., Vol. 68 No 2, pp. 251, 253, 263.

Duss, J. S. (1943:1972) *The Harmonists* (1943) Porcupine Press edn, Philadelphia, (1972) see pp. 2–14.

Encyclopedia Americana (1976) N.Y., Vol. 24, 'The shakers', p. 650.

Godwin, P. (1844:1972) *A Popular View of the Doctrines of Charles Fourier*, Redfield, N.Y., 1844, Porcupine Press edn, Philadelphia, 1972, pp. 51–2.

Hayden, D. (1976) *Seven American Utopias: the Architecture of Communitarian Socialism, 1790–1975*, Harvard U.P. Cambridge, Mass.

Hertzler, J. O. (1965) *The History of Utopian Thought*, Cooper sq. edn, N.Y., p. 314.

McNiff, W. J. (1940) *Heaven on Earth: a Planned Mormon Society*, AMS Press N.Y.

Meinig, D. W. (1965) 'The Mormon cultural region, strategies and patterns in the geography of the American West', *Ann. Ass. Am. Geogr.*, Vol. 55, pp. 191–222.

Melville, K. (1972) *Communes in the Counter Culture*, N.Y.

Nordhoff, C. (1875) *The Communistic Societies of the United States*, Hillary House edn, N.Y. (1961).

Noyes, J. H. (1853:1972) *Bible Communism*, Brooklyn (1853) AMS edn, N.Y. (1972).

Orvis (or **Dwight**) **M.** (1847:1972) *Letters from Brook Farm* (1847) Porcupine Press edn, Phil. (1972) pp. 8, 37, 91.

Richter, P. E. (1971) *Utopias, Social Ideals and Communal Experiments*, Boston, p. 148.

Schlesinger, A. M. (1950) *The American As Reformer*, Harvard U.P. Cambridge, Mass., p. xiii.

Shaw, A. (1884:1973) *Icaria. A chapter in the History of Communism*, AMS Press, N.Y. 1973 reprint, p. 112.

10

The environment in stress

The environment in stress

While Americans have constantly challenged each other, they have been as constantly challenged by their environment. Whatever their mutual relations, by race, religion and class, by sex and age, by city and country, they have all had to relate themselves to that environment. Its wideness stretched them, its harshness hardened them, its richness supported their sense of generosity, its comfort gave them ease, and its beauty uplifted them. Too, its conflicts split them, its variety tempted, and its abundance beguiled.

To the Pilgrims, America offered the chance 'to sow a yet untilled wildernesse with faith and good works'. A hundred – two hundred – years later homesteaders were still breaking into that wilderness to sow it with their ideas. Philip Freneau (Freneau, 1782) wrote: 'For what visible purpose could Nature have formed America when America lay unknown and undiscovered, with all her islands, lakes, mountains, woods, plains, extended shores' if not 'to become the receptacle of civilizing hopes?' Gradually the idea prevailed that America had been preserved, as Walt Whitman said, 'for purpose vast'. Even ordinary men and women were moved by the dream of their part in the country's future.

Yet that part could in fact damage the very foundation of their dreams. The environment became divided with dispute and disfigured with greed. Individual interests, seeking immediate gain, gave little thought to ultimate good. The competition of ethnic groups in a gradation of ghettos, the struggle between classes over 'the dignity of districts' – all exploited geography at the expense of ecology.

In gaining mastery over the environment, Americans still had to master themselves. Otherwise they were going to embroil the environment, on which they depended, in an endless set of value-conflicts. As Swan (1974) has stated '. . . our environmental problems stem from our social values'.

It is fundamental for social geography to take such values into account, for social geography is nothing less than the moral cosmography of a society worked into the landscape; it is the social proclivities of a people made real in land-use priorities: e.g. in whether land should be valued for economic or for social purposes; in whether it should be held for private or public ends. Should it be suborned to race and subsumed under class? Should the thrust and scale of its use be left to *men*; should its control be vested in *age*? American women and the American young are calling into question the right of people to think they have the only such rights.

Environment and human relations

Relationships between races, classes, and other groups have come increasingly to involve the environment on which they are based. Had Whites really tried to share the environment with the Indian, in a way that allowed them both to serve the land and not split it by their mutual divisions, they might have avoided the present resurgence of nativism, or rise of Red Power, that make relations so difficult. If Whites had not assumed that Indians ought to have given way and become 'good Americans', if they could have seen good Americans as embracing the Indian way and thus made room for Indian culture, then conflict could have been lessened and cooperation developed.

Whites will, in fact, have to learn from the Indian. They will have to husband resources; they must soon strike that kind of balance with nature which Indians long ago achieved. As we have seen, the fact that Indians kept so much of their land empty as a reserve against famine and hazard was regarded as a waste. Yet in ploughing up the sod White-man wasted aeons of soil building and brought on the dust storms that ruined – and still can ruin – hundreds of thousands. As Stuart (1938) says: 'In all the vast stretches of time since the American prairies had come into existence as a natural grassland, the western plains had accumulated but four or five inches of precious humus. The supply was not prodigal, far from it. But if it were lost could a man in his short life-time do the work on which Nature had spent thousands of years?' This question was never asked by the pioneers who went ahead breaking up the sod until the tremendous dust storms of the 1930s shocked them into doubt, if not despair. White-man had turned the prairies into a near desert.

Would he not now have to renew them? The prairies came to be seen as a fragile country on the border of drought. To keep them, parts had to be withdrawn from exploitation. Conservation demanded their return to the emptiness of Indian days. A new image had to be created, as this author (J. W. Watson, 1977) has shown: an image that, in a sense, reflected Indian ideas. Indians had been right. Emptiness was a safeguard. Emptiness was something to conserve. In an environment on the razor's edge between hazard and gain, land had to be guarded: some of it had to be kept at rest.

On the other hand Indians held – and hold – land that cried out to be cultivated and could have supported more people at a much higher standard of health and comfort, had only the Indians learned white men's ways and joined the new economy. To stand out against progress in the name of their past, only kept their sons and daughters from the future that America could promise. Nativism might preserve the tribe but it could crucify the individual, and keep him less than his times and the world might make him.

If both White and Indian would cease to think of the supposed right or wrong and learn the good that both could give they would help America to achieve a new set of values. A new social geography would be written in which a balance could be struck between Indian and White to keep them both in balance with nature.

Similarly, in the case of Black and White the old opposition will not work, for merely to oppose whiteness with a blackness still more black is division doubled and doubleness entrenched. In what way could this help America to become the 'new order of man'? Can America really afford to entrench itself in such positions? To use the title of Radford's (1971) article, though in a different sense, this would be a 'journey towards castration'; worse, the way to suicide. The entrenchment of the Blacks in a black town would more than ever establish the Whites in a white town. Should this be the urban geography of the American future? Already there is a ring of white suburbs around a black core in every major American city (see Fig. 10.1): should this be allowed to get even worse? Surely, fundamental environmental issues are here more important than race.

To allow these human divisions would be a dereliction of duty on both sides, towards the environment. The black core would get more cabined and confined, more frustrated, more lop-sided and unbalanced. It would become a region of fixed alienation. At the same time the white ring would become more homogeneous and uniform and unexciting: it would never be jerked out of its standard pattern of middle-class ideas. It could grow into a region of mere mediocrity. Its use of land, though full of landscaped lots and well-planned streets, would be the encapsulation of sameness, from the fringes of Fairbanks to the margins of Miami. Should the urban scene in America be allowed to become the bear-pit of men's pitiful boorishness towards each other? The land should stand up and cry an end to these divisions!

To ignore the essential unity of White and Black in terms of environmental standards can only hurt the sides concerned. For Blacks to isolate themselves through blackism would be in the end to undo black power. The real power of the Blacks must lie not only in their race but in the nation of which they are a part, and, of course, not only in America, but in mankind. And mankind certainly will not be able to put 'men first' if men make

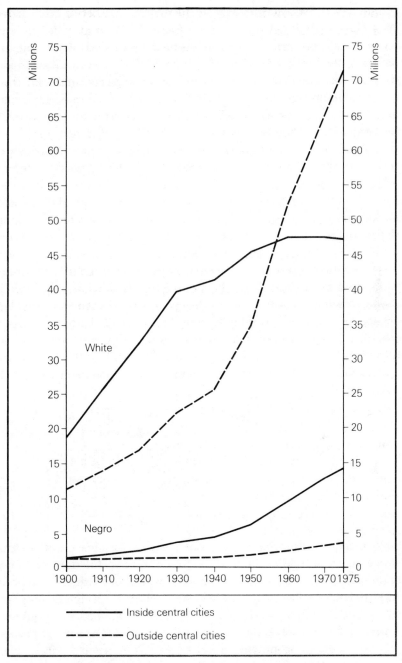

Fig. 10.1 *Population of metropolitan areas by race, 1900–1975.* A white noose around a black core – this is the situation of the American metropolis today. The white population has been declining in the centre city, the negro increasing. Although negro expansion outside the central areas has grown, it is much less than the white expansion out – now the major feature of urban America. Yet both white and black share the same city environment.

themselves the subjects principally of their race, or their cult, their creed or their class, with little concern for the earth. In this respect, Lewis (1970) offers a cogent and powerful argument. A black professor at Princeton, and long a leader of the black movement, he sees black power as a problem as well as a prop for his race. Accepting the value of self-segregation as something which helps to maintain the traditions and morale of a race, he deplores self-apartheid in cutting people off from the main stream of the nation. Although he agrees that as far as the neighbourhood is concerned, each community should have the control over its own institutions, he argues strongly that with respect to the environment as a whole Blacks should participate in country-wide institutions.

The American myth of differences bridged and divisions healed is in the balance. Although no one wants a union out of differences ignored and divisions pasted over, no one wants 'two nations warring in one bosom'. Opposites must be brought to cohere.

In this spirit, Lewis urges black youth to go to white colleges, and work in white businesses – and get to the top! In going to a white college they should really be behind that college, and make the most of it. He cannot accept 'the current attitudes of some of our black leaders to these colleges' which, in effect, destroys the main purpose of a university, i.e. to be the universe of discourse of thinking men. What black power is doing is to break up this universe of discourse, in favour of a fragmented environment – since what it asks is

> that the college should set aside a special part of itself which is to be the black part. There will be a separate building for 'black studies', and separate dormitories and living accommodation for Blacks. There will be separate teachers, all Black, teaching classes open only to Blacks. The teachers are to be chosen by the students – and will, for the most part, be men whom no African university would recognize as scholars, or be willing to hire as teachers.

Such men would not be able to put '*humanity* first', even at centres which, above all, should be devoted to the universe of knowledge, stretching across mankind. If they had their say, division would become more divided. In the end this could only castrate black men from the most significant part of man, which is *thought*, not *blood* – dooming them to be mental eunuchs in a virile America. This is certainly not the way out of the American paradox.

An environment of self-segregation – of separate classrooms, dormitories, cafeterias, sports stadiums, and, beyond the college context, of black shopping centres and black suburbs – if it should ever come about, would be a geography of self-immolation. It would black out the American dream which, from the beginning, was to be 'a city set upon a hill', a place from which light and life were to stream out to the world. Though it is true that the Blacks were, for a long time, not allowed to share that dream, they have been caught up into it by events: their real opportunity is not to shut themselves out from, but to make something more of, America. This is surely their best way of creating something still more, for mankind.

The present questioning, today's quarrel with the most cherished dogmas, the contemporary rebellion against ordered and set ways, must put the American dream in stress; yet this need not represent a set-back for that troubled dream, as many have feared, but may carry it forward to really new things. Men willing to accept and work with a split and unequal world can devise an order that will not merely contain differences but grow out of them. Let the paradox become the paradigm.

The American dream has never had it easy – least of all from Americans. Time and again it has been split by the paradox of opposing claims. But then, any real jump forward in America has come from the creative power of a paradox resolved. As the paradox grows sharper and more divisive, it forces men to find some way out that can be accepted as a common way. The common concern for, and involvement in, the environment is such a way.

The environment in jeopardy

Unfortunately, many of those who differ try to patch up affairs merely by turning away from each other and going their separate paths. They do not work things out together. The geography of separateness has had too long a history in the United States, but space will not now allow it, the environment cannot afford it. Space for flight is over! Parker (1935) claimed that one reason why communitarian societies budded off from mainstem America was that: 'The very expanse of the North American continent . . . invited social experimentation. Land, when not to be had for the asking, was dirt cheap. Natural resources seemed inexhaustible. To the dissatisfied, the gullible, the maladjusted, the adventurous, reformers offered excursion rates to Utopia.' But land is no longer cheap, nor is it inexhaustible. Although in 1862 the nation disposed of western land to the homesteaders free of cost (provided they occupied it for 5 years), by 1960 national land was being sold off at \$15 per acre, and in 1975 at \$283 (*US Statistical Abstracts*, 1976, p. 676). Open land is now everywhere dwindling. Every day 5 square miles is going under city streets or houses. America cannot afford to solve its problems by buying space. A dwindling resource-base must compel maximum community concern and effort. Unable to escape by moving away, America must stand up to its problems. All races, all classes are involved. Indeed, the world itself is caught in how can the world permit a nation which, according to Stapp (1974), 'comprises only 6 per cent of the world's population . . . to produce over 40 per cent of the world's non-human wastes and utilize close to 50 per cent of the world's consumption of natural resources'? It is not on. America must pay more respect to nature.

The American environment has been ravaged as few others have. Sometimes this was done unconsciously, by millions of individuals who cut down the forest to develop their farm, to build their house, to start up and expand their town, and to open up trade through their part in a road, canal, or railway. There was a rapid and widespread attack on the forest and on the life it harboured. The wood was much in need – it supplied housing, furniture, tools, and fuel. For over 200 years it was the basis of a wood-using economy, until coal for fuel, and iron for construction and machines, took over.

Obviously, a lot of this forest had to go. Its replacement was necessary for food, industry, and transportation. But it was cut and used in a most wasteful manner. Much of the cut-over land went into quite inferior and comparatively useless second growth, for lack of immediate reafforestation. A lot of it was so quickly and heavily eroded that it passed for ever into man-made barrens. Huge areas of rock barrens in New England and the Appalachians, and of sand barrens around the Great Lakes and the Atlantic Coastal Plain bear witness, through the permanent scars they have made on the landscape, to the thoughtless and selfish exploitation of man. And clear-cutting on the Pacific coast ranges today continues this highly exploitive system of land-robbing.

The total area of the United States is 2,271 million acres. Of this about two-thirds or over 1,500 million acres was forest. Of this only some 500 million acres is left as timberland – that is to say, a third of the original. Seventy-three per cent of this is in private hands. Although it would be in the ultimate interest of these private developers to treat their forests as tree-farms and to rotate the cutting and immediately plant the cut-out areas, many of the operators still mine the woodlands with disastrous results – not only for the woods, but for the soil from which they have sprung, which gets eroded; and for the rivers flowing through, which become polluted with wood-acids and loaded with silt. The homesteaders, too, in their anxiety to get settled and make a profit, cut down much forest and broke a lot of prairie sod in such a way that erosion and pollution quickly followed. Today, over 230 million acres of land have been so heavily eroded as to have been ruined beyond repair. This is three times as much as the total land area of the United Kingdom!

The freedom of America to make a new order of men has put the land out of order. This was, of course, not intentional. It was done on a bit-by-bit basis through masses of individual decisions. Men thought that there was 'room and enough', as indicated earlier. There was a margin and to spare. No one could see how their particular act or practice could jeopardize the whole. But it did. The damage to wildlife, which could not protect itself, was particularly serious. About 80 per cent of America's wildlife has gone. Once the balance was destroyed between wildlife, forest or prairie and stream whole species went, some of them within a generation or two. The turkey in the eastern forests – beloved of Thanksgiving and Christmas feasts, and of pioneer 'turkey-shoots' – went first, almost completely destroyed. The fated carrier pigeons of the mid-interior woodlands went next – slaughtered by the hundreds of thousands. (One of the most dramatic scenes in American literature is their massacre described in Cooper's *The Pioneers*.) Finally came the buffalo, who ended up a 'heap of bones'. These are some of the worst, but they are only a few among many, examples of how private interest and individual enterprise helped to ruin the American environment, without thought for the total and long-run effects, or of America's need for the wild as a whole.

All too frequently, killing was done not for need, but for pride. Killing for killing's sake became a vogue. The American liked to show off his virility by getting in at the kill. It should be remembered, of course, that he came from European ancestors many of whom had loved hunting, and loved it so much they had made it into a ritual of killing. In Europe, however, hunting was highly organized and controlled, mainly to keep it in the hands of the king and his aristocrats. If the ordinary man went out to hunt, as likely as not he would offend one or other of the many game laws and end up having his hand cut off, or being deported to Botany Bay. It was American to make the sport of kings the thrill of the common man. No permit was needed for rod or gun, and the freedom to kill often ended up in a licence to destroy.

America ruined

A grimmer image took hold of the mind: among the young bloods it became a *fashion* to kill. Washington Irving (Irving, 1865: 1967) in his *A Tour on the Prairies*, describes a buffalo chase in the West which he himself admitted was done for nothing more than wanton destruction. Joining a troop of soldiers that were hunting for 'a supply of provisions' he and some friends rode out to the prairie hoping to have 'plenty of sport'. (Yet he confesses later on that 'I am nothing of a sportsman'. He could not say even *that* much to account for his actions.) He was simply a young easterner delighting in the novelty of the West who 'had been prompted to this unwanted exploit by the magnitude of the game, and the excitement of an adventurous chase'. It was a young man's 'lark', in which instinct and the beat of the blood took over. After a while,

> *we perceived two buffalo bulls descending a slope. The young Count and I . . . urged our horses across the ravine, and gave chase. The immense weight of head and shoulders causes the buffalo to labour heavily up*

hill; we therefore gained rapidly upon the fugitives. The Count fired but missed. The bulls now altered course. As they ran in different directions we each singled one. I was provided with a brace of veteran brass-barrelled pistols. These are very effective in buffalo hunting as the hunter can ride up close to the animal and fire at it while at full speed. I urged my horse sufficiently near when, taking aim, to my chagrin, both pistols missed fire. However, as soon as I could prime my pistols afresh, I again spurred in pursuit of the buffalo.

Irving then describes the exhilaration of a gallop over the open prairie, an experience which brought joy enough even though the buffalo got away.

The young man was not to be daunted. He and his friend set out again. This time they surrounded an unsuspecting herd 'of about forty head, bulls, cows and calves. We quickened our pace, they broke into a gallop, and now commenced a full chase.' A Mr L. was the first to draw blood, who, 'losing ground, levelled his double-barrelled gun and fired a long raking shot'. Since it was into a bunched mass of terrified animals it could hardly miss. In fact 'it struck a buffalo just above the loins, broke its back and brought it to the ground'. This success excited young Irving still more.

Galloping along parallel to the herd, I singled out a buffalo and by a fortunate shot brought it down on the spot. The ball had struck a vital part: it would not move from the place it fell, but lay there struggling in mortal agony.

Dismounting I fettered my horse and advanced to contemplate my victim. Now that the excitement was over I could not but look with commiseration on the poor animal that lay struggling and bleeding at my feet. He lingered in his agony. Death might be long in coming. It would not do to leave him to be torn piecemeal, while yet alive, by the wolves that had already snuffed his blood and were skulking and howling at a distance.

The young hunter therefore dispatched him with another bullet.

'While I stood . . . over the wreck I had so wantonly produced,' Irving goes on, 'I was rejoined by a fellow sportsman who soon managed to carve out the tongue of the buffalo and delivered it to me to bear back to the camp as a trophy.' The rest of the beast was left to the wolves and the ravens. As a result of attacks like this, which, as the author admits, were so often so *wantonly* mounted, the buffalo perished by their millions, and became all but extinct. The geography of the land changed in a generation: a part of the environment had simply been wiped out from the American scene.

Of course wildlife and forests and prairie can be renewed – though only at great cost. But non-renewable resources were hunted out and destroyed in just as reckless ways. Minerals and fuels were cut into with equal savagery. The capitalist system which had begun in Europe, and there too dug into coal and iron with a vengeance, reached its peak in America; mainly because of America's values – the American belief in growth, in expansion, in newness, in labour-saving devices, and a high standard of material comfort. These are all resource-gobbling values. The growth mentality, especially, though it has built up many Americans, has near-ruined much of America. The country has gone through over three-quarters of its oil, two-thirds of its high-grade iron, two-thirds of its copper, lead, and zinc, and over half of its usable coal – and this in only 200 years of its national existence. Its use of oil has been absolutely prodigious: with only 6 per cent of the world's population, America uses 32 per cent of all the world's energy: Western Europe, with 8 per cent of the world's people, only uses 20 per cent – although this, too, is out of all proportion to the population concerned. America is burning up so much of its own oil that it is becoming a major importer. In 1975 home production was a little more than 3 billion barrels, and imports were 2.3 billion (see Fig. 10.2):

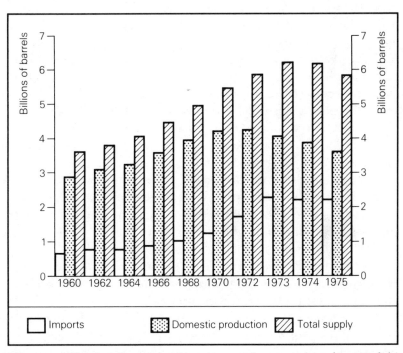

Fig. 10.2 *The changing supply of petroleum, 1960–1975.* American exploitation and consumption of fuel and other natural resources are the highest in the world: American growth is thus a pressure on the world environment, a fact behind the rise of the Zero Growth Society in the USA, pressing for limits to national growth. This is an almost unheard-of thing in the American myth, which took expansion for granted.

These imports had climbed from 0.2 billion barrels in 1950 – or more than a ten times rise! This went with a jump in Btu equivalents from 88 units per head in 1950 to 158 in 1975 (see *US Statistical Abstracts*, 1976, pp. 548–50). The American thirst for energy is quite fantastic, and it is rising sharply with each decade. Americans drive cars that require three times the amount of gasolene per mile that the average European car needs: they use twice as much oil or coal to heat their houses as Europeans do. *US News* (1977) recently noted that the 'typical male adult of the 1970's ... elbowed his way in, saying I want it all – all of it that's good in all aspects of life. This hymn to the "Me Generation" may be taken as one more bit of evidence that, for more and more Americans, self-fulfillment means self-indulgence.. . .' Here is a reckless disregard for the environment which eventually obliged President Carter to intervene.

Resources have been thought of not as part of the national heritage but as individual or company property. Although the individual states were the heritors of 400 million acres of crown land at the Revolution, and the federal government became the repository of nearly 1,800 million acres more of public domain, with fuel and mineral deposits, forest and rangeland to lease, the social values of the day called for the disposal of public land into private hands. Today 58.2 per cent of America is in private hands, operated for private profit, that is, for unique ends, involving unique views and feelings. As Jessie Watson (J. Watson, 1977) says: 'Based on these views and feelings people develop values. Based on these values they make choices. These choices affect the earth; they change the landscape.' Hence the importance of values for social geography. The environment had been valued chiefly for the individual. Indeed, in the 1840s Josiah Warren went so far as to promulgate the doctrine of the 'sovereignty of the individual', with unqualified supremacy over institutions and the state. This paralleled strong and repeated demands for the disposal of public lands for private use. Privatism went with initiative, enterprise, and production. As Adam Smith (Smith, 1776) said – who had championed the end of mercantile controls in the colonies, in favour of individual opportunity – private enterprise was the best way of ensuring the public good. 'Self interest', he wrote, 'when left uncontrolled will necessarily lead proprietors to prefer that species of employment which is most favourable to national industry because it is at the same time most profitable for themselves.'

America has proved the truth of this in the highest standard of living in the world. But that standard has been dearly bought. It has privatized space to such an extent that many have no access to the world of nature which all Americans once enjoyed. Indians were displaced from the space they had treasured and protected. Negroes had to slave over the space Whites parcelled up for themselves. Protestants fought off Catholics from the space they graced. The upper class palisaded space with privilege. The division of space divided the nation. A 'two-valued logic' of 'individual rights against collective needs' so split up the environment that the ecology of wholeness had little chance to make itself felt. Instead, city slums and rural barrens became the life-space of millions.

As Platt (1976) points out, 'By the late nineteenth century land was moving out of the public domain at an incredible pace.' Between the Civil War and the present the dispositions have been – 125 million acres to trans-west railways, 100 million acres of Indian lands alienated for mining, ranching and farming, 300 million acres granted to homesteaders under the Homestead Act, and 240 million acres for other purposes, a total of 765 million acres. On the local scale, developers had used up most of the open spaces in America's cities, both in the city centres and at the city margins.

Deterioration of the urban environment

Americans became very concerned about the matter in the late nineteenth century. The urban environment grew progressively worse. Cities took over all the green space they could in their rush to build roads and put up houses. Apart from the 'meeting-house green' of the New England town, or the 'court-house green' of the Southern town, there were few open spaces left to the citizen. Towns became astonishingly crowded for a country that had such a spread of land. This was in part due to the lack of transportation: there was little commuting from country to town and back again until the advent of the branch-line railroad, in the 1840s–1860s; people had to live close to work, within the town limits. It also resulted from the high price of land as the real-estate speculators subdivided lots as much as they could to sell to status-seeking movers for as great a profit as possible. Even poor immigrants were charged 'the earth' for accommodation: since so few could pay, houses were divided up and lots made narrower and narrower so that rent or mortgage payments seemed minimal – but of course the gain per split-up street or apartment was enormous. All forest within cities and the edge of swamps were filled in and built on. Only a few towns like Boston, with its commons, or New York, with its Battery Park, had any significant open land, and even here the urbanized areas, especially close to docks, warehouses, factories, and offices, became extremely crowded. Row-houses of three or four storeys, split up into apartments, often reached by outside stairs, became the style. These were built along the sidewalk with no front gardens, and had only restricted back yards. Houses with gardens were divided, and their 'backs' built up by tenements reached only through narrow alleys.

Mention has already been made of the way in which the quite generous long lots of the Philadelphia householders became infilled with crowded dwellings along darkened lanes. The merchant on the front street would have his servants, his artisans and their apprentices live in 'the backs'. Later, when the merchant moved to the suburb, his great house was subdivided into rooms, and a rooming-house area would grow up. Later still, speculators bought out these old disordered tangled assemblages of crowded rooms and apartments and sold to developers who tore them down and replaced them with tall, close-set, working-class tenements. Private profit ruled. The old parts of the towns grew more and more dense, noisy, smelly, and ill-lit.

Here was one of the worst examples of a double-standard society – with the lowest standards for the immigrant, the foreign-born, the uneducated, and the poor, in the most crowded part of the city, at and around the city centre, and the highest standards for the Protestant, Anglo-Saxon, native-born Whites who had fled to the suburbs full of peace and light and the grace of space.

In Warner's (1971) account of Philadelphia he mentions that by the end of the eighteenth century the density of housing on excessively divided lots had 'destroyed the hopes of Penn and his surveyors for a "green town"'. A widening abyss separated rich from poor. 'The upper tenth of the tax-paying households owned 89 per cent of the taxable property. Philadelphia was a pyramid of wealth.' This grew worse in the nineteenth century when wealthy developers ' . . . ran up the infamous "Father-Son-and Holy Ghost" three-room house', on the narrowest of subdivisions. 'Row houses on twelve-foot frontages were not uncommon, and building went forward on the most cramped basis.' The results were appalling. 'The crowding of the land exceeded the sanitary capabilities of the town. The streets and alleys reeked of garbage, manure, and night soil, and some private and public wells must have been dangerously polluted.'

The social geography of ill-health

This resulted from the ill-thinking of society. This is brought out most dramatically in one of America's first novels, Charles Brockdon Brown's (Brown, 1887) account of Philadelphia in his *Arthur Mervyn*. In order to gain credit with one of a pair of sisters, Mervyn goes into the then disease-ridden city to rescue the lover of the elder sister. From humble origins in the countryside he moves in among the mansions of the rich, aware suddenly of profound class differences. 'How wide and how impassable was the gulf by which they were separated.' Those 'who had the means of purchasing an asylum in the country had fled the town'. Even in their extremity people did not seem to come together; indeed, panic widened their divisions. The ugly face of individualism showed itself. The very hospital was a scene of selfish disarray. Wallace, the man Mervyn had been seeking, was confined there: he struggled to get out. The attendants 'who were hired, at enormous wages, to tend the sick and convey away the dead, neglected their duty, and consumed the cordials which were provided for the patients. . . .' Wallace imputed the disease 'to filthy streets, airless habitations, and squalid persons'. Mervyn found the whole city

'involved in confusion and panic. Magistrates and citizens were flying to

the country. The numbers of the sick multiplied beyond all example. The usual occupations and amusements of life were at an end. Terror had exterminated all the sentiments of nature. Wives were deserted by husbands, and children by parents. Some had shut themselves into their houses and debarred themselves from all communication with the rest of mankind. Men seized by the disease . . . were denied entrance into their own dwellings; they perished in the public ways. None could be found to remove the lifeless bodies. Their remains, suffered to decay by piecemeal, filled the air with deadly exhalations.. . .'

The memoirs of 1793 were a terrible reflection on new-born America: was this the 'new order of men'?

Meantime the mounds of unremoved garbage increased, and the polluted wells spread the poison. Diseases of water pollution, or of lack of sewage disposal, have in the main gone from the city, with the introduction of public water and sewage, and the proper treatment of the water supply and removal of effluent. However, the diseases of air pollution have increased, particularly with the motor age and the noxious gases emitted by diesel- and gasolene-using machines. In the light of this it is almost amusing to think that the horse was once blamed for urban pollution. As Swan recounts 'horse manure was a breeding site for flies, as well as for tetanus and other pathogenic bacterial growth'. But those days seem almost enviable, bad as they may have been, compared with the smog-filled hours that afflict the motor-polluted city of today. Chronic asthma, bronchitis, pneumonia, and lung cancer are prevailing diseases today – and none more so than in the inner city.

The disordered city with its wear and tear on the nerves is the scene of many mental disorders, such as *anorexia nervosa* among young people – especially among teenage girls in stress – and nervous breakdowns at an older age, associated frequently with the sudden loss of jobs due to technological redundancy, or the sheer pace of city life and its endless round of status competition. City tensions help to increase the incidence of heart attacks, strokes, and diabetes mellitus, and deaths by peptic ulcer and cancer of the bowels. It is interesting to note how the high death rates in the different regions of the United States coincide with those having the greatest number of centre-cites in metropolitan environments (deaths per 100,000):

The mid-Atlantic States (NY, NJ, Philadelphia, Baltimore, Washington) are first for heart, cancer, and diabetes fatalities; and second for cirrhosis of the liver.

- New England (Boston, etc.) is first for pneumonia, second for cancer, and third for heart, diabetes, and cirrhosis of the liver.
- The West Central States (Detroit, Chicago, Milwaukee) are second for heart, cerebro vascular, pneumonia, and bron-

chitis/emphysema, and third for cancer and diabetes.
• The East Central States (Cleveland, Columbus, Cincinnati) are second for diabetes, third for bronchitis/emphysema, and a near-third for heart, cancer and cirrhosis of the liver.

Table 10.1 Death rates per 100,000 by regions by types of disease

	Heart	Cancer	Cere-bro/vascular	Pneu-monia	Dia-betes mellitus	Cir-rhosis of the liver	Bron-chitis/emphy-sema
USA	349.2	170.5	98.1	25.9	17.7	15.8	12.7
New England	372.0	191.0	95.0	33.6	18.8	17.7	11.5
Mid-Atlantic	407.4	194.5	89.8	29.5	20.5	19.2	11.1
East NC	364.8	168.9	97.3	23.4	19.7	14.7	13.3
West NC	376.7	175.3	117.7	30.9	18.0	10.2	14.2
S. Atlantic	337.5	167.8	100.4	25.3	17.8	16.6	12.6
East SC	351.8	164.3	124.0	25.2	17.8	10.4	12.5
West SC	313.0	157.5	104.1	25.4	16.7	11.3	12.2
Mountain	243.0	127.6	72.1	23.4	13.5	14.7	15.3
Pacific	297.3	159.2	89.4	20.7	12.1	20.4	13.4

US Statistical Abstracts, 1976, Table 94, p. 66.

These figures in Table 10.1 point up the widespread degradation in America's urbanized environment. At least some relief from this could be obtained if that environment were opened up and cleaned and made green again and people could get more recreation in areas of light and air. Citizens realized that the rim of 'sin and slum' around the American CBD had to be broken. The suburbs, too, could not be allowed to subdivide all the land at the city's edge and put it under streets and houses. In 1840, while building its waterworks, Philadelphia took in extra land and turned it into Fairmount Park, the first formal effort to create open space for urban recreation in America. In 1863, the huge Central Park in New York was set aside from the private speculation in land moving towards Harlem and Morningside. In the 1890s, the 'city beautiful' idea led to a widespread acceptance of the need for city parks. Spearheaded by Olmsted, parkland was set aside and landscaped in almost every major city. This was a triumph of the collective need against individual interests – nevertheless, the land used was generally what was otherwise unusable, i.e. the bottom of ravines, around swamps, or on rocky exposures. Also much of it was away from the centre-cities out towards the metropolitan fringe. Few slum dwellers could afford to take advantage of municipal benevolence and pay the fare to remote open spaces. The reconstitution of built-over land was needed around the CBD itself – something that few cities felt they could afford.

Although parks continued to be made, they were made largely for those with the means to get to them. Even the parks developed under Roosevelt's New Deal tended to be urban-fringe rather than centre-city ones. By the Second World War urban-fringe parks were so extensive that they were being used by one in twelve of all city people. That war put a halt to further growth and after it, park development increased by only about a fifth the rate of built-over land. Urban freeways became the great competitor for urban land. Eight- to twelve-lane freeways with central dividing boulevards gobbled up peripheral land. Moreover, since they had to run into the heart of the city, they wanted the use of those very river- or creek-bottom sites which had been left for parks: these depressed trenches, so characteristic of the seaboard and lakeshore cities (where the land had risen after glaciation and the creeks had cut themselves into their beds), gave ideal access to city centres without having to cut swathes through housing or fly over existing roads. Many parks were in fact diminished by being turned into parkways – i.e. landscaped speed tracks for commuter traffic. Once again an either/or situation developed, people had to choose *either* car-space *or* play-space. The predominance of the suburban middle-class tax-paying car-owner over the centre-city subsidized slum-dweller left city councils little choice!

The Environment revitalized

It was therefore not until the federal government showed a new initiative, as late in time as 1960, that much was done to ensure the Black, the foreign-born, the urban Indian, and the poor-White of the inner city something of the same opportunity for green space that the middle- and upper-class Americans possessed. Kennedy represented the new mentality, namely that *both* Non-White and White, *both* foreign-born *and* native-born, *both* poor *and* rich had a right to the American environment. 'In every plan for urban redevelopment', the President proclaimed, 'parks and recreation must have their place.' In 1961 Congress amended the existing Housing Act to provide $50 million for the acquisition of urban open space, while in 1965 an Open Space Land Program was linked with the Housing and Urban Development (HUD) administration. Progress was slow. This was one of the many disappointments that led to the negro riots of the 1960s. Appalled by them Congress declared in 1970 'a need for the additional provision of parks and other open space in the built-up portions of urban areas, especially in low-income neighbourhoods'. Since then there has been distinct, though at times interrupted, progress in the situation. Individuals have been taxed to cater for the need of the community.

Meanwhile, in the far vaster non-urban lands, movements have also gone on to give Americans access to the natural environment in every region of the country. It was the beauty and magnificence – and at the same time emptiness – of the Mountain West that made Americans determined to preserve some of their unspoiled scene as a heritage forever. Although a good deal of western land had been leased, especially for ranching and lumbering, Congress authorized the President in 1891 to withdraw a large part of this for 'forest reservations'. This process has gone on until today about 502 million acres are set aside for forest and wildlife (see Fig. 10.3). Access has been made for the public, although in a controlled way, to enable people to enjoy the woods, open range, and alpine pastures as part of their heritage: 164 million acres have been reserved as rangeland. In 1869, the first of America's great national parks, at Yellowstone, was preserved for the nation. Since then, 286 additional parks have been set up in all regions of the nation, covering over 25 million acres: these include 16 national recreation areas, with 3.9 million acres.

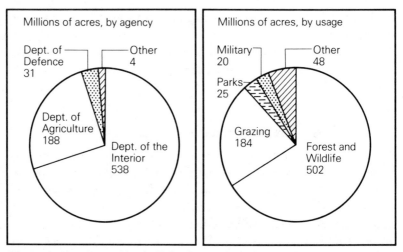

Fig. 10.3 *Land owned by the Federal government, 1975.* The national bank of land, owned by the American people, which had dwindled rapidly in the late eighteenth and through the nineteenth centuries, is again being built up – a triumph for American concern for the community as a whole.

A major step forward in public initiative came when Eisenhower established the Outdoor Recreation Resources Review Commission (ORRRC) in 1958. Its statute was based on the will to 'preserve, develop, and assure accessibility to all American people of present and future generations such quality and quantity of outdoor recreation resources as will be necessary and desirable for individual enjoyment and to ensure the spiritual, cultural and physical benefits such outdoor recreation provides'. In 1963 Congress passed the Outdoor Recreation Act and set up a Bureau to carry its measures into effect. Progress in public responsibility was rapid. In 1965, the Land and Water Conservation Act was authorized to fund the acquisition of public land and the supply of public facilities for the enjoyment of the environment. In

1969 came the really influential National Environmental Policy Act to look at the total needs for the revival of the American environment. This insisted on an environmental impact survey before any new development could take place and coordinated plans for different kinds of land-use, so that a view of the whole could be obtained.

The test of concern has always been self-sacrifice. Americans are now taxing themselves, and that means sacrificing some of the money they would have spent on individual interests, to spend on the public good. A case in point is the spending on pollution (see Table 10.2). Only a decade ago there was virtually no expenditure for the abatement of water or air pollution.

Table 10.2. Federal and state obligation for pullution control (in billions of dollars)

	Water			Air		
	1960	1970	1975	1960	1970	1975
Federal	–	0.7	5.2	–	0.2	0.3
State	–	0.1	0.6	–	0.02	0.07

The mind of America is changing. There is now a very strong public commitment to the revival and maintenance of the environment. People care. Moreover, they participate. Americans have gone out into the country as never before. Whereas in 1950 the number of visits to the national parks came to 33 millions, by 1975 this had grown to 238.8 millions. Day visits to state parks had climbed from 114.3 millions to 482.5 millions in the same period. Altogether 205.6 million people had gone out into the countryside on one or more visits! Of these 7.7 millions had moved into wilderness America to camp in remote areas where they could really be at one with nature, and 26.7 millions had gone on nature walks to get into the heart of the woods.

This fully justified the Wilderness Act of 1964 which empowered the country to preserve for ever the really wild parts of America as a means of keeping that balance between people and the land which was so necessary for a new wholeness in the nation.

America restored

The recreative powers of nature became increasingly acknowledged and have been widely sought, from the end of the nineteenth century. An example of this is seen in Marquand's (1937: 1958) *The Late George Apley*. This story, already referred to, starts about the end of Thoreau's generation and runs on into the 1920s. It thus covers a period in which the family 'camp' in the woods was at the height of its influence, profoundly affecting both the people and the land. It tells of a wealthy and patrician family in Boston, the

Apleys, who try to keep not only their fortune, but their traditions, going, over the changing years. One of their most constant and unfailing sources of strength is their camp in the woods. To this they return again and again, as a spring of constant regeneration, since they feel that it keeps them down-to-earth, self-reliant, adaptive, sane, and free. Here colour, class and creed do not matter; what counts is a man's ability to get on terms with nature.

The camp itself has an Indian name, *Pequod*, borrowed from the Pequod Tribe that early resisted civilization – believing in the integrity of its own, natural, ways. (Incidentally, how different Marquand's *Pequod* of refuge was from Melville's *Pequod* of revenge: the change of symbol is most significant.) In Marquand the heart of civilization is linked up with the heart of the wilds. The camp is far up in hardly accessible, rugged, back-country uplands, 'on a jewel of an island nestled in the clear blue waters of one of Maine's wilderness lakes'. It originated from a canoe trip in September when the maples would have been a vibrant red and the birch a rich gold.

> *We were weary indeed as the canoes neared the golden bow of beach that fringed the wooded slopes of Pequod Island, but it was a carefree, happy weariness. As we went for a dip in the lake, while the guides busied themselves expertly with putting up tents, cutting soft beds of balsam boughs and preparing trout, coffee, and flapjacks for supper, we were alone in a Wilderness of woods and water, alone save for the mournful call of the loons and the splash of an occasional fish.*

They were completely away from traffic and business and the whole façade – and the need to keep up the façade – of the city, and at once George Apley decided to buy the island as his refuge and strength.

This is but one example of the millions of individuals in America who have staked their claim in the wilderness as a means of regenerating themselves, and in this way helped to regenerate the wild as a vital part of the American landscape.

At first Apley thought of his wilderness island as 'a haven for *men*, since he was under the illusion that its facilities were too rough and ready to appeal to the fairer sex'. However, the women and children would not be shut out, they too felt the need for regeneration. Soon a large central lodge had been built from trees cleared away from the beach, and a pier constructed, and boats brought into the wild. 'Everyone arriving at Pequod Island dock recalls the sign, made in rustic cedar twigs, "All ye who step upon this pier, leave the world behind".'

Actually that ideal was hard to maintain; the retreat became a rendezvous, cottages were built around the main lodge, and guests were invited up for the summer. The place became virtually a *Chatauqua*, except that it was visited only upon invitation. 'Poetry, philosophy, music, art and diplomacy, all have passed beneath the giant pines which guard the door.' As a result, George Apley whose 'love for the woods and solitude became more and more pronounced', organized a group within the group at Pequod Island, known as the 'camping crowd'. With its canoes and tents this lot left the island for days, and sometimes for weeks, for untouched beaches and streams. Here the host, with like-minded friends, could get away to what they longed for – 'the dripping water from a canoe paddle, the scent of balsam, the sweet smell of pond lilies and mud, and the weariness of a long carry'.

Later, when the son, John Apley, wanted to spend his holiday yachting at Bar Harbour, he was urged not to neglect the wilderness retreat. The father, George, wrote to him, saying, 'What worries me about your not going to Pequod Island is that I am afraid you are neglecting a certain duty which you owe to others. Our little community at Pequod Island requires the co-operation of everyone to keep it together.'

The circle has come full round. The descendant of those Puritans who had at one time abjured nature now felt it was a duty to retire there, year by year, and keep up the wilderness habit. Boston, which had once hacked away the trees, now felt the trees were part of a heritage that had to be maintained. This change in mind, changed the whole land, and kept bits of Maine and Vermont and the Green Mountains and the Berkshires going, that might otherwise have ended up as cut-over barrens or deserts of erosion.

With this new attitude to nature, nature could take on a different role in the land. It was seen to be as important as the city, indeed, to help the city redress its wrongs. If given the chance, nature could put to rights what injuries the city had done; it could restore a balanced world, a whole environment. In this, it *is* tremendously important. Indeed, few things are of greater importance. Hence the nation-wide effort to improve the countryside, and gain back from it the renewing many people had lost.

The matter is becoming more and more urgent. As the cities have moved out into the country, the countryside has grown less effective. It has itself been tainted. The camp in the woods has become an outpost of the house in the city. George Apley recognized this, and it worried him. To try to prevent city ways invading the wilderness he insisted 'there should be no drinking of liquor and no smoking'. But city habits prevailed. 'I had thought on first coming to Pequod Island', he wrote to a friend, 'that we might get away from things, that we might have a moment's breathing space . . . I suppose this was rather too much to hope for. It sometimes seems to me that Boston has come to Pequod Island.' It was for this reason he formed his own breakaway group to get off to go to Maine, 'it became his habit to arise each Saturday morning at four o'clock in the spring and autumn to bicycle to Caleb Goodrich's woods in Milton [a small place in the Boston surrounds] where he could gratify his love of nature and solitude'.

For many Americans, Boston has gone to Pequod. Their own little camp in the wood has become citified, to some extent or other. Consequently, there has been the cry for true wilderness areas, beyond the impress of man. Many are not even content with national or state parks because these only preserve a semblance of nature, not nature itself. Such parks have their lodges and cafés, their gasolene stations and roads, their caravan sites and tenting places, all marked out and fenced off, with every city convenience. The idea of truly wild areas is now taking over, with wilderness parks where man can really get to grips with nature.

If this cannot be arranged, asks the writer, Hardin, how will the youth of America test itself? As urban guerillas, in race riots and class wars that ravage the nation? But if there were true wilderness parks, then people could learn to lose themselves in, – more, unite themselves with, – nature, and thus renew the oldest of human relationships, that between man and the earth. Consequently, Americans have begun to preserve the wilderness, before it should disappear from their midst. 'In wildness', said Thoreau (1854:1966) 'is our preservation.' The Thoreau II movement of today, stressing Thoreau's claim, together with the Wilderness Society, have come back to this: hence its value for twentieth-century geography.

Thoreau was no romantic; he recognized that to stay in the country could be soul-destroying where 'the better part of man is ploughed into the soil for compost', and the sheer struggle for existence could crowd out life. However, he wanted to break man from having 'no time to be anything but a machine'. The main advantage of country existence would be 'to learn what are the gross necessaries of life', and get at and keep the fundamentals – the *real* fundamentals, 'not the sunrise and the dawn, merely, but Nature herself!'

Thoreau kept asking how much better off people were who broke their health and ruined their peace of mind (trying to get clothes and houses and equipment far beyond their real need) than the savages who, having the necessities, could live the life they liked. In fact, since in America, 'the luxury of one class is counterbalanced by the indigence of another', it was 'a mistake to suppose that . . . the condition of a very large body of the inhabitants may not be as degraded as that of savages'. In many respects it was worse, and Americans could well take a leaf from the Indian's book of living. This respect for the Indian as a man to be emulated, being the man of nature, was in itself significant; to so many Puritans he had been nothing better than 'a limb of Satan'. (Here was a marked change; though, coming in 1854, it was too late to save anything but a remnant of the Indian race. It is strong today, however.)

Fortunately for Thoreau there was (near Concord where he had lived) a pond in the woods which was in the no-man's-land between two towns, and so had not been caught up into the toils of the speculator and the developer. He took up life here until he had sorted himself out. 'I went to the woods', he wrote, 'because I wished to live deliberately, to front only the essential facts of life . . . I did not wish to live what was not life. I wanted to live deep and suck out all the marrow of life.' Few could do as he did and take years out to find in the wisdom of woods the meaning of their days. Nevertheless, many followed him to this extent, they sought out some wild spot, and put up a cabin there, and took their family into retreat with them, for an annual holiday. To this day millions of Americans stream out of their cities every summer and try, by going into the woods, once again to recapture something of the simplicity and refreshment found at the hand of nature. Here they wear the fewest clothes, live in a log hut, chop their own wood, cook over an open fire, canoe up river, fish in pool or lake, and go for walks along nature trails, looking for a loon's nest or a beaver's lodge.

As a result, woods are at a premium. There is a desperate attempt to preserve them. People buy up sections of farm wood lots or, in the case of run-down places, take the whole farm over and replant it in forest. Second-growth scrub beside logging rivers or lakes, where logging companies have cut out the timber beyond replacement, will sell as well as city property, even if there are only logging roads in. A whole new geography has come to spring up, centred in the restoration of the tree, after the frontier onslaught had virtually destroyed the forest. In helping to re-create man, nature was itself recreated.

The environment and mindscape America

The change in appreciation of the environment is due to a change in attitude to it. Of great significance is the fact that the year after the Environmental Policy Act there came, in 1970, the Environmental Education Act. The leaders of the country realized that practice depended upon ideas. The American nation could never unite in trying to keep land and people in balance until the American mind could overcome its differences and create a new approach to individual and community. As Morrissett and Wiley (1971) say, '. . . with the divisiveness of present issues, such as war, poverty and racial discrimination, the country feels a need for some significant issue which can "bring us together"'.

That need inspired new views of education which tried to change it from the transmission of information to the creation of ideas (see Fig. 10.4). To study the environment meant to look at it in the round. It involved learning the values of White and Indian or White and Black towards each other and to the land; it meant perceiving the values of different religious groups, or of different social classes embroiled in the struggle for space; it had to see what women, and youth, and age expected of the world or could concede to society: it had to set a new value on values. Indeed, 'the roots of the environmental problem' and of our need to adjust to it, lie in our value-system. 'Through various social mechanisms we determine what things are to be valued and

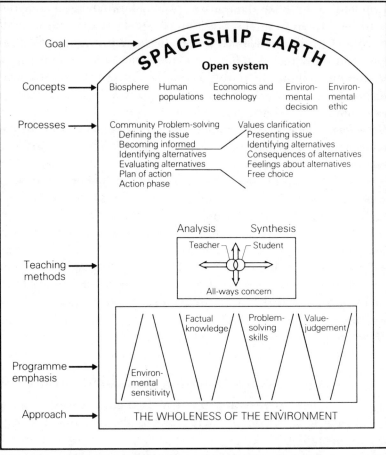

Fig. 10.4 *Space-ship Earth*. 'Space-ship Earth', featured in a new environmental educational model, stresses the need for all nations, races, classes, and creeds to recognise their dependence on each other in their dependence on the environment. Travelling together they should pay more attention to the earth which is the ultimate vehicle of their progress.

what things are not, whose values are to dominate and whose are to be subordinate, and which values will be given support and which will be discouraged.' An education that leads to this kind of debate is essential today. Social geography can help to further it, because it shows how values have kept the environment in balance or thrown it out of kilter, and, above all, because it looks at the *total* impact of these values upon the landscape. It is a major way of providing 'the holistic approach to problem solving' seen as a principal need in modern education. It provides the three main approaches demanded by the National Schools Public Relations Association (1971) in its publication *Environment and the Schools*, namely (1) How the environment operates, the basic ecology; (2) how man uses his environment, the technical skills; and (3) how man values his environment, the cultural frame. 'To cope with the problems of pollution, land misuse, and deterioration of aesthetics, one must learn in systems of interacting factors.. . .' This is the key.

In the environment, all things cohere. And the realization of this has been one of the great new forces to revolutionize America or, perhaps one should say, to keep the revolutionary American going. The challenge of the environment has been repeated in every generation, but has never been to the fore so much as today. Whatever the Indian or the Black may think of the White, this does not now so affect their future as what they all think of the environment. The class struggle cannot mean as much as the struggle for the environment. The growth of cities, the health of people, and their education and prospects, all relate to the environment. This is the encompassing thing that will draw all together, whatever their differences. The way in which nature, even when harmed, tries to bind everything together in the grand ecology of terrestrial unity, has worked upon the hunger of human nature for wholeness.

Yet this is difficult to achieve. It means having to contain coexisting difference, that is to say, holding in one hand White and Non-white, upper and lower class, authoritative age and rebel youth, as the ecosystem holds tearing down and building up, predator and prey. To quote Bruce Hutchison, though out of context, the ego system is easier than the ecosystem. The 'I am right, they are wrong' world is the easiest to accept. This was why in the Salem of the Puritans, those who differed were burned as witches. 'The Salem tragedy', according to Miller (1959), 'developed from a paradox. It is a paradox in whose grip we still live . . . for the balance has yet to be struck between order and freedom.' The tempting ease of choosing a right or wrong system which led the Puritans to believe 'they held in their steady hands the candle that would light the world' has remained with America since. 'We have inherited this belief and it has helped and hurt us.' It has helped in giving America a sense of mission and in providing it with a code of discipline. But it has hurt in making America too self-righteous and too self-centred. As a result America has often been moved to deny to Americans *their* idea of *their* freedom where these have countered America as a whole. This was the danger that led to the Salem witch-hunt, and, in modern times, to McCarthy's Committee on Un-American Activities. But, as Miller insists, America cannot be run on the 'plane of heavenly combat between Lucifer and the Lord'.

The Lucifer/Lord confrontation long put Protestant against Catholic, Gentile against Jew, White against Black, and the upper against the lower classes in cities divided and divided yet again, marked by the geography of competition and conflict. It is difficult to get away from the I–They mentality which splits the American city up into its ethnic ghettos and class districts with little regard for the environment that contains them – unless we think environmentally, unless we put the ecosystem first. Ghettos must be broken down. Black, Jew, Catholic, the foreign-born, the poor must have their values considered, their choices known. Human nature can go beyond a nature which leaves each to find its level. In a city developed as a whole environment, to bring out the whole man in us, each should have the equality to live where he chooses – not cooped up where he is shoved. This choice should not relate to a person's power to choose, but to his right to choose. It should not depend on the economic gradient – on a man's power to earn the level of his choice, but the public grace to give him the choice of his level. The whole of urban space must be socialized. Blacks have as much right to the suburbs as Whites; the poor to a 'room with a view' as much as the well-to-do. Mass development of the suburbs for the poor should match the vast private housing 'estates' for the well-to-do. The city must get away from the dualisms of one group *against* another, of one *better* than another, of one *more privileged* than another, to both groups in living association with each other. Each must be balanced in terms of striking a better balance with the environment.

It is unfortunate, as Pole (1967) remarks, that the American historians of all but the present generation have read into history an essentially two-sided view of happenings. He instances Beard who saw the American story as very much a 'dichotomy of opposed forces'. The broad and rough outline of a division discernible in the later eighteenth century, between mercantile and agrarian interests, became for Beard a precursor of the class war.. . . In lining up the two sides Beard assumed that the mercantile and moneyed interests, because 'capitalist', were conservative, and by inference opposed to the democratic principles of American progress; which meant that the agricultural interest was the popular and democratic side in the struggle. As a result of 'yielding his powerful intellect so easily to the idea of a recurring dichotomy' in American politics Beard 'by-passed . . . the immense weight of landed interest that was thrown behind the Constitution . . .', a fact that ought to have opposed a dualistic interpretation of events.

Alastair Taylor (Taylor, 1969) has a good deal to say along such lines. America grew up, as he points out, in the heyday of a 'two-valued logic'. This went back to 'Kant's celebrated antinomies in a number of dichotomies, such as freedom versus organization, individual rights as against collective needs, linear theories of progress versus the cyclical *Weltanschauung* of a Spengler'. Polarization was seen in the landscape in terms of the open range and the fenced-in lot; private property and communal holdings; owner and tenant; the city versus the country; protected industry versus free trade; the Gold Coast and the Slum. A two-valued geography grew up, that cleft the American scene. Views about these things were held with the finality of 'Newtonian or Euclidean absolutes'. Hence the difficulty in bridging the gap between the poor and the rich, White and Black, private enterprise and public control. However, 'Newtonian absolutes have been replaced by Einstein's model of relativity and Riemannian geometry'. If in the physical sciences 'we have seen how the Quantum and Relativity theories have supplied us with a new world-view of reality', representing a 'fundamental shift of thought', then in the social sciences we should be prepared for 'the dismemberment of two-valued forms of orientation, as expressed in Aristotelian logic, or Hobbesian . . . either/or sovereignty and war/peace modalities'. Taylor goes on to claim that 'the growing discrepancies between formal, traditional precepts and actual, societal performance reflect a dangerous ideational lag in our present society'.This is manifested, for example, in the traditional educational system that supports 'two-valued orientations, and behaviour patterns emphasizing either/or action rather than multi-relation transactions'. He would argue that we must find a new context for the American dream: we must move on to the world of the multiverse, of relativities, and discontinuities; he calls 'for the construction of a new model of reality'.

This is a very difficult position to take; many say that it implies no firm standards and is simply a permission for more permissiveness. They are concerned about the breakdown of the home, the changing views of sex, the scorn for private property, the liberties people take with tradition, and the challenge against authority. These are very disturbing matters. They make many want to go back to a right or wrong state. But let them go back far enough; let them hear the sermon Robinson preached to the Pilgrim Fathers as they were about to set out for America. It is a sermon that has done more for American geography than almost any other force, because it urged men to follow the light that was *yet to break forth*. And isn't that what the whole American experiment has been about? Is this not the drive that is trying to create new relationships between the sexes, and the ages, between White and Indian, White and Black, Protestant, Catholic and Jew, the élite and the common man, and between all these and their environment? Here is the compelling thrust in American thought which is remaking the American landscape. Of course this means shattering many former and often cherished concepts. And, because the breakaway is so severe, because it may take the form of extreme movements, like the anarchist or free-love communes already described, or simply the far-out views of disaffected groups, many reject it and want to 'get back to the basics'.

Such values, however distressful – invoking as they do futures of change and as well as calling on the bulwarks of the past – are of deep concern to geographers, because they are the making of geography: they are writing the future into the landscape in forces and forms that have got to come to terms with the past; they are creating a new scene in which, as never before, man has the burden of the whole environment upon him to make an environment of wholeness.

Fortunately Americans are aware of this. They also know that America has held together tensions as fierce as these before and out of them made a great jump forward. Watergate has shown that Americans do have a profound sense of right and are willing to follow it to the very overthrow of their President. This has resulted from their passion for equality and love of liberty, the twin pillars of their state. Liberty may have bred conflict, but equality has called for cooperation; and out of these America coheres.

In his Inaugural Address President Carter spoke of his hope to further 'The American Dream'. He spoke as if it were a living thing, environing the life of all Americans. There is an environment of the mind as real as sticks and stones which, given scope, can remake the environment of the land. Mindscape America is not a figment: it is the image of America worked out in the American scene. This is not a contrived thing, but real, but powerful. The American image came out of the American way, out of Northern faith and Southern adventure, out of the Revolution that each man felt in himself and all advanced, out of the West won, the country torn in two by civil war, the nation finding itself again, the power of the individual, the claims of the community and the mission that sent America into the world: we are dealing with one of the great realities of all time, like the rise of the Greeks, the march of Rome, the spread of Christianity, the birth of Western civilization, and what President Wilson called 'the swarming of the English' – a swarming that carried these great movements to the American shore. America contains all these in it – the glory that was Greece, the grandeur that was Rome, and the greatness that was Britain; and yet is more, is a 'new order of men'.

It is from this new order that the American scene is constantly reborn.

References

*Brown, C. B. (1887) *Arthur Mervyn, or the Memoirs of the Year 1793,* McKay, Philadelphia, Vol. 1, pp. 48, 157, 173, 161, 129–30.

Freneau, P. (1782) *The Philosopher of the Forest,* 1782, quoted in Nye, R. B., and Grabe, N. S., (eds.) *American Thought and Writing,* Houghton Mifflin, Boston (1965) p. 191.

*Irving, W. (1865:1967) *A Tour on the Prairies* (1865) Pantheon edn, N.Y. (1967) pp. 153, 165, 191.

*Lewis, W. A. (1970) 'Black power and the university', *Dialogue,* Vol. 3, No. 2, pp. 87–9, 95.

*Marquand, J. P. (1937:1958) *The Late George Apley,* (1937) Collins edn. (1958) London, pp. 156, 159, 161.

Miller, A. (1952:1959) *The Crucible,* 1952, Bantam Classic edn, 1959, p. 5.

Morrissett, I. and **Wiley, K. B.** (1971) *The Environmental Problem and the Environmental Education Act of 1970,* U. of Colorado Press, Boulder, p. 1.

National Schools Public Relations Association *Environment and the Schools,* Education U.S.A., N.Y., p. 17.

Parker, R. A. (1935) *A Yankee Saint: John Humphrey Noyes and the Oneida Community,* Putnams, N.Y., p. 145.

Platt, R. H. (1976) 'The federal open space programs: impacts and imperatives', in Adams, J. S. (ed.) *Urban Policymaking and Metropolitan Dynamics,* Ballinger's, Cambridge, Mass., p. 333.

Pole, J. R. (1967) 'The American past: is it still usable?' *J. Am. Stud.,* Vol. 1, No. 1, Apr., p. 66.

Radford, F. L. (1971) 'The journey towards castration', *J. Am. Stud.,* Vol. IV, No. 2, Feb., pp. 227–32.

Smith, A. (1776:1843) *The Wealth of Nations,* Wakefield edn, London (1843) Vol. 1, intro. cxxxv.

Stapp, W. B. (1974) 'Historical setting of environmental education', in Swan, J. A., and Stapp, W. B. (eds) *Environmental Education, Strategies Towards a Livable Future,* Wiley, N.Y., p. 47.

Stuart, D. (1938) *The Canadian Desert,* Ryerson, Toronto, pp. 6–7.

Swan, J. A. (1974) 'Some human objectives for environmental education', in Swan and Stapp, op. cit., p. 34.

Taylor, A. M. (1969) 'Integrative principles and the educational process', *Main Currents in Modern Thought,* Vol. 25, No. 5, May–June, p. 127.

Thoreau, H. D. (1854:1966) *Walden,* 1854, Norton Critical edn, N.Y., 1966, pp. 3, 61–2.

US News (1977) *US News and World Report,* Vol. lxxxii, No. 2, 23 May, p. 61.

*Warner, S. B. (1971) *The Private City, Philadelphia in Three Periods of its Growth,* Philadelphia, U. of Pennsylvania Press, pp. 16, 19, 181, 11, 16.

Watson, J. (1977) 'On the teaching of value geography', *Geography,* July. July, p. ooo.

Watson, J. Wreford (1977) 'Images of Canada' *Bull. Can. Stud.,* Vol. 1, No. 1, p. 12.

White, S. E. (1920) *The Forest,* Doubleday Toronto, p. 5.

---

*The sequence of page numbers at the end of the reference corresponds to the sequence of quotations in the text.

Index